Deepening Your Ministry Through Prayer and Personal Growth

.

LIBRARY OF CHRISTIAN Leadership

Deepening Your Ministry Through Prayer and Personal Growth

30 Strategies to Transform Your Ministry

Marshall Shelley, General Editor

MOORINGS
Nashville, Tennessee
A Division of The Ballantine Publishing Group, Random House, Inc.

Library of Congress Cataloging-in-Publication Data

Deepening your ministry through prayer and personal growth : 30 ways to
  transform your ministry / Marshall Shelley, general editor. — 1st ed.
      p.   cm. — (Library of Christian leadership)
    ISBN: 0-345-39599-9
    1. Clergy—Religious life.   I. Shelley, Marshall.   II. Series.
  BV4011.6.D44   1996
248.8'92—dc20   96-4782
                                                                 CIP

First Edition: May 1996

10   9   8   7   6   5   4   3   2   1

Contents

Section 1: Deepening Your Ministry Through Prayer

Part 1
Making Time

Part 2
Moving In

Part 3
Exercising Discipline

Introduction

If we don't put in the hours when no one's looking, we can't expect decades of fruitful ministry.

—ED ROWELL

Nolan Ryan is the patron saint of aging baby boomers.

His twenty-seven-year reign as a major league pitcher inspired all who want a long, productive career. When he retired at age forty-six, his fastball still made the rookies step back in disbelief.

Everyone who talked with Ryan during his final season wanted to know the secret of his longevity.

"My secret is mostly just a lot of hard work," he told reporters. His conditioning routines had changed little over nearly three decades: aerobic conditioning on the stationary bike increased his endurance; weight training kept tendons and muscles strong and flexible; ice therapy after each start quelled inflammation and promoted healing. For Ryan, every moment of glory on the mound was the distillation of hours of sweat in the training room. When it came to conditioning, there was never an off-season.

Nor is there an off-season for pastors and church leaders.

Our ability to minister effectively is acquired through regularly scheduled hours of toil in the gym of the soul. Those still throwing heat after decades of ministry have adhered to two major conditioning strategies: staying close to God and keeping a keen edge on ministry skills. Ministry tends to pull us away from our spiritual center, and the constant pressures of ministry tend to dull the practice of it.

Deepening Your Ministry Through Prayer and Personal Growth helps a leader both stay close to God and sharpen ministry skills. Both require conditioning—or, as Nolan Ryan put it, a lot of hard work. If we don't put in the hours when no one's looking, we can't expect decades of fruitful ministry.

The contributors to this volume share the time-tested theology of the spiritual disciplines. If you sit close enough to any one of them, you will hear the rumbling of a hungry spirit, one never satisfied with enough of God. It's not that they never struggle, but that they *do*, in fact, struggle. We believe their wisdom will strengthen you for the seasons of ministry yet to come.

—Ed Rowell
Associate Editor, *Leadership*

Contributors

Greg Asimakoupoulos is pastor of the Evangelical Covenant Church of Naperville (Illinois). Before that he pastored Crossroads Covenant Church in Concord, California. He is coauthor of *The Time Crunch*.

Roger Barrier Jr. is senior pastor of Cases Adobe Baptist Church in Tucson, Arizona. He has written for a number of periodicals and was a contributing author of *The Power and the Glory*.

Steve Brown is president of Key Life Network, Inc., and Bible teacher on the national radio program "Key Life." He is also professor of communications and practical theology at Reformed Theological Seminary in Orlando. He formerly pastored Key Biscayne Presbyterian Church in Florida. He has authored books such as *When Being Good Isn't Good Enough* and *How to Talk so People Will Listen*, and coauthored *A Voice in the Wilderness*.

Jim Cymbala is pastor of the Brooklyn Tabernacle in Brooklyn, New York. The church is home to the Brooklyn Tabernacle Choir, which is directed by his wife, Carol. The Brooklyn Tabernacle has planted several churches in other parts of New York City and features a Tuesday night prayer service attended by more than 1,000 people each week.

Ed Dobson is pastor of Calvary Church in Grand Rapids, Michigan. Before that he served as vice president for student life at Liberty University in Lynchburg, Virginia. With Jerry Falwell and others, he has written *The Fundamentalist Phenomenon,* and with Ed Hinson, *The Seduction of Power.* He is also the author of *Starting a Seeker Sensitive Service.*

Maxie Dunnam is president of Asbury Theological Seminary in Wilmore, Kentucky. Before that he pastored Christ United Methodist Church in Memphis, Tennessee. He has been an editor with *The Upper Room* and has served churches in California, Georgia, and Mississippi. Among his many books, mostly on spiritual growth, are two volumes in *The Communicator's Commentary* series. He is also coauthor of *Mastering Personal Growth.*

Mark Galli is managing editor of *Christian History* magazine and the *Preaching Today* tape series. Before that he pastored congregations in California and Mexico. He is coauthor of *Preaching That Connects.*

Wayne Gordon is founder and copastor of Lawndale Community Church on the west side in Chicago, Illinois. He is also founder and president of the Lawndale Christian Development Corporation, an economic and housing arm of Lawndale Community Church. He has written *Real Hope in Chicago.*

Em Griffin has been professor of communications at Wheaton College in Wheaton, Illinois, since 1971. He has written *A First Look at Communication Theory, Making Friends and Making Them Count,* and *The Mind Changers: The Art of Christian Persuasion.*

Dave Hansen is pastor of Belgrade Community Church in Belgrade, Montana. Before that he pastored yoked congregations in western Montana. He has written *The Art of Pastoring.*

Kent Hughes has been pastor of College Church in Wheaton, Illinois, since 1979. He is author of *Disciplines of a Godly Man, Disciplines of Grace,* and *Liberating Ministry from the Success Syndrome,* and coauthor of *Mastering the Pastoral Role.*

Bill Hybels is founding pastor of Willow Creek Community Church in South Barrington, Illinois. He is the author of, among others, *Descending into Greatness* and *Rediscovering Church*, and coauthor of *Mastering Contemporary Preaching*.

Charles Killian has been professor of preaching and drama at Asbury Theological Seminary in Wilmore, Kentucky, since 1970. He has written several dramas including "Francis Asbury on the Kentucky Frontier" and "Wesley on Wesley—I Believe."

Gordon MacDonald is pastor of Grace Chapel in Lexington, Massachusetts. Prior to that he served Trinity Baptist Church in New York City and was president of InterVarsity Christian Fellowship. His many books include *Ordering Your Private Word*, *The Life God Blesses*, and *Mastering Personal Growth*.

John Maxwell is founder and president of Injoy, an international leadership development institute. Before that he served as pastor of Skyline Wesleyan Church in San Diego, California, for fourteen years. He has written, among others, *Developing the Leader Within You* and *Developing the Leaders Around You*.

Louis McBurney is founder and medical director of Marble Retreat, a counseling center for clergy in Marble, Colorado. He serves on the advisory boards of *Leadership, Marriage Partnership* magazine, and Called Together Ministries. He has written *Every Pastor Needs a Pastor, Counseling Christian Workers*, and *Families Under Stress*.

Don McCullough is president of San Francisco Theological Seminary. Before that he pastored Solana Beach Presbyterian Church in Solana Beach, California. He has written *Finding Happiness in the Most Unlikely Places* and coauthored *Mastering Personal Growth*.

Steven L. McKinley is pastor of House of Prayer Lutheran Church in Richfield, Minnesota. He is the author of *I'm Glad You Asked* and coauthor of *The Time Crunch*.

Terry Muck is professor of comparative religion at Austin Presbyterian Theological Seminary in Austin, Texas. Before that he was editor of *Leadership* and executive editor of *Christianity Today*. He has written, among others, *Alien Gods on American Turf, The Mysterious Beyond*, and *Theology and Ministry in a Global Age*.

John Ortberg is teaching pastor at Willow Creek Community Church in South Barrington, Illinois. Before that he pastored Horizons Community Church in Diamond Bar, California. He has written articles for both scholarly and popular journals. He is coauthor of *Dangers, Toils, & Snares*.

Ben Patterson is dean of the chapel at Hope College in Holland, Michigan. Before that he pastored Presbyterian congregations in New Jersey and California. He is contributing editor to *Christianity Today* and *Leadership*, author of *Waiting: Finding Hope When God Seems Silent*, and coauthor of *Mastering the Pastoral Role* and *Who's in Charge?*

Eugene H. Peterson is the James M. Houston Professor of Spiritual Theology at Regent College in Vancouver, B.C. His many books include *The Message: The New Testament in Contemporary English* and *The Psalms: The Message*.

Lorne C. Sanny has been on staff with The Navigators for more than fifty years. During thirty of his years there, he served as international president, general director, and chairman of the U.S. Board of Directors. Though semiretired, he continues to serve The Navigators as a consultant.

Gary V. Simpson is senior pastor of the Concord Baptist Church of Christ in Brooklyn, New York. Before that he served Calvary Baptist Church in Morristown, New Jersey.

Fred Smith Sr. is a business executive living in Dallas, Texas. He is a recipient of the Lawrence Appley Award of the American Management Association. He is a contributing editor to *Leadership* and serves on the board of directors of *Christianity Today, Inc.* He has written *You and Your Network* and *Learning to Lead*.

Barbara Brown Taylor is rector of Grace-Calvary Episcopal Church in Clarkesville, Georgia. Her books include *Gospel Medicine, The Preaching Life*, and *The Seeds of Heaven*.

William H. Willimon is dean of the chapel and professor of Christian ministry at Duke University in Durham, North Carolina. He has served United Methodist pastorates in Georgia and South Carolina. His numerous books include *Peculiar Speech: Preaching to the Baptized*, *The Intrusive Word: Preaching to the Unbaptized*, and *A Voice in the Wilderness*.

Section 1:
Deepening Your Ministry Through Prayer

I don't want to dispense mimeographed hand-outs that describe God's business; I want to witness out of my own experience. I don't want to live as a parasite on the first-hand spiritual life of others, but to be personally involved with all my senses, tasting and seeing that the Lord is good.

—Eugene Peterson

PART 1

Making Time

1

A Driven Pastor's Pursuit of God

Feeling close to God is important. It makes our relationship with God fulfilling and our faith contagious.

—WAYNE GORDON

Our church had met in a storefront for five years when we decided we needed more room. For several years, we had eyed the property across the street, a building that needed major remodeling. We offered $25,000 and finally settled on a price of $35,000.

Any mortgage would seriously tax our church budget, and the cost of remodeling still lay ahead. We needed to paint inside and out, erect walls for office space and classrooms, fix the roof, and lay new carpet. To save money I served as general contractor and carpenter. We were anxious to move in, so the remodeling was a high priority for the church and my daily schedule. After a quick morning devotion—a fast reading of a psalm and a "Bless me today, Lord!"—I rushed to the job site, where I hammered nails, called subcontractors, took estimates, and directed volunteers, often until eight o'clock at night.

Only after that, when I was done with the building project for the day, did I start my pastoral work: writing sermons, visiting in homes and at the hospital, and phoning leaders to plan services.

After a few weeks of this schedule, I paid the price. I wasn't just tired; my body screamed for rest. I felt emotionally distant from my wife and children, and they were obviously unhappy about not getting more of my time. Worst of all, I felt as though God were a star system away.

But I also felt I had to finish the project soon. To reach the neighborhood as we had envisioned, with a medical clinic, gym, and larger facilities for Sunday services, we had to sacrifice. I kept telling myself, *I have to pay the price.* So I kept pushing.

Around that time, I bought *Ordering Your Private World* by Gordon MacDonald. (I didn't have the time to read, but I knew I needed help!) The book stopped me in my tracks. As I read one page in his book, I was sure MacDonald had been looking over my shoulder for the past several months:

> A driven person is usually caught in the uncontrolled pursuit of expansion. Driven people like to be a part of something that is getting bigger and more successful. . . . They rarely have any time to appreciate the achievements to date. . . . Driven people are usually abnormally busy. They are usually too busy for the pursuit of ordinary relationships in marriage, family, or friendship . . . not to speak of one with God.

The scales fell from my eyes. I had pursued the building project like someone who was driven, not called. But that was only the symptom of a deeper problem.

I realized that I knew a lot about God—I had a master's degree in Bible—but I didn't know God intimately. Like stars and planets in the night sky that I only occasionally lifted my head to wonder at, God was distant. But I wasn't content with that, so in the fall of 1985 I launched out on a journey toward a deeper walk with God.

Quest for intimacy

Elder Christian statesmen like John Stott and John Perkins inspire me because they show that intimacy with God can keep growing throughout our lives, that greater intimacy is indeed a journey. Since that fall, I have gradually discovered a deepening sense of closeness with the Lord. Perhaps some of what I have learned can help you.

Follow your feelings. Pastors often must tell Christians not to follow their emotions (they are the caboose, and all that). But intimacy is a feeling. Though we can't base our assurance of salvation on emotions, feeling close to God is important. It makes our relationship with God fulfilling and our faith contagious.

What helps me feel closer to God? For years the mainstay of my daily devotions was Bible study. Although vital to true knowledge of God, Bible study doesn't normally foster intimacy for me. The key for me is waiting quietly on God until I sense his presence.

Get born again. Bill Leslie, pastor of LaSalle Street Church in Chicago for several decades, felt burned out at one point in his ministry, so he went to a Catholic retreat center. He talked to a nun about how he felt. She listened patiently, and then she said, "What you need is a personal relationship with Jesus Christ."

Ouch! Bill was a card-carrying evangelical. That experience jarred him and convinced him he needed to deepen his relationship with the Savior.

Ministry is more than constructing buildings and leading people to Christ. It is knowing God and being the person he wants me to be. Out of that flows ministry. When asked what the greatest commandment was, Jesus didn't begin, "Love your neighbor as yourself." Rather, "Love the Lord your God with all your heart and with all your soul and with all your mind" (Matt. 22:37 NIV). I wasn't exempt from this command just because I was doing ministry. I needed to make first things first.

Follow the cycle of intimacy. Knowing God is a process that can no more be exhausted than the exploration of the universe. There is always another blazing aspect to discover in God. John 14:21 describes the stages in the cycle: "Whoever has my commands and obeys them, he is the one who loves me. He who loves me will be loved by my Father, and I too will love him and show myself to him" (NIV).

Stage one: if we love God, we obey his commands. Stage two: if we obey his commands, he reveals himself to us. Stage three: when he reveals himself to us, we know him better and love him more. Then the cycle repeats itself, with our love and knowledge of God growing ever deeper and stronger.

Unless accompanied by obedience, prayer and Bible reading cannot bring intimacy. At one point in their history, the Israelites

rigorously practiced spiritual disciplines. They were fasting, worshiping in the Temple, seeking the Lord. But God told them, in
Isaiah 58, that he had another kind of fasting in mind. <u>They</u>
<u>needed to follow the spiritual discipline of obedience: to stop</u>
<u>oppressing their workers, to feed the hungry and set prisoners</u>
<u>free. G</u>od promised to come near those who obeyed him.

Of course, no one obeys perfectly, but deliberate, ongoing dis-
obedience breaks the cycle of intimacy as surely as eating the
apple sent Adam and Eve packing from the Garden of Eden.

Journal morning thoughts. I am not a natural writer. Journaling is the last spiritual discipline I gravitate toward. But a number
of writers I had been reading recommended the practice, so I
decided to try it. I've never stopped. Ten years later I'm still
journaling nearly every day. While the streetlights are still shin-
ing bright on Ogden Avenue, I wake up, walk the cracked and
vaulted sidewalks to church, crank up the footrest on my easy
chair, and sloppily write in a spiral notebook things (unlike John
Wesley) I never want anyone to read.

The thoughts I have when I wake, shower, and shave are the
first thing I record in my journal. Early morning thoughts are
significant. Worries, anger, new ideas, plans—they cluster at
dawn, before the press of daily events, and in my journal I process them. My journal is one place where I can be completely
honest with God.

Where I journal, pray, and read Scripture is important. On
Saturdays I have tried to wake up early and journal at home, but
even though I'm up before my family, it doesn't work. I don't get
the same settled feeling in my spirit. I'm restless. My best times
with God come when I'm at my right place: my office.

Don't unnecessarily upset family rhythms. For one six-month
period, I fasted one day a week. My family eats together every
night, so on fasting days I sat at the table and talked. That was
awkward. Then I tried cloistering myself in the bedroom to read
and pray during meals. "For a while I'm not going to eat with
everyone on Mondays," I explained to the kids (trying not to
sound super-spiritual). "While you're eating, I'm going to be
alone with God because I want to know God better." My spiritual
quarantine upset everyone. My wife was frustrated at having to

handle the meal and children alone, and the kids wanted to see me.

After six months the fasting hadn't helped me feel significantly closer to God, but it had increased family stress. That spiritual discipline finally went out the window.

I still believe in the benefits of fasting (which I have since concluded benefits me most when I fast in three- to five-day stretches). Fasting over important decisions helps me stay focused. I have never come down from Mount Sinai with tablets in my hands, but I usually get a deep, settled peace.

I also fast about specific needs. When I taught high school, I met with another coach in the athletic equipment room during lunch hour; instead of eating, we prayed for the troubled marriage of a friend. After nine months, that marriage had recovered.

My most refreshing spiritual discipline is keeping an agreement made with my wife years ago. We have promised each other to take a week away together every year with no children, no agenda; we want to simply enjoy each other. We pray and read the Bible together, rest, and play tennis. It is the highlight of our marriage and my spiritual life.

Get quiet and make time. To have intimacy with God in my quiet time, I can't do without two things: (1) quiet and (2) time.

As a student at Wheaton College, I was a fellowship fanatic. I loved being with people. One year I went on a wilderness retreat. Retreat organizers told us to bring only three things besides our clothes and toiletries: a Bible, a notebook, and a pen. For three days they required participants to spend their time alone with God. I had never spent half a day away from people and alone with God! I quickly learned how dependent my relationship with God was on others. I also learned that spending quantity time with God enhances intimacy, and that I could enjoy the quiet and the luxury of time with God alone.

There is no substitute for time. I can't rush intimacy. When I have been away from my wife for several days, five minutes of conversation at the dinner table does not restore our sense of closeness. We need one or two hours together. What we discuss isn't as important as spending the time with each other.

I have a friend who talks about how much he enjoys "wasting

time" with God, that is, spending unstructured, unhurried periods with the Lord. Although I often use a prayer list, I also like following no agenda, just as one of my favorite activities with family and friends is just hanging out together. Fellowship with God has to be led by the Spirit and informed by the concerns and feelings on my heart at the moment.

In some of the most intimate moments my wife and I have shared, we haven't said anything; we sit or lie together, holding hands or arm in arm, enjoying each other's presence. So it is with the Lord. "Be still, and know that I am God" (Ps. 46:10 NIV) is a verse that shapes my time with God as much as any other. Such stillness energizes me. Along with journaling, my greatest sense of closeness to God comes when sitting in silence before him until I feel his presence.

Differences for pastors

Bringing up the subject of "spiritual disciplines" usually brings up guilt in people. We all feel we could do more in this area. In addition, pastors are often troubled because they feel that the pressures of pastoral life encourage them to cheat God.

I believe, however, that we need to accept that our practice of spiritual disciplines will be different than the practice of our parishioners. In particular, there are three areas that trouble us, but here's how I deal with them.

First, I've come to accept that pastoral life is a ride on the Screaming Eagle. One day I'm ministering to a young man in prison for murdering a storekeeper; the next day I perform a wedding; the next day, a funeral. We can talk about balance and order, but pastoral life isn't balanced or ordered!

I've decided I'm not going to feel guilty when I miss a day of devotions. If I don't do them before 7 A.M., they don't happen, or at least they don't have the same benefit. When I can't fit in my quiet time, I feel cheated. I miss my time with the Lord. But if I am legalistic about spiritual disciplines, they no longer are spiritual disciplines for me, just mere duty.

Second, I merge daily devotions with sermon preparation. I

know some consider that a problem, but it works well for me. I often read and meditate daily on my preaching text for the coming Sunday. My best preaching is a reflection of how I'm growing and what God shows me in my times with him.

Third, I allow myself to think about church during my quiet time. For some, this becomes a temptation to refuse to get personal with God, to keep playing pastor even in his presence. But I am a pastor, and so much of what I do is pastoral. Often as I wait in God's presence, ideas come to my mind like a meteor shower, and many are from the Lord. I write them down in full when the inspirations come and sometimes act on them immediately.

Recently, as I was praying, the name of one woman in our church came to me. I wasn't sure why, but I sensed I was supposed to call her. When I did phone, she told me she had been struggling for several days. She desperately needed someone to talk to. She was shocked that I called just when I did.

Closing the open door

It's no surprise that my spiritual lows come when I'm busy, preoccupied, focusing my attention on everything but God, and my spiritual highs come on "Sabbath" days of rest and relaxation. God instituted the Sabbath not only because the human body needs physical rest, but more so because human activity frustrates intimacy with the Creator.

That means that at times I've had to take forceful steps to make this happen.

As a people-person and activist, I've prided myself on having an open-door policy. So for years, people regularly interrupted my devotions, but it didn't bother me much. When I started my journey of knowing God, I knew something had to change; I had to find uninterrupted time with God. So I started coming to church earlier for my morning devotions.

Then people who wanted to see me learned a good time to catch me was early in the morning. Still, I kept my door open and kept coming in earlier and earlier to be alone.

One early morning as I was in my office praying, a drug addict named Norman, to whom I had been ministering for months, came to my door and said, "I don't have any money for the train. Can you give me a ride to work?"

"I'll give you some money," I said.

"I'll be late for work. I need you to give me a ride."

He pressed his plea, and so finally I drove him. When I returned to the office, I was never able to resume my devotions.

I woke early the next morning looking forward to my devotions. I settled into my chair at the office and began reading the Bible. Minutes later Norman showed up again at my door. Same request. Again I refused. He begged me, and once again I grudgingly interrupted my time with the Lord to drive him to work. Once again I couldn't resume my devotions later in the day.

The next morning, Norman reappeared at my open door. "I'm not driving you to work," I said firmly. "I have a commitment."

"Coach, you have to! I'll be fired if I don't get there on time."

"That's too bad. I have a commitment."

Norman pleaded and pleaded with me. Finally I said, "Okay, okay, I'll drive you to work, but if you come to my door tomorrow, I'm not driving you. You'll just have to lose your job."

The next morning I was not surprised when Norman stuck his head in my office (with that kind of persistence, how could he not succeed in life?!). But this time I held firm. Angrily he rushed out to take the train, and he didn't lose his job.

That experience was a turning point for me. Though contrary to my nature, I started saying no to people to guard my time with the Lord. I now close and lock my outer office door during devotions. When someone knocks, I don't answer, nor do I answer my phone. I have told the congregation, "If you come knocking on my door early in the morning, I'm not going to answer. I need to be alone with God. I don't want to know about God, I want to know God."

Just a couple of years ago, I found myself deeply discouraged about the work at the church. Frankly, I debated quitting ministry at Lawndale. So, feeling like the despondent Elijah when Jezebel had designs on his prophetic skin, I went off by myself to a retreat. I fasted, prayed, and waited for three days to hear from God.

There were no tremblors or bolts of lightning, but when the three days were up, the tide had come back in. I sensed God saying, *Be still. Know that I am God. You don't have to solve all of Lawndale's problems or save everyone you meet. Love me, and we'll work together. Just keep going.*

Returning home, I talked it over with my wife, and we decided to stay. My eight-year journey in pursuit of intimacy with God is what enabled me to work through that dark night of ministry. Often finding time for God is difficult in the midst of church life, but closeness with God is the basis for lasting ministry.

2

The Pastor's Sabbath

If we do not regularly quit work for one day a week, we take
ourselves far too seriously. The moral sweat pouring off our brows
blinds our eyes to the action of God in and around us.

—EUGENE H. PETERSON

Question: "Do you take a day off?"

Answer: "Unthinkable! In a world where a cobalt bomb might detonate any moment, how can the very people entrusted with the Word of Life to this doomsday population take a day off?"

This interchange took place in a seminary classroom while I was a student. The answer came from a prominent pastor whom, I thought, I had every reason to admire and therefore emulate. Thus, when I became a pastor, I practiced what had been impressed upon me: long hours, seven-day weeks, year after year. Most of my friends and mentors did the same. The only alternative I could imagine was sloth, by far the deadliest of the ministerial sins.

After a few years, pressure from my wife and children got me to take an occasional break. I began to realize I worked far better and got more done in six days if I had a change of pace on the seventh. Remarkable! The arguments and evidence mounted: I was persuaded to take a regular day off.

Then I noticed something (why it took so long I'll never know): my practice was not at all the same as the biblical practice of Sabbath-keeping. I had more or less assumed I was being biblical, but actually I stood in stark and utter contrast. My day off was basically utilitarian, a secularized Sabbath, making it possible to get more done on the other six days. It was also a common-sense contribution to family harmony and emotional health.

At that point I set out to keep a genuine Sabbath.

No other behavioral change has brought so many unintended but welcome benefits to my life of faith and my work as a pastor.

Daily and weekly rest

Sabbath means "quit." "Stop." "Take a break." The word itself has nothing devout or holy in it. It is a word about time, denoting our nonuse thereof, what we usually call "wasting time."

The biblical context is the Genesis week of creation. Sabbath is the seventh and final day, in which "[God] rested *[shabath]* . . . from all His work which He had done" (Gen. 2:2 NASB). As we reenter that sequence of days when God spoke energy and matter into existence, we repeatedly come upon the refrain "And there was evening and there was morning, one day. . . . And there was evening and there was morning, a second day. . . . And there was evening and there was morning . . ." (Gen. 1:5–31 NASB)—on and on, six times.

This is the Hebrew way of understanding day, but it is not ours. Our day begins with an alarm clock ripping the predawn darkness and closes, not with evening but several hours past that, when we turn off the electric lights. In our conventional refer-ences to day, we do not include the night except for the two or three hours we steal from either end to give us more time to work. Because our definition of day is so different, we have to make an imaginative effort to understand the Hebrew phrase *eve-ning and morning, one day*. More than idiomatic speech is in-volved here; there is a sense of rhythm.

Day is the basic unit of God's creative work; evening is the beginning of that day. It is the onset of God speaking light, stars, earth, vegetation, animals, man, woman into being. But it is also the time when we quit our activity and go to sleep. When it is evening, "I lay me down to sleep and pray the Lord my soul to keep" and drift off into semiconsciousness for the next six or eight or ten hours, a state in which I am absolutely nonproductive and have no cash value.

Then I wake up, rested, jump out of bed, grab a cup of coffee, and rush out the door to get things started. The first thing I discover (a great blow to the ego) is that everything was started hours ago. All the important things got under way while I was fast asleep. When I dash into the workday, I walk into an operation that is half over already. I enter into work in which the basic plan is already established, the assignments given, the operations in motion.

Sometimes, still in a stupor, I blunder into the middle of something that is nearly done and go to work thinking I am starting it. But when I do, I interfere with what has already been accomplished. My sincere intentions and cheerful whistle while I work make it no less a blunder and an aggravation. The sensible thing is to ask, "Where do I fit? Where do you need an extra hand? What still needs to be done?"

The Hebrew evening/morning sequence conditions us to the rhythms of grace. We go to sleep, and God begins his work. As we sleep he develops his covenant. We wake and are called out to participate in God's creative action. We respond in faith, in work. But always grace is previous and primary. We wake into a world we didn't make, into a salvation we didn't earn.

Evening: God begins, without our help, his creative day. Morning: God calls us to enjoy and share and develop the work he initiated.

Creation and covenant are sheer grace and there to greet us every morning. George MacDonald once wrote that sleep is God's contrivance for giving us the help he cannot get into us when we are awake.

We read and reread the opening pages of Genesis, along with certain sequences of Psalms, and recover these deep, elemental rhythms, internalizing the reality in which the strong, initial pulse is God's creating/saving Word, God's providential/sustaining presence, God's grace.

As this biblical rhythm works in me, I also discover something else: when I quit my day's work, nothing essential stops. I prepare for sleep not with a feeling of exhausted frustration because there

is so much yet undone and unfinished, but with expectancy. The
day is about to begin! God's genesis words are about to be spoken
again. During the hours of my sleep, how will he prepare to use
my obedience, service, and speech when morning breaks? I go to
sleep to get out of the way for a while. I get into the rhythm of
salvation. While we sleep, great and marvelous things, far beyond
our capacities to invent or engineer, are in process—the moon
marking the seasons, the lion roaring for its prey, the earthworms
aerating the earth, the stars turning in their courses, the proteins
repairing our muscles, our dreaming brains restoring a deeper
sanity beneath the gossip and scheming of our waking hours. Our
work settles into the context of God's work. Human effort is
honored and respected not as a thing in itself but by its integration into the rhythms of grace and blessing.

We experience this grace with our bodies before we apprehend
it with our minds. We are attending to a matter of physical/spiri-
tual technology—not ideas, not doctrines, not virtues. We are
getting our bodies into a genesis rhythm.

Sabbath extrapolates this basic, daily rhythm into the larger
context of the month. The turning of the earth on its axis gives us
the basic two-beat rhythm, evening/morning. The moon in its
orbit introduces another rhythm, the twenty-eight-day month,
marked by four phases of seven days each. It is this larger
rhythm, the rhythm of the seventh day, that we are commanded
to observe.

Sabbath-keeping presumes the daily rhythm, evening/morn-
ing—we can hardly avoid stopping our work each night, as fatigue and sleep overtake us. But the weekly rhythm demands
deliberate action. Otherwise, we can go on working on the seventh day, especially if things are gaining momentum. Sabbath-
keeping often feels like an interruption, an interference with our
routines. It challenges assumptions we gradually build up that
our daily work is indispensable in making the world go.

But then we find the Sabbath is not an interruption but a
stronger rhythmic measure that confirms and extends the basic
beat. Every seventh day a deeper note is struck—an enormous
gong whose deep sounds reverberate under and over and around
the daily percussions evening/morning, evening/morning, eve-

ning/morning: creation honored and contemplated, redemption remembered and shared.

Reasons for remembering

In the two passages where the Sabbath commandment appears, the commands are identical but the supporting reasons differ. Exodus says we are to keep a Sabbath because God kept it (Exod. 20:8–11). God did his work in six days and then rested. If God sets apart one day to rest, we can too. There are some things that can only be accomplished, even by God, in a state of rest. The rest/work rhythm is built into the very structure of God's inter-penetration of reality. The precedent to quit doing and simply be is divine. Sabbath-keeping is commanded so that we internalize the being that matures out of doing.

The reason given in Deuteronomy for remembering the Sabbath is that our ancestors in Egypt went four hundred years without a vacation (Deut. 5:15). Never a day off. The consequence: they were no longer considered persons but slaves. Work units. Not persons created in the image of God but equipment for making bricks and building pyramids.

Lest any of us do that to our neighbor or husband or wife or child or employee, we are commanded to keep a Sabbath. The moment we begin to see others in terms of what they can do rather than who they are, humanity is defaced and community violated. It is no use claiming "I don't need to rest this week and therefore will not keep a Sabbath"—our lives are so intercon-nected that we inevitably involve others in our work whether we intend it or not. Sabbath-keeping is elemental kindness. Sabbath-keeping is commanded to preserve the image of God in our neighbors so that we see them as they are, not as we need them or want them to be.

Every profession has sins to which it is especially liable. I haven't looked closely into the sins that endanger physicians and lawyers, woodworkers and potters, but I've had my eye on the snare from which pastors need deliverance: it is the sin of revers-ing the rhythms. Instead of grace/work we make it work/grace.

Instead of working in a world in which God calls everything into being with his word and redeems his people with an outstretched arm, we rearrange it as a world in which we preach the mighty work of God and in afterthought ask him to bless our speaking; a world in which we stretch out our mighty arms to help the oppressed and open our hands to assist the needy and desperately petition God to take care of those we miss.

That, of course, is why so few pastors keep a Sabbath: we have reversed the rhythms. How can we quit work for a day when we must redeem the time? How can we pause when we have a fire in our mouth? How can we do nothing for a whole day when we have been commanded to be urgent in season and out of season, and there is never a season in which the calls for help do not exceed our capacity to meet them?

Perhaps that is why the Sabbath is *commanded* not *suggested,* for nothing less than a command has the power to intervene in the vicious, accelerating, self-perpetuating cycle of faithless and graceless busyness, the only part of which we are conscious being our good intentions.

Of all the commandments, not one is treated with such disregard by pastors as this one. We are capable of preaching good sermons on it to our parishioners, and we take great care to provide them a Sabbath of good worship and holy leisure. But we exempt ourselves. Curious. Not many of us preach vigorously on the seventh commandment and then pursue lives of active adultery. But we conscientiously catechize our people on the fifth commandment and without a blush flaunt our workaholic Sabbath-breaking as evidence of an extraordinary piety.

Pure preaching but Pelagian practice

Sabbath: uncluttered time and space to distance ourselves from the frenzy of our own activities so we can see what God has been doing and is doing. If we do not regularly quit work for one day a week, we take ourselves far too seriously. The moral sweat pouring off our brows blinds our eyes to the action of God in and around us.

Sabbath-*keeping*: quieting the internal noise so we hear the still small voice of our Lord. Removing the distractions of pride so we discern the presence of Christ "in ten thousand places,/Lovely in limbs, and lovely in eyes not his/To the Father through the features of men's faces" (G. M. Hopkins).

Sabbath-*keeping*: separating ourselves from the people who are clinging to us, from the routines to which we cling for our identity, and offering them all up to God in praise.

None of us has trouble with this theologically. We are compellingly articulate on the subject in our pulpits. It is not our theology that is deficient but our technology—Sabbath-keeping is not a matter of belief but of using a tool (time), not an exercise for the mind but the body. Sabbath-keeping is not devout thoughts or heart praise but simply removing our bodies from circulation one day a week.

We are, most of us, Augustinians in our pulpits. We preach the sovereignty of our Lord, the primacy of grace, the glory of God: "By grace are ye saved . . . not of works, lest any man should boast" (Eph. 2:8–9 KJV). But the minute we leave our pulpits we are Pelagians. In our committee meetings and planning sessions, in our obsessive attempts to meet the expectations of people, in our anxiety to please, in our hurry to cover all the bases, we practice a theology that puts moral effort as the primary element in pleasing God.

The dogma produces the behavior characteristic of the North American pastor: if things aren't good enough, they will improve if we work a little harder and get others to work harder. Add a committee here, recruit some more volunteers there, squeeze a couple of more hours into the workday.

Pelagius was an unlikely heretic; Augustine an unlikely saint. By all accounts Pelagius was urbane, courteous, convincing. Everyone seems to have liked him immensely. Augustine squandered away his youth in immorality, had some kind of Freudian thing with his mother, and made a lot of enemies. But our theological and pastoral masters agree that Augustine started from God's grace and therefore had it right, and Pelagius started from human effort and therefore got it wrong. If we were as Augustinian out of the pulpit as we are in it, we would have no difficulty keeping Sabbath.

How did it happen that Pelagius became our master?

Our closet Pelagianism will not get us excommunicated or burned at the stake, but it cripples our pastoral work. And it is catastrophic to the church's wholeness and health.

Making good nonuse of time

The technology of Sabbath-keeping is not complex. We simply select a day of the week (Paul seemed to think any day would do as well as any other—Rom. 14:5–6) and quit our work.

Having selected the day, we also need to protect it, for our workday instincts and habits will not serve us well. It is not a day when we do anything useful. It is not a day that proves its worth, justifies itself. Entering into empty time, nonfunctional time, is difficult, for we have been taught that time is money.

Our secularized age is so fragmented that no consensus in the details of Sabbath-keeping is possible. We cannot prescribe a practice for each other. But lest the command dissolve into a fog of good intentions, I will risk autobiography. The risk is that someone will try to imitate the details of my practice, or (more likely) will say, "That's sure dumb; I don't see the point of that" and dismiss the whole business on the basis of my inept practice. I excuse my example with Thoreau's precedent: "I should not talk so much about myself if there were anybody else whom I knew as well. Unfortunately, I am confined to this theme by the narrowness of my experience."

Monday is my Sabbath. Nothing is scheduled for Mondays. If there are emergencies, I respond, but there are surprisingly few. My wife joins me in observing the day. We make a lunch, put it in a daypack, take our binoculars, and drive anywhere from fifteen minutes to an hour to a trailhead along a river or into the mountains. Before we begin our hike, my wife reads a psalm and prays. After that prayer there is no more talking—we enter into a silence that continues for the next two or three hours, until we stop for lunch.

We walk leisurely, emptying ourselves, opening ourselves to what is there: fern shapes, flower fragrance, birdsong, granite outcroppings, oaks and sycamores, rain, snow, sleet, wind.

We have clothes for all weather and so never cancel our Sabbath-keeping for reasons of weather any more than our Sunday churchgoing—and for the same reason: we need our Sabbath just as much as our parishioners need theirs. When the sun or our stomachs tell us it is lunchtime, we break the silence with a prayer of blessing for the sandwiches and fruit, the river and the forest. We are free to talk now, sharing bird sightings, thoughts, observations, ideas—however much or little we are inclined.

We return home in the middle or late afternoon, putter, do odd jobs, read. After supper I usually write family letters. That's it. No Sinai thunder. No Damascus Road illuminations. No Patmos visions. A day set apart for solitude and silence. Not-doing.

Being-there. The sanctification of time.

We don't have any rules for preserving the sanctity of the day, only the commitment that it be set apart for being, not using. Not a day to get anything done but a day to watch and be responsive to what God has done.

But we do have help. Sabbath-keeping cannot be carried out as a private enterprise. We need our congregation's help. They need our help to keep their Sabbath; we need their help to keep ours. From time to time I say something like this to my elders and deacons: "The great reality we are involved in is God. Most of the people around us don't know that and couldn't care less. One of the ways God has provided for us to stay aware of and responsive to him in a world that doesn't care is by Sabbath-keeping. At regular intervals we all need to quit our work and contemplate his, quit talking to each other and listen to him.

"God knows we need this and has given us a means in Sabbath—a day for praying and playing, simply enjoying what is, what he is. One of my tasks is to lead you in the celebration of Sabbath each Sunday. But that is not a Sabbath for me. I wake up on Sunday morning with the adrenaline flowing. It is a workday for me. Monday is my Sabbath, and I need your help to observe it. I need your prayers; I need your cooperation in not involving me in administration or consultation; I need your admonitions if you see me carelessly letting other things interfere with it. Pastors need pastors too. One of the ways you can be my pastor is to help me keep a weekly Sabbath that God commanded."

And they do it. They help. I don't think there are many congregations who would not help us do it if they knew we were committed to it and needed their help to carry it out.

My wife has been keeping, off and on, a Sabbath journal for many of the years we have been doing this. The journal is labeled, "Emmaus Walks." You wouldn't be greatly impressed, I think, if you read the sporadic entries. Bird lists, wildflowers in bloom, snatches of conversation, brief notes on the weather. But the spareness records a fullness, a presence. For Sabbath-keeping is not primarily something we do, but what we don't do.

We got the phrase "Emmaus Walks" from Douglas V. Steere, who told us the story of an old Lutheran retreat master he once knew, very Prussian, whose speech was thick with German gutturals. He specialized in men's retreats. As the men would come into the lodge, he would make them open their suitcases, from which he would confiscate all the whiskey. Then he would pair them up and send them off on what he called *ee-mouse* walks.

Steere told us that for a long time he wondered what *ee-mouse* walks were, and then realized one day that the old Prussian drillmaster was sending his men out on *Emmaus* walks: two disciples walking and talking together and Jesus, unrecognized, with them. But afterward they knew: "Did not our heart burn within us, while he talked with us by the way, and while he opened to us the scriptures?" (Luke 24:32 KJV).

It is this kind of unobtrusive alteration in perception that happens quietly but cumulatively in the practice of Sabbath-keeping.

3

How to Spend the Day in Prayer

The test of such a day is not how exhilarated we feel when the day is over but how it works into life tomorrow.

—Lorne C. Sanny

"I never thought a day could make such a difference," a friend said to me. "My relationship to everyone seems improved. Why don't I do it more often?"

Comments like these come from those who set aside a personal day of prayer.

With so many activities—important ones—clamoring for our time, real prayer is considered more a luxury than a necessity. How much more so spending a day in prayer!

The Bible gives us three time-guides for personal prayer. There is the command to "pray without ceasing"—the spirit of prayer—keeping so in tune with God that we can lift our hearts in request or praise anytime through the day.

There is also the practice of a quiet time or morning watch—seen in the life of David (Ps. 5:3); of Daniel (Dan. 6:10); and of the Lord Jesus (Mark 1:35). For the growing, healthy Christian, this daily time specified for meditation in the Word of God and prayer is indispensable.

Then there are examples in the Scripture of extended time given to prayer alone. Jesus spent whole nights praying. Nehemiah prayed "certain days" upon hearing of the plight of Jerusalem. Three times Moses spent forty days and forty nights alone with God.

How to go about it

Having set aside a day or portion of a day for prayer, pack a lunch and start out. Find a place where you can be alone, away from distractions. This may be a wooded area near your home or your backyard. An outdoor spot is excellent if you can find it; but don't get sidetracked into nature studies and fritter away your time. If you find yourself watching the squirrels or the ants, direct your observation by reading Psalm 104 and meditating on the power of God in creation.

If an outdoor spot isn't available, try a quiet corner of a library.

Take along a Bible, a notebook and pencil, a hymnbook, and perhaps a devotional book. I like to carry with me the booklet *Power Through Prayer* by E. M. Bounds and read a chapter or two to challenge me with the strategic value of prayer.

Even if you have all day, you will want to use it profitably. So lose no time in starting, and start purposefully.

Divide the day into three parts: waiting on the Lord, praying for others, and praying for yourself.

Waiting on the Lord

As you wait on the Lord, don't hurry. You will miss the point if you look for some mystical or ecstatic experience. Just seek the Lord, waiting on him. Isaiah 40:31 promises that those who wait upon the Lord will renew their strength. Psalm 27:14 is one of dozens of verses that mention waiting on him, as does Psalm 62:5, "Find rest, O my soul, in God alone; my hope comes from him" (NIV).

Wait on him first to realize his presence. Read through a passage like Psalm 139, grasping the truth of his presence with you as you read each verse. Ponder the impossibility of being anywhere in the universe where he is not. Often we are like Jacob when he said, "Surely the LORD is in this place; and I knew it not" (Gen. 28:16 KJV).

Wait on him also for cleansing. The last two verses of Psalm 139 lead you into this. Ask God to search your heart as these verses suggest. When we search our own hearts, it can lead to imaginations, morbid introspection, or anything the enemy may want to throw before us.

But when the Holy Spirit searches, he will bring to your attention what should be confessed and cleansed. Psalms 32 and 51, David's songs of confession, will help you. Stand upon the firm ground of 1 John 1:9 and claim God's faithfulness to forgive whatever specific thing you confess.

If you realize you've sinned against a brother or sister, make a note of it so you won't forget to set it right. Otherwise, the rest of the day will be hindered. God won't speak to you if there is something between you and someone else that you haven't planned to take care of at the earliest possible moment. As you wait on God, ask for the power of concentration. Bring yourself back from daydreaming.

Next, wait on God to worship him. Psalms 103, 111, and 145 are wonderful portions to follow as you praise the Lord for the greatness of his power. Most of the Psalms are prayers. Or turn to Revelation, chapters four and five, and use them in your praise. There is no better way to pray scripturally than to pray Scripture.

If you brought a hymnbook, you can sing to the Lord. Some wonderful hymns have been written that put into words what we could scarcely express ourselves. Maybe you don't sing well— then be sure you're out of earshot of someone else and "make a joyful noise unto the Lord." God will appreciate it.

This will lead you naturally into thanksgiving. Reflect upon the wonderful things God has done for you and thank the Lord for these: for your own salvation and spiritual blessings, for your family, friends, and opportunities. Go beyond what you thank the Lord for daily.

Prayer for others

Now is the time for the unhurried, more detailed prayer for others that you don't ordinarily get to. Trace your way around the world, praying for people by countries. Here are three suggestions:

First, ask for specific things. Perhaps you remember or have jotted down various needs people have mentioned. Use requests from missionary prayer letters. Pray for spiritual strength, courage, physical stamina, mental alertness, and so on. Imagine yourself in the situations where these people are and pray accordingly.

Second, look up some of the prayers in Scripture. Pray what Paul prayed for other people in the first chapters of Philippians and Colossians, and in the first and third chapters of Ephesians. This will help you advance in your prayer from the stage of "Lord, bless so and so and help them to do such and such."

Third, ask for others what you are praying for yourself. Desire for them what the Lord has shown you.

If you pray a certain verse or promise of Scripture for a person, you may want to put the reference by his or her name on your prayer list and use this verse as you pray for that person the next time. Then use it for thanksgiving as you see the Lord answer.

Prayer for yourself

The third part of your day is prayer for yourself. If you are facing an important decision, you may want to put this before prayer for others.

Again, let your prayer be ordered by Scripture and ask the Lord for understanding, according to Psalm 119:18. Meditate upon Scripture you have memorized or promises you have previously claimed from the Word. Reading a whole book of the Bible through, perhaps aloud, is a good idea. Consider how it might apply to your life.

"Lord, what do you think of my life?" is the attitude of this portion of your day of prayer. Consider your main objectives in the light of what you know to be God's will for you. "My food," said Jesus, "is to do the will of him who sent me and to finish his work" (John 4:34 NIV). Do you want to do God's will more than anything else? Is it really your highest desire?

Then consider your activities—what you do—in the context of your objectives. God may speak to you about rearranging your schedule, cutting out certain activities that are good but not best, or some things that are entanglements or impediments to progress. Strip them off. You may be convicted about how you spend your evenings or Saturdays, when you could still get the recreation you need but make better use of your time.

As you pray, record your thoughts of your activities and use of time, and plan for better scheduling. Perhaps the need for better preparation for your Sunday school class or a personal visit with an individual will come to mind. Or the Lord may impress on you to do something special for someone. Make a note of it.

During this part of your day, bring up any problems or decisions you are facing and seek the mind of God on them. It helps to list the factors involved in these decisions or problems. Pray over these factors and look into the Scriptures for guidance. You may be led to a promise or direction from the passages with which you have already filled your mind during the day.

After prayer, you may reach some definite conclusions upon which you can base firm convictions. It should be your aim in a day of prayer to come away with some conclusions and specific direction—some stakes driven. However, do not be discouraged if this is not the case. It may not be God's time for a conclusive answer to your problem. And you may discover that your real need was not to know the next step but to have a new revelation of God himself.

In looking for promises to claim, there's no need to thumb through the Bible looking for new or startling ones. Just start with the promises you already know. Chew over some old familiar promises the Lord has given you before, ones you remember as you think back. Pray about applying these verses to your life.

I have found some of the greatest spiritual rewards from a new realization of old promises, ones I already knew. And the familiar promises may lead you to others. The Bible is full of them.

You may want to mark or underline in your Bible the promises the Lord gives during these protracted times alone, and put the date and a word or two in the margin beside them.

Variety is important during your day of prayer. Read a while, pray a while, then walk around. A friend of mine paces the floor of his room for his prayer time. Rather than get cramped in one position, take a walk and stretch.

As other things pop into your mind, simply incorporate those items into prayer. If it's a business item you must not forget, jot it down. Have you noticed how many things come to mind while you are sitting in church? It will be natural for things to occur to you during your prayer day that you should have done, so put them down, pray about them, and plan how and when you can take care of them. Don't just push them aside, or they will plague you the rest of the day.

At the end of the day, summarize in your notebook the things God has spoken to you about. This will be profitable to refer to later.

Two questions

The result of your day of prayer should answer two questions Paul asked the Lord on the Damascus road (Acts 22:6–10 NIV). Paul's first question was, "Who are you, Lord?" The Lord replied, "I am Jesus." You will be seeking to know him, to find out who he is. The second question Paul asked was, "What shall I do, Lord?" The Lord answered him specifically. This should be answered or reconfirmed for you during the part of the day when you unhurriedly seek his will for you.

Don't think you must end the day with some new discovery or extraordinary experience. Wait on God and expose yourself to his Word. Looking for a new experience or insight you can share with someone when you get back will get you off the track.

True, you may gain new insight, but often this will divert your attention from the real business. The test of such a day is not how exhilarated we are when the day is over but how it works into life tomorrow. If we have fully exposed ourselves to the Word and come into contact with God, it will affect our daily life. And that is what we want.

Days of prayer don't just happen. Besides the attempts of our enemy Satan to keep us from praying, the world around us has plenty to offer to fill our time. So we have to make time. Plan ahead—the first of every other month or once a quarter. Do it soon! You too will probably ask yourself, "Why not more often?"

PART 2

Moving In

4

Fatal Omission

*Our prayer is our work! Only when that is true for us will our
work be prayer.*

—BEN PATTERSON

Great baseball catcher Yogi Berra played a game in which the
score was tied with two outs in the bottom of the ninth inning.
The batter from the opposing team stepped into the batting box
and made the sign of the cross on home plate with his bat. Berra
was a Catholic, too, but he wiped off the plate with his glove and
said to the pious batter, "Why don't we let God just watch this
game?"

That is good theology when applied to the outcome of a baseball game. It is terrible theology when applied to the way we live
our lives and carry out the work of the church. Worse than that,
it is fatal.

But too often that is precisely the outlook we bring to our
vocation as Christian elders, deacons, and pastors. God is in attendance at the game, but only as our honored spectator. Our
prayers are merely ceremonial functions: tips of the hat, verbal
recognition over the loudspeaker between innings, or requests to
throw out the game ball. God may even have the best seat in the
stadium, but he rarely, if ever, gets on the playing field.

Am I overstating things a bit? Not if I am to believe half of
what I hear from my colleagues about the weight and frequency
assigned to the role of prayer in their work. Prayer is always
getting nudged aside, neglected, or perfunctorily performed as
more pressing concerns take center stage. Many of us feel we just

have too much to do to make time to pray. That is the problem. At bottom, we don't believe we are really doing anything when we pray—other than pray, that is.

It is this attitude I would like to address, for I believe it is one of the most subtle and pernicious forms of worldliness in the church today. Why don't we believe we are getting anything done when we pray? Two reasons: the world's view, and the world's pace.

The world's view

The world's view is basically a philosophical issue. It is the view of secularism: the view that this material world is all there is; that we live in a closed system of cause and effect with nothing outside; that official reality is only what is accessible to our senses. The secular worldview is what Peter Berger called a "world without windows." There can be no such thing as prayer in that kind of world.

Of course, any Christian can see that that worldview is at odds with faith. For the church, however, what is more significant than secularism as a formal philosophical system is secularism as a sociological phenomenon. For secularism as a sociological reality, says Os Guinness, is the notion that religious ideas, institutions, and interpretations are losing practical social significance.

For instance, it is fine to pray in your support group, for it can be a warm exercise in intimacy. But pray as a means of doing the business of the church? When we must get something done, we need to start talking, writing, telephoning, spending, budgeting, mobilizing, organizing, and mailing. Those kinds of things take time. So prayer gets preempted. It is a pleasant luxury that would be wonderful to spend more time on, if only we did not have so many necessities pressing in. After all, we must complete the budget and formulate policies and act on the proposals from the fellowship committee.

God's view couldn't be more in opposition to that fatuous notion. Our battle is not with those so-called necessities, but "against the rulers, against the authorities, against the powers of this dark world and against the spiritual forces of evil in the heavenly realms" (Eph. 6:12 NIV).

We therefore fight our battle with truth, righteousness, the gospel of peace, faith, salvation, and the Word of God. And we "pray in the Spirit on all occasions with all kinds of prayers and requests" (Eph. 6:18 NIV).

That places our work in a totally different perspective, doesn't it? That demands an entirely different agenda of what things must get done, does it not?

What if every church business meeting began with a reading of that passage from Paul? What if we pastors, elders, and deacons really believed we were in the midst of a raging spiritual battle in which the stakes, the territory being fought over, are none other than us and our people? What confidence would we place then in our organizational charts, lines of accountability and authority, budget reports, and plans for the Labor Day picnic? My hunch is we'd all be too frightened not to pray. We'd all become foxhole Christians. Can there be any other kind?

It isn't that those business items are trivial; they are to be included in the responsibilities of Christian leaders. They are, however, trivial in comparison to our vocation to be men and women of prayer. To paraphrase Calvin Coolidge's famous remark about the business of America being business, the business of the church is to pray.

The world's pace

The world's view leads to the world's pace. There is a sign reputed to be on the Alaskan Highway that says, "Choose your rut carefully. You'll be in it for the next 200 miles." The view that sees the material reality as all there is, or at least all there is that is worth bothering with, creates a pace that is frantic at times, monotonous at others.

I read an article that created a great deal of anxiety in me. It was entitled "If You Are 35, You Have 500 Days to Live." Subtract the time you will spend sleeping, working, and tending to personal matters such as hygiene, odd chores, eating, and traveling.

In the next thirty-six years you have 500 days of leisure. If this world is all there is, then none of us should waste our time praying. We should literally be grabbing for all the gusto we can get.

We see precisely that all around us. Yet, as leisure time increases, so do the problems of emptiness, boredom, and restlessness. We have, as a culture, a frantic determination to relax, unwind, and have fun. Where an earlier generation may have been compulsive about work, we are compulsive about what we do with our leisure time. Martha has become the patron saint of American recreational life.

Of course, this affects the church. Activists that we are, we all feel there is so much to do and so little time to do it. A sign of our times, religiously, is the fact that Hans Küng's otherwise brilliant theological work *On Being a Christian* did not have a chapter in it on prayer. When asked about its absence, he apologized and admitted it was a serious oversight. But, he explained, at the time of writing he was so harassed by the Vatican and busy trying to meet his publisher's deadline that he simply forgot. That is my point exactly. Prayer is always the first thing to go when we get caught up in the world's pace. And only prayer can deliver us from that pace.

We would do well to take our clues from St. Benedict of Nursia. He founded his Benedictine order as a reaction to the worldliness of the sixth-century church. His slogan was *Ora Labora,* from the Latin *ora,* pray; and *labora,* work. He taught his followers that to pray was to work, and to work was to pray. Following that rule, the Benedictine order broke down the artificial dichotomy between work and prayer. From there they also bridged the gap between the manual arts and the liberal arts, the physical and the intellectual, and the empirical and the speculative. A great tradition developed in which learning, science, agriculture, architecture, and art flourished. Much of what is thought of as beautiful nature in Europe today, particularly in France, was created by the Benedictine monks who drained swamps and cleared forests.

We must learn that prayer is our chief work. Only then can our work become prayer: real service, real accomplishment, real satisfaction. This simple truth alone explains why so many workers in the church find themselves exhausted, stretched to the breaking point, and burned out.

The apostle Paul, when writing to the church at Colossae, wanted to encourage them by telling the things being done on their behalf. He mentioned one of his colleagues, Epaphras, whom he described as "always wrestling in prayer for you, that you may stand firm in all the will of God, mature and fully assured . . . he is *working hard* for you" (Col. 4:12–13 NIV, italics mine). Epaphras's hard work for the church was his earnest prayers on their behalf!

How often has our telling someone we'll pray for them been a cop-out? Meaning we won't do anything that really matters, anything concrete, or meaning we want to maintain a safe distance from them and their need.

Our prayer is our work! Only when that is true for us will our work be prayer: real worship, praise, adoration, and sacrifice. The classical postures of prayer, arms stretched out and hands open, or head bowed and hands folded, are gestures of openness and submission to God. They express perhaps the greatest paradox of prayer: that only when we give up on our human efforts can God's work begin and, mysteriously, human effort can come to fulfillment. As Dr. Hallesby puts it in his book *Prayer,* "Wherever we touch his Almighty arm, some of his omnipotence streams in upon us, into our souls and into our bodies. And not only that, but, through us, it *streams out to others."*

Ora labora.

5

A Heart Close to God

At the heart of ministry is a heart close to God.

—Maxie Dunnam

After I finished seminary in the late 1950s, I organized a new church in Gulfport, Mississippi. From one perspective, it was a huge success. With rapid growth, a new building, and suburban prosperity, the church was the Cinderella of our conference.

But increasingly I was miserable. I felt like an organization man, not a man of God. In the midst of a thriving church setting, I felt far from God. For a while I thought seriously about leaving the ministry. In retrospect, I see I was running on my own power, relying on my own resources. But I didn't know how to do otherwise. There was no question about my commitment to Christ or my call to preach. It was a matter of power, spiritual power: the inner resources for living with a strength not my own. My relationship with God was hardly more than a formality.

Few things are as hollow as a relationship intended for passion that instead is marked by mere duty. When the heat of a couple's romance and honeymoon is cooled by concerns over mortgage payments, child raising, and household chores, the relationship becomes drudgery: husband and wife don't kiss each other at the door; they make love as a matter of routine; they stare past their dinner plates with nothing to talk about.

So it is in ministry. A love relationship, which is what God intends us to have with him, is necessary for a vital ministry. At the heart of ministry is a heart close to God.

More than a feeling

While serving the church in Mississippi, my spiritual rebuilding began. A major step in my pilgrimage came several years later when I found myself with another dilemma—and an opportunity to get closer to God.

I was in California, pastoring another church. I was increasingly getting invitations from across the country to lead conferences and retreats on the subject of spirituality. Then I received two invitations, each to join a parachurch ministry, one as the leader of a retreat center and the other as a staff member of a mission organization. I found myself perplexed: Should I remain in pastoral ministry or move into the parachurch service? What would I do with the rest of my life? I took a retreat to pray through and find direction.

The result was as dramatic as my conversion experience: I felt the Lord telling me to stay put, to remain a pastor. With as much confidence as I've had about anything, I refused both invitations and continued pastoring the California church. In that period, I felt as close to God and as centered in his will as I've ever felt. It illustrates what it means to me to be close to God: at the core, it means having an internal sense of harmony with what God wants me to do.

Early in my spiritual journey (and to some degree now), I depended on the feeling of God's nearness. Though feelings are wonderful and beneficial, I don't want to be dependent on them. Instead of considering how I feel at the moment, I try to discern how centered I am in God's leading. For example, when I pastored in Memphis we elected our first black mayor. Unfortunately, people voted along racial lines, Memphis being 52 percent black. To help unify our city, I felt the white community needed to show our support for our newly elected mayor. So I persuaded the pastors of some of the largest white churches in town to pay for and sign an open letter of support in the local newspaper.

We took some heat for doing that. A few members resigned from my congregation, and the mail and calls from outside my church were pretty tough. That dampened my emotions. Frankly, I didn't feel particularly close to the Lord at the time. I knew, however, I was doing what was right. That certainty assured me that I was with God even though I did not feel close.

Even when I don't know God's will, if I'm at least seeking it earnestly, that is enough. A man and woman who struggle to "get on the same page" often feel closer after they've worked through their difficulties. Waiting on God does the same for me.

I identify with a friend who, after being asked to consider becoming a candidate for bishop in the Methodist church, said, "I'm in the middle of that decision right now, and I'm not getting any direction, but I'm feeling close to the Lord because I'm struggling. I'm dependent. I feel in resonance with the Spirit; while I don't have an answer, I'm where God wants me to be because I'm focused on him."

Distant warning

If feeling close to God is not a sure indicator of one's closeness, neither is a feeling of distance to be equated with a poor relationship with God. So I must have some other signs that signal the strength of our relationship. Here, for me, are some signs the relationship needs help.

I have no heart for ministry. This is key for me. In fact, I'm more concerned about losing my appetite for ministry than I am about burnout; loss of heart can be so spiritually deceptive. A pastor who has lost appetite may perform well, do everything required with finesse and professional skill, and succeed at keeping the church going. But there's no excitement. There's no sitting on the edge of one's seat to share something great God has done recently.

Furthermore, there's no heart for doing the hard thing and no burning concern for missions or outreach, unless the church rolls start to suffer. The void in the pastor's heart may not even be perceived and certainly not confessed.

My church members in Mississippi thought everything was tremendous—after all, we were the fastest growing church in the local Methodist conference. Because the church was doing well, they thought I was doing well. With all the "success" surrounding me, I was tempted sometimes to ignore my inner warning signals and assume that was as good as ministry was going to get.

Although this is perhaps the largest and brightest warning light we should notice, others less ominous are worthy of our attention.

I feel depressed about my spirituality for a significant period of time. In late 1991, I was confronted with a major decision about the course of my ministry. Although I spent extended time daily in prayer and Scripture reading, for two months I was unable to sense any direction from God. I finally got to the point where I was simply numb, unable to progress in my thinking about the decision. I knew then that something was wrong.

My decisions are not well thought through. In this regard, my wife serves as a barometer of my relationship with God. She has an uncanny way of asking the questions that show I've not given enough thought and prayer to certain decisions. She also shows me how I take a simple decision and complicate it, sometimes because I'm seeking to evade God's way of doing something.

My emotions are on edge, inappropriate. I've discovered that the way I respond to telephone calls can be a signal. When I begin to think, *Oh no, another phone call,* or start procrastinating returning phone calls, it's time to stop and assess what's going on. It's likely I no longer have the spiritual resources to meet the demands of my calling.

I have a chronic problem with sleeplessness. Sometimes sleeplessness is God's way of getting our attention. I have been awakened by God to receive some message that I haven't received during my working day. Some of my most meaningful times of prayer and spiritual reflection have come in the early hours of the morning.

But chronic sleeplessness is often a sign to me that I'm not only overworked but also working on my own steam, without depending on God's power.

One recent month was particularly hectic. I spent ten days in Russia, followed by three days at home—one of them a Sunday with full preaching responsibilities—and then two weeks in a demanding denominational General Conference. Though in the weeks following I had time to recover physically, I was still waking up in the middle of the night. That signaled my busyness had affected me spiritually.

Role danger

Just as marriage can both enhance and detract from the romantic passion between a man and a woman, so the pastoral role is both a boon and a bane to spirituality. We are wise to be alert to its possibilities. Being a pastor hinders closeness to God in at least two ways.

First, busyness. Shopkeeping chores, as Eugene Peterson so aptly describes church administrative tasks, and constant interaction with people, all to keep an organization humming, take time, attention, and enormous amounts of energy. That often leaves us little concentrated time to spend with God. If we do attend to the spiritual disciplines in such a ministry, we often do so less because we desire closeness with God and more because we are supposed to: it's our job, all duty and no delight. We can conduct spiritual disciplines like a factory worker punches the clock. We pursue spirituality as a military man pursues stripes on his uniform.

Second, the professional side to ministry. Pastors, in order to do their jobs well, need to learn certain professional skills: how to conduct meetings, how to be diplomatic in all kinds of situations, how to juggle family and ministry, how and when to take community responsibilities. In addition, if we seek to expand our ministry by serving larger and larger parishes and provide increased security for our family, we have to build relationships in the denomination and, probably, attain another advanced degree.

In the process of jumping through all the hoops toward becoming a "professional," though, we may begin losing our passion for prayer. Although no one makes a deliberate decision to eliminate prayer or to stop depending on the Holy Spirit, walking on the path of pastoral professionalism has a way of making us feel less dependent on God.

Hazardous tools

Some of the benefits associated with being a pastor can enhance our relationship with God—or, if misused, can actually
damage it. For instance:

Scheduling freedom. Pastors, more than most professions, have
the ability to set their own schedules. Except for Sunday morning
worship and the monthly board meeting, our time is pretty much
ours to manage.

In some church settings, if we are content to do so, a pastor can
cover the required bases without working especially hard. Pastoral ministry can be the most demanding work or the most
cushy work on earth, depending on what we make of it.

Lots of affirmation. When we do our jobs well, especially
when we respond with compassion to our people, they will affirm
us lavishly. But the amazing thing is we often don't have to do
well for people to praise us. No matter how poorly we do, in fact,
there are always some kindhearted souls in the congregation who
will tell us we're doing great. Whether the praise is due or not, if
we hear enough of it, we may assume that we're God's person,
that all is well with us, when nothing could be farther from the
truth.

Regular contact with the sacred. Whether it's leading a Bible
study or preaching a sermon, opening a meeting in prayer or
closing worship with a benediction, baptizing people or serving
Communion, we're constantly handling holy things. But continual absorption in spiritual things breeds a dullness toward the
sacred. Unless we are humble and pay full attention to what we
are saying and doing, the holy can become routine, and that can
lead to a spiritual dullness that is hard to sharpen.

Relationship builders

Fortunately these spiritual hazards are balanced by the unique
opportunities ministry offers to the spiritual life.

We are regularly confronted with our need for God. My daughter is a hospital chaplain. She became well acquainted with an
older woman who was a cancer patient. One day my daughter

went into her room and sensed she was near death. At a loss what to do, she sat beside the woman's bed and prayed silently for her. Almost unconsciously she began to caress the woman's hair. After a while she started singing to her, singing an old lullaby my wife and I sang to our children when putting them to bed.

In the middle of her singing, my daughter felt a presence in the room and assumed someone had come in the room behind her. She was embarrassed about her singing and hesitated to turn around, but when she did, nobody was there. Kim quickly realized she had sensed the presence of Christ.

Such life-and-death situations, in which human limitations are so apparent, remind us of our utter dependence on God and our need for prayer.

Constant contact with the holy. This, as I mentioned, can be a challenge, but it is also a blessing when approached in the right attitude. For me that means humility.

Take my preaching, for instance, an opportunity to study God's Word and proclaim it to others. To keep this holy event from becoming routine, I'm intentional about being confessional in my preaching. I have found that if publicly I'm fairly vulnerable about my shortcomings and my desires to walk more fully in God's will, that puts demands on me to follow through.

Interaction with "saints." I regularly call on several people in our church for prayer and advice; I especially value their spiritual insights and discernment. One is an older woman with a vocation of intercession. Another is a young couple with a special freshness about their walk with God. In many ways I look to these people as models of spiritual maturity. In my role as pastor, I am privileged to speak with such people often, and that only encourages my spirituality.

Drawing nearer

I have found six things especially helpful in keeping me close to God. Granted, we are each different when it comes to spirituality, but here is what has worked for me.

Attend to the emotional. Pastors can be hindered spiritually by emotional and personality hang-ups. For example, when I first moved to California, I became increasingly insecure about myself. Having been raised in poverty, I felt I lacked education and sufficient exposure to the finer things of life. I felt inferior to others, and that hampered me both emotionally and spiritually. Eventually, I sought a professional counselor and attended a therapy group, which turned things around for me. Getting my emotions straightened out really helped me spiritually: I was able, for instance, to accept God's acceptance of me, no matter my background, and that freed me to start using the gifts I did have for his service.

Practice spiritual disciplines. I often find it helpful to hear how others do this so that I can fine-tune my approach. Here's my procedure: I get up at 6 A.M., put on a pot of coffee (the first discipline!), and go to my study, which is in my home. I begin with intercession for those on my prayer list. Devotional reading follows; often I use a devotional guide along with the Scriptures. Then I spend time in reflection, pondering what I've read, examining my life, listening to the Lord.

Naturally, sometimes this morning time is tremendously rewarding and exciting, with things popping off the page and insights coming left and right. At other times it's dry and seemingly fruitless. But overall, it's worked for me.

Retreats. I schedule two personal retreats a year as "regular maintenance" for my soul, one around my birthday, and another about six months later. In addition, I sometimes need an unscheduled time away to break through a prolonged dry period. Short retreats of one day are usually sufficient.

Practice the presence. When I don't feel God's presence, I've learned the importance of practicing God's presence. For me this most often means sharing God's presence—his love and goodness—with someone else.

A woman in our church was admitted to the Mayo Clinic to await a liver transplant. I wanted to convey the presence of God to her, but I hesitated at first because at the time I wasn't feeling God's presence in my own life. I didn't want to sound artificial to her. But I decided not to wait until I was "in the mood," and I deliberately phoned her to assure her of God's presence in her situation. I practiced God's presence by reaching out to someone else.

John Wesley encouraged Christians to practice "acts of mercy" partly because in many ways we act our way into Christlikeness more than we pray, study, or worship our way into Christlikeness. So by practicing the presence, I incorporate it into my life.

Keep stretched. After preaching and administrating a church for a few years, I face the danger of feeling I'm in control, that I can through mere technique bring about effectiveness and success. To counteract that, I welcome ministries that take me out of my control zone.

On Sunday nights our church holds healing services, where we partake of Communion, anoint people with oil, and pray for them. It's something that has not been usual in my tradition, so I'm on a learning curve as to how to minister through it effectively. Besides, when praying for the sick, I can't feel anything but dependent on God.

Nurture relationships. John Wesley used the term *conferencing* to describe intentional reflection and sharing with others about what God is doing in your life. The most important person with whom I do this is my wife, but I also conference regularly with others.

Two questions I find helpful when meeting with others are: (1) When this week did you feel closest to God? and (2) When did you have a discipleship opportunity, the chance to experience growth yourself or to help others grow, but ignored it? The first question leads to a greater awareness of our experience and relationship with God, and the second sensitizes us to opportunities for growth.

Once in a while I ask my family and fellow workers for feedback. I ask what, in their view, is going well with me and what things I should be cautioned about. Especially when I'm making decisions about God's direction for my life, consulting others helps me accurately hear from God. With big decisions, I can easily get sidetracked by my emotions and desires. In the throes of one major decision, I called a friend and during our conversation asked, "Do you think I'll be happy if I do this?"

"You don't have any right to ask that question," he replied.

That shocked me. But the more I thought about it, the more I saw his point; the question was not happiness but rather fruitfulness and meaning and obedience. I needed to hear that.

I'm happy when the church I serve grows, when ministry expands, when what I do is "successful." But I've learned to see that as secondary. What really sustains my life and ministry is God. The closer I am to him, the more fruitful and satisfying my work is for him.

6

Thankful in a Thankless World

*If we gauge gratitude by the way God has worked in our lives,
then nothing the world withholds can dispel our thanksgiving, and
we can even rejoice in the pettiness of those around us.*

—TERRY MUCK

An old man wistfully reads the Hebrew Scripture's promise of a Messiah to come. Night after night he reads until the light or his energy wanes. Each night he prays, *O, that I could see the Messiah before I die!*

Silence is his only answer. Still he prays.

Then one night he prays and, instead of silence, God answers: *I have heard your prayer. You shall see the Promised One.*

Not sure he has heard correctly, the old man continues his yearning prayer on the nights that follow—yet the answer grows stronger, more firm. *You shall see him. You shall hold him and touch the Messiah.*

Simeon's joy was great. He was probably already an old man when God told him he would not die until he had seen the Messiah. The promised coming of the Savior was ancient, and few really believed it anymore. For a man of Simeon's age, it was too much to hope for. Yet God said it would happen—and the promised day did come.

In the temple Simeon took the baby Jesus in his arms and said, "Sovereign Lord, as you have promised, you now dismiss your servant in peace. For my eyes have seen your salvation, which you have prepared in the sight of all people" (Luke 2:29–30 NIV).

Simeon's experience is the paradigm of true thanksgiving. What better reason for giving thanks to God than the fact that we

have all been given the chance to see the Savior? We have not
held the baby Jesus in our arms, but we have been given the joy
of holding him in our minds and hearts. If every other facet of
our lives were negative—if we were poor, homeless, and friend-
less—we would still have this reason to be thankful: the fact of
Jesus Christ.

Our human nature being what it is, however, very often we
find the fact of Jesus Christ is not enough to help us maintain an
attitude of thanksgiving. Gratitude is one of the most difficult
emotions to express and maintain.

Perhaps our culture is partly to blame. Gratitude is particularly
hard when everything comes easily, when our relative wealth
makes us think we can, by birthright or the sweat of our brow,
get whatever we need. Why should we be thankful when we've
earned it on our own?

For Christian leaders, the problem is even more complex.
Leaders are victims to all the gratitude-limiting pressures of a
wealthy society, but as helping professionals they also suffer the
ingratitude of those they serve, both lay workers and fellow leaders. Christian leaders are assailed from two directions: a sated
society and a sometimes thankless Christian community.

Victims of prosperity

Wealth is not a worldwide phenomenon. Other cultures still
have to struggle to earn their daily bread, to keep their families
warm and safe. Westerners who live in those cultures for even a
short time discover new meaning to the word *gratitude*.

Missionaries are typical.

Franklin and Phileda Nelson went to Burma as missionaries in
the 1940s. They served there eight and a half years before the
government closed the country to further missionary work. They
returned to the United States where Franklin served several
churches in various pastoral roles.

While in Burma they worked among remote tribes, and Franklin found his sense of gratitude for God's providence rekindled:

In the Burmese hill country, the only way to get to remote villages was by "shank mare." (That's walking, in case you've never heard the phrase.) It was not at all uncommon for me to walk twenty miles a day in the dry season. When I got back to the States and worked as a pastor and church leader, I rarely walked a mile a day; the telephone and car made walking unnecessary.

In Burma, if one of us got sick, the nearest hospital was ten days away. In the States, medical care is minutes away. In Burma, we'd go months without bread. Once we asked our daughter Karen to say grace before a meal, and she said, "Why do I have to pray for my daily bread when I don't ever get any?" I have often coveted that experience for our youngest daughter who never had to wonder where her food came from. It's hard to have that sense of helplessness and humility so vital to prayer when you sit down to your daily bread and don't even think about how you got it.

I don't in any way blame people here for not knowing what God can do. We're victims of our prosperity. But I sometimes wish we had a few more hard times so people could experience firsthand how wonderful it is to be totally dependent on God.

Thankless followers

One denominational official lamented that for him one of the hardest things about leadership has been developing lay and professional leaders in churches, only to have them quickly forget "from whence cometh their help" and turn their backs on their benefactors as soon as they begin to make it on their own.

I asked my father, who recently retired after thirty-five years of teaching at a Christian college, if he had any regrets about his fruitful professorial career.

"I guess it would have to be the lack of gratitude by students," he said. "I never had very high expectations about students thanking me. They are in school at a difficult age—late teens and early twenties. Their identity crisis makes it a hard time psychologically for expressing thankfulness. But I did notice a steady decline over the years in what gratitude there was. It was almost as if students were never taught to be thankful. And even though I didn't expect much gratitude, I missed it all the same."

Gratitude is one of those curious emotions that grows or shrivels in direct proportion to the amount we receive from others. Pastors, especially, seem to get caught in the middle of a two-flank attack: our wealthy society discourages it, and the nature of the pastoral task often seems hopeless, helpless, and thankless. Over the past generation or two, a subtle devaluation of the pastoral role has occurred that rivals the devaluation of the dollar. In the same span that has seen the dollar shrink in buying power by almost half, the role of the pastor in the local community has probably shrunk even further. The natural respect once shown is a thing of the past. The gratitude that goes with respect is even less.

Interestingly, you don't find many pastors publicly bemoaning their reduced status. But in terms of their functioning in the community, in terms of their spiritual lives, the danger is that cynicism about the task can subtly creep in and rot the roots of thankfulness.

God-based gratitude

What's the solution? Perhaps to focus on the natural opportunities of Christian leadership, not its shortcomings. The call to ministry is not strictly parallel to other professional career paths. God guides his chosen leaders in profound ways. We sometimes feel frustrated with our inability to discern God's will for our lives. The factor most often overlooked in such cases is that gratitude for guidance is actually one of the things that increases its intensity. Recognition that God has directed in the past is what increases the volume of his voice in the future.

Some helpful insights for gratitude can be found in Deuteronomy 26, which outlines three elements to thanksgiving. The first is a concrete expression of thanks. "Take some of the firstfruits of all that you produce from the soil of the land . . . and [the priest shall] set it down in front of the altar of the LORD your God" (vv. 2–4 NIV). God says that when the Israelites arrive in the land

and have conquered it and are living there, they must present to the Lord the firstfruits from each annual harvest. They are to take it in a basket and hand it to the priest at the temple.

It is almost paradoxical but still true today: giving increases gratitude. Psychologists tell us that the human mind grasps the concrete far more easily than the abstract. By giving a concrete expression of thanks, the abstract reality (our feeling of gratitude), the crucial part, becomes more real to us.

Sometimes the concrete gift is prayer itself. Gib Martin, pastor of Trinity Church in Burien, Washington, said, "Bonhoeffer wrote that the Psalms were God's gift to the church, and when we have nothing else to give God, we can give those back to him in the form of prayers. I have tried that and reaped the benefits."

The second element is to remember difficulties God has seen you through. Verses five to nine say that after the priest has accepted the gifts in the name of God, the people should recite a brief history of their being freed from Egypt and given a new fertile land. In this illustration, the children of Israel remember what it was like to live in Egypt. For us it is the remembrance or recognition of what we are like without God. After all, that is the crucial factor. What is it like not to hold the Messiah in our hearts and minds? Bleak, desolate, hopeless.

One Christian leader said she uses the harder times of her life to combat current crises: "I'm a person who is always ready with plan B or C if plan A doesn't work out. I think my experiences have forced me to develop that attitude. I once had three major surgeries in three months. I had no control over what would happen with my life then. Remembering those brick walls helps me understand God's sovereignty and the potter-clay relationship."

Perhaps for today's Christian leaders, fellowship needs are greater than any other. Most local churches, for example, are one-person pastorates, and most are operated in entrepreneurial fashion. Fellowship languishes under such conditions. No camaraderie with staff, no employer to unload on, no evaluation sessions to tell you how it's going. Ministerial associations usually turn into bragging rather than brainstorming sessions. The minister feels cut off from the warmth of peer support.

Again, Franklin Nelson's experience on the mission field is instructive:

> Like the pastorate in the States, the mission field can be lonely. I remember when our first daughter was born. Several days after her birth I had to visit some villages. It would take two weeks. After a couple of days out I began to feel sorry for myself. I was alone, climbing steep hills, no one to talk to and tell about my new daughter.

> I asked the Lord for some sign that he was with me. I didn't know what I wanted him to do because I didn't know what would help me. As far as I knew, it was impossible to cheer me up. But I asked God to do it anyway.

> The middle of that afternoon I came to a village. It was a new Christian village that was just beginning to get grounded spiritually, so I didn't expect the warm welcome of old friends. But to my surprise, they came out en masse singing a welcome song. I hadn't planned on spending the night there, but they asked me to. They took me to a hut they had cleaned up very nicely. I decided to stay. This overwhelming hospitality and love, totally unexpected, answered my prayer. It was simple, something we expect almost as a matter of course back home. But it was just what I needed at that time.

Remembrances of God's love in good times and bad can stimulate our gratitude.

The third element is to be grateful for what the Lord has made out of us. After reciting the litany of our once-lost-now-found status, the Lord says to "rejoice in all the good things the LORD your God has given to you and your household" (v. 11). Like Simeon who held the baby Jesus and rejoiced, we should be ever aware that God has worked, is working, and will continue to work in our lives.

For Christian leaders, then, the key to developing a deep thankfulness is not to base our gratitude on the uncertain status of wealth and prosperity or the fickle gratitude of those we serve.

The Christian leader's gratitude must be based on a deep satisfaction in ministries faithful to God's will.

Gordon Johnson pastored College Avenue Baptist Church in San Diego. Before coming to California, Gordon had been dean of a Christian college and had held several pastorates. He said:

> Gratitude for me comes only when I focus strictly on what God has done in my life. For example, I pray for guidance more often than anything—and God has always answered. When I was serving a church in Chicago, I had two job offers at once. One was to become dean of students at a Christian college. They asked first, and after interviewing there, I was pretty convinced I would go if the college trustee board approved the call. I went back to Chicago and preached in my church on Sunday morning. After the service representatives from another church in the area came up and asked if they could take me and my family out to dinner. We had no other commitments, so I agreed. At dinner they asked me if I would come to pastor their church. I was thrown into a terrible confusion. Why is God doing this? What is he trying to tell me?
>
> That week an official letter of invitation came from both the church and the college. I prayed about both at length and finally wrote a letter of acceptance to the college and a letter of rejection to the other church. My wife typed the letters, and I remember sitting on the edge of my bed that evening looking at them both. I felt sick, plagued by inner doubt. *You're just getting emotional about this,* I thought. Get them in the mail and that will give you some peace.
>
> I walked to the corner mailbox and dropped the letters in. But when I got back home, I felt sicker and sicker about the whole thing. About eleven o'clock that night I called the post office to see if I could get the letters back. "Too late," they said. They had already gone.
>
> The next morning I called the college president and asked if he would please ignore the letter he was about to receive from me. I did the same with the pastoral search committee. Then I got on a train and went back to the college for one more look. By the end of that visit, I decided being dean of students wasn't for me, and I

turned down their invitation. I also declined the invitation from the other church.

Looking back, I think God used the invitation from the church to get me to rethink the way he was working in my life.

Had Gordon not asked the fundamental question of What is God trying to tell me in this? his prayer for guidance might have been the much more self-centered—*Please, God, which of these offers will be the best for me?*

If we gauge our gratitude on worldly wealth and opportunity, we may someday find ourselves in Franklin Nelson's shoes in Burma with no worldly wealth to celebrate. If we gauge gratitude on the thankfulness of those around us, human nature will disappoint us. Nine of ten healed lepers ran away without even thanking Jesus.

If, however, we gauge gratitude by the way God has worked in our lives, then nothing the world withholds can dispel our thanksgiving, and we can even rejoice in the pettiness of those around us because we can say, "Lord Jesus, thank you for the opportunity of working with these your children so obviously in need of your love."

To those who seek, God provides the grace to be gracious.

PART 3

Exercising Discipline

7

The Disuse, Misuse, Abuse, and Proper Use of Prayer

When I've done my best, only then in prayer can I peacefully accept failure and success and, with Kipling, "treat those two impostors just the same."

—FRED SMITH SR.

Prayer alone will not produce a leader. Paul was a leader but leading in the wrong direction before he learned Christian prayer. Chuck Colson was a great leader in politics before he ever prayed.

But neither can someone be a competent Christian leader without prayer. As healthy plants require rain, so powerful leadership requires prayer. Prayer and Christian leadership unite to bring the blessings of God.

Disuse

Leaders face unique temptations in the area of prayer, and the first is to let it fall into disuse. When spiritual leadership becomes anemic or arrogant through lessened prayer, then prayer gets pushed farther and farther down the organizational agenda. Inevitably comes a leanness of soul even in times of outward success. A current writer says it well: "If I am so successful, why do I feel so phony?"

The problem is, success often lessens our urgency for prayer. As a work gains momentum, the needs in prayer change but not the need for prayer. An organization on a roll needs prayer for direction; a struggling work needs prayer for support to keep it alive. But both organizations need prayer just as much.

Misuse

Busy leaders can sometimes misuse prayer. For example, using prayer for persuasion is a misuse. I served on a corporate board whose president always started the morning meeting with a devotional. Late one night, giving his "good-night prayer," he thanked God for the devotional I was to give the next morning, which he knew he had not mentioned to me. I felt no disrespect to God to interrupt and say, "God, you know I didn't know about this and I'm not going to stay up all night preparing." Everyone laughed after they got over the shock of my interrupting his "prayer." He was not praying; he was making an announcement.

Recently I heard a speaker ask the audience to pray while he spoke. I think this too can be a misuse, for a preacher should ask people to listen, not pray.

Neither can improper lead time be overcome with prayer, for only once do we know of the sun standing still. Leadership through great sermons and Sunday school lessons will not come without preparation, no matter how sincerely we pray. Sermons are preceded by prayer but developed through work. Study to be informed; pray to be wise.

Nor can we pick the wrong people and make up for their incompetence with prayer. Prayer will not turn a donkey into a racehorse, no matter how much we prefer the racehorse to the donkey.

Finally, when leaders become hesitant to make a crucial decision, prayer can be misused as a pious way to procrastinate. Who can criticize a leader who asks for more time so he can pray— even though he is really hiding his fear and indecision? A leader needs to face his fears and indecision, not cover them with a prayer shawl.

Abuse

Stepping over a fine line from misuse is abuse. I see a difference between the two. Misuse comes from ignorance, while abuse comes from the wrong attitude and motive.

I have heard leaders instruct God to bless their plans. This, to me, is abuse, for it is proper to request something from God but not to instruct him.

Sometimes a leader lets followers listen in while he thanks God for telling him what the organization is supposed to do. Often such prayers claim knowing God's will in order to line up followers. I once heard a leader ask for discussion of a program that according to him was the will of God. I refused to enter the discussion, for it is not mine to argue with the will of God.

Prayer is not a substitute for intelligent effort, careful planning, efficient selection of people, or adequate financing. A Christian business leader resigned from a college board because of the repeated calls for "seasons of prayer" to get the college out of financial difficulties. The businessman believed in prayer but not as a substitute for responsible financial management. He told me the board was never given any financial statements or operating figures; in fact, none existed other than the depleted bank account and the unpaid bills. As leaders, we have no right to pray for what we can do, for God has already supplied that need.

Proper use

As important as these dangers in prayer are, however, as leaders we must accent the positive powers of prayer properly used. When I became chairman of the board of Youth for Christ, I remember hearing the old-timers talk about the tremendous blessings that accompanied all-night prayer.

What is the responsible use of prayer?

To ask God to do what we can't do. For example, we cannot permeate our projects with his Spirit, and so we ask him to. Often we are unaware of the need to change direction, so we ask God for wisdom to be given at the right time and to guide us in the right direction.

Other responsible uses of prayer include these: to recognize God as the ultimate leader; to seek his will together, being willing to do it when it appears; to dedicate ourselves before God to our maximum effort.

I have found that proper leadership prayer involves four steps, which often overlap:

1. *Positioning.* Prayer positions me. It reminds me I am not the ultimate leader; the Lord Jesus is. I am a steward, not the owner. Sometimes kneeling physically helps me with this step.

2. *Shifting into neutral.* Prayer becomes most effective when I get fully into "neutral," where I will accept divine leadership. This is the most difficult part of my prayer life.

Leaders usually are strong-willed, opinionated persons who feel awkward and uncomfortable in neutral. It is so much easier to ask God's approval of what we want to do than to say "Thy will be done" and truly mean it.

I've found I must still my thoughts, honestly separate my interest from the ministry interest, and then test in my mind and spirit various options and how they feel to me. If there is time, I let the options simmer overnight or longer. Then I repeat the options, and if one seems to serve the cause better than the others, I know I am ready to get out of neutral and put the machine in motion with a clear conscience.

3. *Dynamic peace.* Tournament golfers settling over a crucial putt block out the amount of money on the putt and think only of making a pure stroke. Often as leaders we must block out our fear of failure or our second-guesses as to what we have decided.

Prayer helps us find a dynamic peace—not a sleepy peace but an exhilarating peace. There is confidence in dynamic peace, and confidence lets me concentrate fully upon the task. Prayer does not improve our basic skill, but it gives us concentration that permits us to do our best.

4. *Acceptance.* When I've done my best, only then in prayer can I peacefully accept failure and success and, with Kipling, "treat those two impostors just the same." A leader prays himself into the conscious presence and will of God so that he accomplishes "my utmost for his highest" and hears the welcoming benediction, "Well done, good and faithful servant."

8

Runaway Mind

My discovery that the human spirit is our organ for God-consciousness gave me not only the power to survive but the energy to thrive in the ministry!

—ROGER BARRIER JR.

I am cursed with a runaway mind. Some call me a worrywart. Others brand me as overly anxious. I'm constantly wondering *What if?* Maybe I inherited the tendency from my mother. More than likely, though, I did it to myself. Maybe it doesn't matter where I got the tendency.

One Saturday night I found myself sitting in tears behind the couch in our den. Sunday morning sermons were fast approaching, and I was in no shape to preach. Something was wrong. My emotions were frayed. I had four ulcers. I had high blood pressure. I had to cry out for help.

Relief techniques

The first call I made was to the head of our church's counseling center.

"I've been waiting for this," he said. "I've already arranged for you to see a counselor who specializes in executive-level stress."

During our fourth session, my new counselor mentioned my tendency to worry. He predicted that, unless I got help, my out-of-control mind could one day destroy my ministry. Ministerial stress is bad enough, he said, without adding self-induced anxiety to it.

"You have what I call a runaway mind," he began. "Every thought initiates a physical circuit of chemical changes in the brain. The more we think the same thought over and over again, the deeper we entrench that circuitry. I like to think of it as a racetrack with horses going around and around. The more we worry, the harder it is to stop the horses."

My counselor equipped me with all sorts of mental tricks for dealing with anxiety. One was to worry as hard and as much as I wanted for ten minutes—but only for ten minutes. After that I had to put my worries into an imaginary file cabinet and move on. This has often brought relief.

A second approach was to imagine the most idyllic scene. Immediately I pictured an oak near a stream in central Texas. Now, when my mind fills with anxiety, I mentally go to the shade of that tree. The water is cool, and the breeze is steady. In my mind I've erected hammocks, napped on pallets, enjoyed picnics, and read books under that tree. When tension strikes in the ministry, a few moments under that tree quiet my heart.

Aided by such techniques, my runaway mind began to come under control, and I got through the crisis. But I soon discovered willpower alone isn't enough.

Slowing the pace

We live in a society of frantic activity. Pastors often seem to be the most hurried, harried people I know. Seventy work-hours per week were normal for me when I began pastoring. My fatigue—and worry—increased daily. My near collapse showed me my pace could not last forever. Fortunately, I had wise leaders who helped slow me down.

As a result, we developed a plan limiting every minister at our church to a fifty-hour workweek (including Sundays). The plan includes time compensation, because stress is cumulative. If some weeks require more than fifty hours, the ministers must balance with fewer hours over the next several weeks. In addition, our pastors must be home seven nights out of every fourteen. Each of us must take off a full twenty-four-hour day each week. It took several months, even years, for some of us to adjust. But we did it.

Soon after implementing the plan, several of our ministers' wives quietly thanked me. They were seeing more of their husbands than they ever thought possible.

As my pace slowed, my overactive mind slowed too. My runaway thoughts were easier to corral. But I had more to learn.

Spirit to spirit

Slowing my work life was one thing, but quieting my mind was another. It's hard to listen for God's still, small voice when I'm thinking about tomorrow's lunch appointment, or next Sunday's sermon, or the balance in my checkbook, or Deacon Jones's surgery that I forgot. On and on go the thoughts. I can travel from my driveway to the rings of Saturn in seconds.

I found some help when I discovered that our brains run at different speeds. When we're in a deep sleep, for example, the brain runs at zero to three cycles per second (the delta wave). As it speeds up to four to seven cycles per second (the theta wave), the brain moves toward increasing levels of wakefulness. The alpha wave, at eight to thirteen cycles per second, is best for our creative and contemplative side, for communing with God and hearing him speak.

Most Americans, however, spend the bulk of their waking hours in the beta-wave level of brain activity. This speed (fourteen to twenty-five cycles per second) is perfectly suited for baking casseroles, going to meetings, and solving problems. However, as we approach the levels above twenty-one cycles per second, we find ourselves operating in a hassled, hurried, frenzied state. I do some of my best worrying here.

Part of the problem is the rapid-fire sensory images of our society, which overload our circuits. Remember when television commercials lasted a full sixty seconds?

Now they last for fifteen with four or five visual images flashing at us per second! The visual and auditory bombardment reminds me of the radio jamming during the Cold War. No wonder we can't hear God's voice!

The journey out of extreme beta-wave living began when my wife and I were sitting at a red light in Pittsburgh. She asked, "Have you ever heard a sermon about the human spirit?"

I hadn't, and I didn't know much about it. So we began to study the Scriptures. I was intrigued by Paul's statement in 1 Corinthians 14:15 (NIV): "I will pray with my spirit . . . [and] with my mind; I will sing with my spirit . . . [and] with my mind." And in 1 Corinthians 2:10–13, Paul writes how the Holy Spirit expresses spiritual words to our human spirit—the Holy Spirit to our spirit.

The study changed my life. I discovered that the human spirit is our organ for God-consciousness, the seat of our communion with God, the deepest part of our innermost being. In this I discovered not only the power to survive but the energy to thrive in the ministry! It gave me access to spiritual power like never before.

Paul encourages us in 2 Corinthians 10:5 to take every thought captive for the glory of Christ. That is essential advice for controlling a runaway mind. But to shut out the distracting noises, I had to acquire new skills to focus my listening habits. I began by sitting quietly in meditation for minutes at a time. Soon minutes turned to quarter-hours, then half-hours, and occasionally an hour. I concentrated on praying slowly through the Scriptures. Then I would sit quietly and listen for God's Spirit to speak.

I believe this is part of what Paul meant when he testified to praying "with [his] spirit." I still pray with my mind—working through a prayer list and consciously considering the things for which I pray. But when the list is complete, I quiet my mind and begin to pray in my spirit. Again and again, God prompts me in my innermost being to pray for people and situations that would normally never come to mind. The most precious times in my life are when God speaks through the Holy Spirit to my human spirit.

The calm in the storm

I no longer need to find a special place to quiet my mind and listen for God. The practice has become a habit I can enjoy at any moment.

Several months after I began the practice of gaining control over my mind, I was leading a particularly difficult elder meeting. My anxiety increased with the tension in the room. Opposite viewpoints were being expressed—and with force. My mind was awash with worry about the outcome. I felt nervous and uncomfortable. I had been here before.

Suddenly, I quieted my mind like I had practiced and sought God deep within. Right in the middle of the fireworks of that elder meeting, the peace of God washed over me and calmed my heart. I was amazed at what God had begun to do in my life.

Later, I began to see how God could speak to me for the sake of ministry. A young mother in our congregation was diagnosed with a life-threatening brain aneurysm. I stopped outside her hospital room and prayed for ministry wisdom. As I was praying, I had an impression deep within my spirit that she was going to be fine. I sensed that God told me she would survive with no complications and be able to raise her children.

She was awake and conscious when I entered. "Surgery is scheduled for Monday," she said. "The doctors must wait for the swelling to go down. There is no guarantee that the artery will hold until then." Fear filled her eyes.

I relayed carefully what I sensed God had told me moments before. Then I stepped out and said, "This sickness is not unto death. Whether the doctors need to operate on Monday or not, you are going to be fine. Be at peace."

I prayed for her healing and recovery with no "ifs, ands, or buts." Over a decade has passed since then, and she has watched her daughters grow up and marry.

The above story is unusual. Usually I have no idea what God intends to do when I pray for the sick. It is not that I do not ask; God seldom tells me. But occasionally, deep in my inner spirit, I sense his peace, and then I am able to pass it on to someone else.

God's voice patterns

Over the years I have developed a checklist to help me distinguish when God is speaking to me. I don't want to be led by my own imaginings. I certainly don't care to be fooled by Satan's temptations, accusations, or deceit.

The following list is not complete or foolproof. No one point, of course, is sufficient in itself to prove or disprove the voice of God. But these principles have helped me discern more accurately the voice of God.

God tends to speak gently. Remember how God spoke to Elijah? God was not in the whirlwind, earthquake, or the fire. "And after the fire came a gentle whisper" (1 Kings 19:12 NIV), and God spoke in the whisper.

Whenever the voice within me drives and demands like a pushy, used-car salesman, God is not speaking. Many times I have discovered that my drivenness to minister for God has more to do with my own agenda than the prompting of God. Either self or Satan tends toward compulsive clamor and loud demands.

God is never pushy; he seldom urges sudden action without giving us time to reason through the issues.

God's voice produces freedom. In Matthew 11:30, Jesus says, "For my yoke is easy and my burden is light" (NIV). How often I hear, "God gave me this heavy burden to reach this city for Christ." I used to pray for big burdens like that—but not anymore! The city needs to be reached for Christ, but the burdened attitude may be more of a hindrance than a help. Satan loves to put people into bondage; God loves to set us free.

God tends to speak while we are consciously seeking him. I remember shaving one morning when I heard this voice tell me that the way to expand our church was to buy the six neighboring houses, bulldoze them, and use the land for parking.

What a disaster that turned out to be! It had not been God's voice. Remember the tenth commandment: "Thou shalt not covet thy neighbour's house" (Exod. 20:17 KJV).

Later, while listening for God's Spirit, I sensed his leading in another building matter. This time I followed the promptings, and God opened several doors for us to purchase and pay off many acres of land.

Both self and Satan often inject thoughts or impressions into my mind when I'm not seeking God. But God's voice usually is heard when we're diligently listening for it.

God speaks with truth. I often say in moments of despair, "I'm no good" or "Nobody loves me" or "I can't do anything right." These are half-truths that come from either self or Satan, but not God.

In marriage counseling, I often meet Christians convinced that God has told them to marry a nonbeliever. That runs counter to God's Word. Whatever voice or prompting they hear is not God; God will never—and cannot—contradict his Word.

God convicts of specific sins. John 16:8 teaches that the Holy Spirit convicts the world of sin, righteousness, and judgment. When God convicts us of sin, the sin is usually specific: "Yesterday at 4:00 P.M. you did such and such." I know exactly what I did and when I did it. Self or Satan, on the other hand, brings a haunting guilt not tied to specific sins. I've often felt accused or had a nagging feeling of guilt. *Why do I feel so guilty?* I think. I don't know; I just feel guilty. These feelings are not from God's Spirit. Often they are from the "accuser of our brethren" (Rev. 12:10 KJV).

God does not confuse. When the trumpet of God sounds, it does not play confusing melodies. When I finished seminary, I began looking to pastor full-time. While I was headed out the door to fly to Denver to candidate at a church, the phone rang. The call was from a pulpit committee in Tucson.

While talking on the phone, I had a deep impression that I was to pastor the church in Tucson. I hung up the phone, turned to my wife, Julie, and said, "We are going to pastor in Tucson."

"I know," she replied. "God told me the same thing while you were on the phone."

Within two weeks, we had moved to Tucson, and we've been there ever since. Since then, I've felt that clarity in other settings. When I feel confused or uncertain about something major, I tend to wait until God's will can be discerned more clearly. Satan, not God, is the author of confusion.

Today my runaway mind is under much better control than the time when I was crying behind the couch. I still worry more than I'd like. But I no longer wonder whether I will survive ministry. I have fingernails again. My ulcers are gone. My blood pressure is down. I know how to relax.

Just ask my wife.

9

Disciplines for the Undisciplined

The greatest need of unstructured people is to accept and celebrate who we are in Christ.

—CHARLES KILLIAN

I grew up with a profound sense of inadequacy at practicing spiritual disciplines.

I remember weeping myself to sleep many nights as a boy, apologizing to God for failing to read enough of the Bible, for not praying enough, or for just not being the person I thought I should be. I saw God as a referee in a black-and-white-striped shirt, ready to call a technical or throw me out of the game. At best, I saw him as a taskmaster shouting, "Back to the yoke. You haven't measured up yet."

I wanted so much to earn the smile of God's approval, and as hard as I worked for it, I never sensed God say, "Good boy, Chuck." I felt as if I failed the test of what a spiritual person should be.

I was raised in a good home; my mother took us to church twice on Sunday and once during the week. Her heart was right, but there was a certain rigidity about our faith. We were scrupulous about religious activity, and every time an altar call was given, I responded. I went forward so many times to be born again I ended up with stretch marks on my soul.

I remember one evening when our small church was holding revival meetings. The evangelist preached that we were the ones who nailed Christ to the cross. That image stuck in my mind, and that evening I cried myself to sleep, apologizing to God for killing his Son.

I didn't understand the unconditional love of God that motivated Christ's sacrifice, that my sin was completely covered by the Atonement, and that grace meant God was neither angry with me nor blaming me for the death of his Son.

For the next thirty years, I labored under perfectionism. This played into my understanding of spiritual disciplines. I always seemed to be a brick short of a load. Regardless of how much or how often I prayed, it was never good enough.

The turning point for me came during a "dark night of the soul" as I realized what my perfectionism was doing to my work, my family, and myself. I began to explore the meaning of grace. For years I had asked, "God, what can I do to be holy?" I struggled, sweated, manipulated, and worked to please God. But I never escaped feeling like the bad little boy who helped kill God's Son.

What finally brought stability and peace to this unstructured person, who today is still somewhat unstructured—and delighted to be so—was the realization that my salvation was Christ's work, not my own. I couldn't save myself, only he could. It was liberating to realize I no longer had to "do" in order to please God, but could simply "be" in Christ, which included my devotional life.

I was forty before that happened, but once I realized what grace was all about, I began to laugh with a holy laughter. My desire to please God through the practice of spiritual disciplines was replaced by a desire to become conformed to the image of Christ. I no longer felt God was holding a whistle or ready to charge me with a foul for failing to measure up in my prayer life or Bible study.

New image

In my long journey to grace, I learned that I was not alone. Many pastors—but not all—struggle in the same area. For some pastors, practicing spiritual disciplines comes naturally. They get up at 5:30 A.M., read five chapters of Scripture (translating one from the original languages), then pray for an hour before their morning run. They journal daily, fast twice a week, and take an annual retreat to a monastery for a week of silence.

For other pastors, perhaps most, it's not that simple. While they pray frequently, both publicly and privately, most of the time their prayers are on the run. They struggle to read the Bible cover to cover in one year, despite the latest systematic reading program they ordered in the mail. They live with persistent feelings of inadequacy over their devotional lives.

Some of the guilt pastors feel results from a distorted view of God.

My wife, Jane, helped me see the true meaning of grace. During one particularly difficult time in our lives, I came home and found our oak coatrack standing in the middle of the hallway. It was covered with yellow ribbons.

A note attached to the tree read, "So what if it's not a real oak tree? Any old tree will do. I love you." Her unconditional love and acceptance broke through to me. I saw for the first time that God loved me in the same way my wife did. It was a marvelous realization.

Naturally spontaneous

When a pastor has difficulty maintaining daily spiritual disciplines, many regard that as the sign of a spiritual problem or character flaw, and for some that may be the case. But for others the explanation may be their basic temperament. Structure comes more naturally to some personality types than others. Some people naturally prefer order and discipline, while others prefer a more spontaneous and unstructured approach to life.

In their book *Prayer and Temperament: Different Prayer Forms for Different Personality Types,* Chester Michael and Marie Norrissey suggest a relationship between our basic temperament and the type of spirituality or prayer that works best for us. I've certainly found that true in my pilgrimage. I am an "unstructured personality," and I have discovered there is more to spirituality than discipline.

Our personality structure is a gift from God, and we ought to celebrate its strengths and potential rather than agonize over its weaknesses and shortcomings. Learning to do that, however, hasn't been easy for me.

The unstructured and the structured person are both healthy and balanced if their life is in Christ. For me to understand and accept my resistance to structure is a measure of balance. I will always be that way to a certain degree, and I need to thank God for the way he made me, even as I struggle for bringing more order to my life. The structured person will always be striving to some degree to break out of a box.

As a result, today my definition of the spiritual disciplines includes but goes beyond the traditional fasting, Bible study, and prayer. It involves any activity that helps me better understand the nature of life in Christ.

For example, when the Mona Lisa was on tour in Washington, D.C., I found myself sitting transfixed for nearly half an hour, engaged by this moving portrait. I sensed I was in the presence of greatness.

How did that help me in my walk with Christ? Two weeks later when I was working on a sermon about the divine mystery and presence that invades us and draws us to God, my experience in Washington, D.C., helped me explain the concept of mystery and presence to my congregation.

I don't mean to suggest God is present in paintings; that's pantheism. But I try to be continually sensitive to the surprising places where God can meet me and teach me more about life in Christ. Engaging in that type of ongoing spiritual observation of life, the "God-hunt" as David Mains calls it, is one form of spiritual discipline.

Unstructured people still should pray, study, and fast on a regular basis, but they shouldn't be in bondage to any particular method or regimen. As soon as maintaining the method becomes more important than knowing Christ himself, it becomes idolatry.

I don't have the same degree of discipline in prayer that John Wesley did. I don't get up at 4:30 or 5:00 A.M. as he did. But I do get up early enough to be alone and spend an hour of quiet in the presence of God, away from the telephones, the noise, and the confusion of life. It's such a peaceful time, and I'm reluctant to bring it to an end.

Prayer shouldn't be restricted to a certain length of time or time of day. It encompasses the totality of life. Jesus said we ought always to pray and never faint. So I'm always praying, whether I'm preaching, teaching, loving my wife, or counseling a student. When I communicate with God even as I go through the routines of life, there's a holiness and sanctity to these moments.

Forced weakness

There is a danger, however, of such a devotional life becoming too experiential and subjective. That's where spiritual accountability is important. While unstructured people resist expectations, they need to put goals and structure in place. A soul mate or friend needs to love me enough to say, "Hey, Chuck, you're copping out. You need to get back to the program."

Like most unstructured people, I resist structure until it's forced on me. One hallmark of my personality is that I don't usually see what God is doing until he's done it. That was the case when I was asked to take an interim pastorate in a neighboring state, while continuing my teaching load. It lasted four years. During that time, I virtually never used an old sermon; everything I preached was fresh that week. The pressure of that situation created a need for a fresh discipline of Bible study, meditation, and prayer that proved enormously beneficial.

While I still try to avoid what I consider the bondage of the predictable, my devotional life was enriched by the structure forced on me by that assignment.

The effort we make to overcome the weaknesses of our personality types does have value. I was the adviser for a student in the doctor of ministry program who wrote his dissertation on the relationship between obesity and spirituality. He studied an aspect of his personality that had given him tremendous difficulties.

When graduation day arrived, I stood next to him and couldn't believe my eyes. In just one year, he had lost ninety pounds. For him, controlling his eating became a spiritual exercise.

You be you

Pastoral ministry presents unique challenges and opportunities for the undisciplined personality.

Pastors who struggle with consistency in their devotional lives may feel like hypocrites when they preach about spiritual disciplines. But we all preach beyond our experience to some degree, particularly if we're preaching the need for radical discipleship to Christ. I don't know anyone who is the full embodiment of what that means. But if we preach desire rather than attainment, we aren't being hypocritical. If I want more structure, even though I haven't attained all that I want, I can legitimately preach.

I used to see the ministry as a place where I could be God's workman. "Watch me today, Lord, and tell me what you think." Now I realize what happens in authentic ministry is the exact opposite. God says to me, "Hey, Chuck, come along and watch *me* work today." Whatever measure of spiritual consistency I achieve is the result of God at work. I don't have to have a spiritual walk that matches someone else's expectations; I just have to be in Christ and allow him to do his work.

The downside to our pietistic tradition in the Western church is that devotionally minded people can become lost in themselves. My spiritual development should not be just for my own sake, but for the sake of the church as well. It is the church that calls me into ministry, that confirms my ordination. It is the church that Jesus is coming for someday.

Those of us who like to fly our own kite need to remember that we don't exist for ourselves but for the glory of God and for the good of the church. That's why growth groups, Bible studies, and Christian education can all have a vital part in building up the spiritual life of the unstructured person.

The greatest need of unstructured people is to accept and celebrate who we are in Christ.

The story of Suszi of Anitole has helped me. As he lay dying, he called one of his disciples to his bedside and whispered, "I shall soon stand before the Great Tribunal. I will not be asked, 'Why weren't you one of the prophets?' or 'Why weren't you Moses?' No, on that day I will simply be asked, 'Why weren't you Suszi? You would have made a good Suszi if you had just let go.' "

My desire is not to be another Praying Hyde or Martin Luther. I simply want to make a good Chuck Killian. That's all God is asking of me.

PART 4

Enlisting Others

10

The Most Challenging Prayer Partner

I'll never forget the relief I felt when my wife said, "I just want a spiritual companion, not a leader."

—Louis McBurney

A sick feeling takes over the pit of my stomach. The pastor's wife I'm counseling has just brought up a topic I'd rather avoid. Nancy is registering hurt at the hands of her pastor-husband—and nailing me in the process.

"I remember how excited I was when we fell in love, and I realized I was going to be married to a minister," she says. "I had always prayed for a godly husband, a man who would be a spiritual leader for me and our children. I was sure Joe would be God's answer to those prayers. We even prayed together on our dates. It gave me such a secure feeling.

"I just don't know what happened. After we married, all of that stopped. Oh, sometimes we still pray together or read the Bible, but only if I insist. That doesn't feel right. I want him to take the leadership for our spiritual life together."

I'm gulping hard and nodding knowingly—too knowingly. I've heard my wife echo similar concerns. One of my frequent failures: not taking initiative for spiritual closeness in marriage.

Why is spiritual intimacy with my wife so easy to avoid?

Reasonable excuses

I've discovered I'm not alone. Most of the ministers we counsel at Marble Retreat also struggle with this problem. Some common explanations have emerged.

The first is the professional exhaustion defense. It goes something like this: "I have to keep up this mask of religiosity almost all the time. From morning till night I'm 'the minister.' I can't just be me. I'm always the one called on to pray everywhere I go. The only other guy who has prayed at Kiwanis in the past four years is Father O'Roarke. Men in the locker room at the health club apologize for cussing in front of me. I'm always expected to have scriptural answers for every question and deliver them with a loving smile.

"I get sick of it. Home is the only place I can relax and be real. I want to share spiritual things with my wife, but quite frankly, when she says, 'Can't we pray together?' I feel attacked. Then I feel guilty. Then I feel angry. Then I just want to escape."

I can't use this excuse, however; I'm a shrink, not a man of the cloth.

However, the second one, the hypocrisy factor, does fit. My wife, Melissa, sees me offering sound spiritual counsel to others, but she knows I'm no saint. Sometimes I'm reluctant to pray with my wife because of this rationale:

"Melissa knows the real me. It's fine to offer holy solutions and wise biblical advice to others, but I can't get away with that at home. She knows I'm not very disciplined. She's seen my temper. She puts up with my pouts.

"She remembers the ways I've hurt her through the years by my selfishness or lust or thoughtless actions. She knows what I've been like as a father to our children. I'd feel like a total hypocrite expounding some Scripture verse to her or offering some pious prayer. She'd crucify me.

"No, it's safer to just play the game. She knows me too well. Maybe someday when I get my act together . . ."

Of course, the problem with that is, I'll never get my act together. I need at least one place I can let down and be real. That seems more necessary than devotions.

The third factor is the spiritual-dwarf syndrome. Many ministers believe, often accurately, that their spouse is a spiritual giant compared to themselves. They feel dwarfed by her deep faith. She doesn't seem to agonize with the same gut-wrenching doubts and questions as he.

Her quietly committed prayer life shines compared to his hasty, often desperate prayers fired off on the run. The Word really seems to speak to her. Ages have passed since he has even read the Scriptures to find God's message for himself, and she wants him to be her "spiritual leader"?

How can he risk the vulnerability that spiritual union would bring? She'd find out how shallow he really is. He feels less dwarfish behind the pulpit. Better stay there. It's definitely safer.

The other day a pastor friend told me, "I hate it when my wife asks me what the Lord has been saying to me. I've been feeling so spiritually dry I'm not sure the Lord even remembers me. He seems to talk to her all the time, and that just makes it worse. I'm ashamed for her to know how far ahead of me she is spiritually."

Entering into real spiritual togetherness is a distinct threat to him.

Holy disharmony

Another obstacle to spiritual intimacy is holy disharmony. Distinctive belief differences or style preferences may create dissonance when you try to pray, worship, or interpret Scripture together. Rather than unifying, it divides. You both agree with Paul that your joy would be complete if you were only of one mind, but that's about all you agree on. Common areas of disagreement include preference for time of day, interpretation of Scripture, devotional style, and issues of trust.

Melissa is a morning person, for example. For her, the most meaningful devotional experiences are flooded by the first rays of the rising sun. I'm pretty convinced, however, that God doesn't wake up till midafternoon. I'm sure the splendor of starlight was created to bathe our expressions of worship. That difference seems trivial until we try to adjust our biological clocks to find a time for devotional togetherness.

If your devotional time together includes reading Scripture, you may find tension in how you interpret what you read. One of you may thoroughly enjoy a lively debate, discussing various interpretations. The other may shrink from such encounters, preferring to find a practical application or an inspiring devotional thought. It is easy for a win-lose dynamic to emerge that quickly poisons the wellspring of shared spirituality. For example, a couple at our retreat just had a doozy of a battle over what Ephesians 5 means regarding a husband's giving himself up for his wife. Her list of ways that apply was much longer than his.

Another difference is style. When praying together, this includes the volume of words, the use of the language of Zion versus the vernacular, who does the praying, what resources are chosen, and what physical posture is preferred. Listening to public prayers in church, I realize the importance of these elements. Just as in corporate worship liturgy, our private devotional styles create a sense of comfort. If our mate's style is too divergent from our own, the feeling of genuine contact with God may be destroyed.

A friend of mine told me once that he couldn't pray with his wife. By the time they finished, he felt his prayer had been rated like an Olympic diver. He usually got only about a 6.0. His wife went on to a 9.5 performance.

The issue of trust encompasses concerns about what to ask God for or depend on yourself to do. Whether God wants to heal our physical illness may raise anxiety. How to seek God's will is often understood differently. Should we take risks in life trusting God to provide for our plans or should we not extend ourselves beyond the provisions God has already provided?

Most of the aspects of trust carry intense emotion, since this is such a foundational element of our personality. Taking a cautious approach seems to be showing a lack of faith for more adventuresome souls, while to more "practical" believers leaps of faith seem irreverently presumptuous.

Is it wise to confess?

Another obstacle is the fear of confession. "Confess your sins to one another so you may be healed" sounds pretty good delivered from the safety of a pulpit. Applying it with your mate is a different matter. Just how confessional can you be without creating hurt or anger or doubt?

I want to be totally open with Melissa, but at times I'm reluctant to disclose all of the sins of my thought life. Can she hear about my lust without feeling rejected? She faces the same dilemma. Can I face her admissions without defensiveness?

Quite honestly, I'd rather confess to God or to my buddy Doug than to my wife.

Let me mention a final, common explanation of why pastors avoid spiritual intimacy with their spouses: spiritual stone-throwing. At times, the only time marriage partners feel safe to confront each other is in prayer or through Scripture.

One pastor's wife told me recently, "I hate to have prayer with John. He begins right away to beseech the Almighty to reveal to me my sins: 'Lord, help Susan with her laziness. Reveal to her how she can be more organized. Create in her a spirit of submissiveness so she can be the godly woman you want her to be. Protect her, Lord, from the evil influences of television and the covetousness that stalks her in the mall.'

"I come away from our prayer time together feeling flagellated and condemned. I think I'd rather be slapped in the face than deal with the guilt he heaps on me disguised as prayer. One of these days, I'm going to pray that the Lord will reveal to him his judgmental attitude and lack of love. In the meantime, I don't want family devotions. Thanks, but no thanks!"

Digging out

So what's to be done? Most clergy couples agree they need the sense of spiritual oneness. Wives particularly crave the feeling of closeness nurtured in those moments of bondedness before the Lord. Avoidance or a frustrated acceptance of failure doesn't bring much peace.

You don't have to remain stuck, though, in the ditch of spiritual estrangement. Here are some steps Melissa and I have found helpful for ourselves and others.

1. *Identify the problem.* Clear an afternoon or evening in your schedule to discuss this area of your relationship. Allow no interruptions, and covenant together to make understanding (not agreement) your goal. Enter the time without your usual agenda of proving who's right and who's wrong. Believe me, you both are—right *and* wrong.

Since who is in control is such a common marital conflict, it's particularly important to take conscious steps to avoid that dynamic. Lay ground rules giving each person time to speak and the responsibility of listening.

I frequently observe marital breakthroughs, when couples suddenly release their old perceptions and assumptions. I hear, "Oh, so that's how you've been feeling," or "I didn't realize you wanted *that.*" When defensiveness is abandoned, it's possible to hear and really understand each other.

Trace the history of your spiritual relationship, recalling the times it went well and the times it didn't work for you. Then try to identify how you've felt inside about having a time of spiritual conversation.

Try not to let time demands be the rationalization. As difficult as it is, I find most people make time for the things that reward them. Push beyond your busy schedules, and search for deeper problems.

Your goal is to understand each other in a nonjudgmental way. You may be uncomfortable with how your mate feels, but accept her perception as the truth from which she acts.

2. *Clarify expectations.* I used to believe Melissa wanted me to be something I'm not. She would talk about her desire for me to be more of a spiritual leader. That sounded pretty overwhelming. So rather than risk embarrassment or failure, I'd avoid even trying. I interpreted her expectation as wanting me to lead in deep discussion of the Scriptures or to expound on some dramatic vision the Lord had given me (a fresh one for each day, of course).

When I finally told her what I thought she craved, she was

flabbergasted. I'll never forget the relief I felt when she said, "Oh, that's not what I want. I just want a spiritual companion, not a leader."

Compare your childhood experiences with family devotions. Most of our expectations germinate in the rich soil of the family garden. The seeds of a disciplined but oppressive system may bear blossoms in marriage that look like weeds to a mate whose family had a freer style. Families who had no devotional patterns at all can create either a hunger for times together with God or a fearful resistance. When your childhood memories clash, then the bouquets of togetherness can lose their fragrance.

Often our expectations are totally unrealistic or simply indescribably vague. We may have developed an image of what spiritual sharing is supposed to look like from some conference or a book we read, but never stopped to define it clearly with our mate.

When our vision doesn't materialize, we get bummed out. Nothing leads more quickly to frustration and disappointment than unmet expectations. When those ideals are present as a hidden agenda and not spelled out clearly, you can predict failure.

3. Renegotiate a contract. When I had a clearer idea of Melissa's expectations, I felt more comfortable working toward an agreement. What would "spiritual companionship" look like to her? What were specific things I could do that would invite her into my soul-life?

As it turned out, what she'd been wanting was much easier than what I'd been assuming. We began to spend a short time at breakfast reading Scripture (usually a paragraph or maybe a chapter), then praying together briefly about our individual concerns. It also helps when I talk about how the Lord is working in my heart. At times we get together for a longer period of prayer or discussion, usually when life's pressures seem to be closing in.

For Melissa the keys were two: that I would show enough interest to initiate spiritual conversation and that I let her peek inside my mind and heart. The first is accomplished by my reaching for the Bible when we finish breakfast. That's not too hard. The second is satisfied by my letting her know my prayer concerns. Looking back, it's sad we made such a difficult problem out of such a simple task.

4. Avoid criticism. You can be sure you're going to blow it somewhere along the way. You'll get busy or be angry with each other, or somebody will have the flu, and then you won't do it the way you intended. When that happens, refuse to place blame and judgment *anywhere*. That's deadly.

A couple at our retreat struggled with bringing some positive change into their lives. Just yesterday, Joe said, "I've discovered I'm really resistant toward trying to change. I find myself feeling a lot of anxiety. I'm afraid that I won't be able to do it right, and then Sue will point out my failure. When that happens, I think, *What's the use?* and look for somewhere to run."

Whatever you do, don't get into a courtroom debate over whose fault it is, or who wants to quit. You can express your sadness that your time has been interrupted. "I really miss our spiritual time together" is enough. You might ask, "How can we get things going again?" If some of the old resistance has redeveloped, start over identifying the causes. Focus on yourself and what you may have contributed. Then apply grace to each other where it's needed.

5. Celebrate your steps toward spiritual oneness. Every time Melissa tells me how good she feels when I initiate sharing, I get a renewed commitment to the process. Our unity is reinforced each time we tell others about the importance of having a soul mate as our spouse—for example, when we're with friends and I tell them that Melissa and I were praying together for them the other day, or when she says, "Louis and I were just reading that Scripture recently."

Those comments are ways we let each other know how satisfying our spiritual closeness is.

Ours has been a rocky pilgrimage to this area. But we're finding a new sense of freedom and safety. Our growing spiritual oneness is helping us enjoy more fully the other dimensions of our lives together, whether long walks hand in hand or our sexual intimacy. It's still not easy, but the strength and joy we experience together make the struggle worthwhile.

11

Contagious Prayer

Effective ethical influence is best served by giving the group plenty of space. It's okay to try to persuade. But never short-circuit the other's freedom to respond.

—EM GRIFFIN

We met the train at three o'clock Sunday afternoon. I went in my official capacity as president of our university chapter of InterVarsity. Joyce, our vice president, was with me. We'd received word that our new IVCF field rep would visit our group that night. We'd been told to pick her up at the train station and spend time with her until the meeting.

To say we were apprehensive is putting too heavy a cast on the situation. But our executive board was used to flying solo. We hadn't seen a staff person for six months, and we weren't sure exactly what it was we were supposed to do with "our leader" until seven o'clock. It turned out that our vague unease was well founded.

As she stepped off the train, she announced, "My name is Angela Thompson. Please call me Angie because we're going to be very close. I'm ready to give you the counsel and advice you've been needing this past year."

We took her to the student union for coffee. She told us she felt Christians shouldn't purchase anything on Sunday so she'd pass. But, she said, we could feel free if we wanted some. As we sat down at the table, she leveled me with an intent gaze and asked, "How's your quiet time?"

Angie meant well, but it was a long four hours.

It would be easy to read these paragraphs and conclude that I see any attempt to influence someone else's devotional life as misguided, foolish, or wrong. Not so. I've told the story of Angie because it introduces the topic of a leader's legitimate attempts to persuade others. As I recall my own spiritual journey, I can see the influence others have had on me. Three separate people have had an impact on my quiet time with Christ, each through a different process of persuasion.

Identification

I became a Christian through the influence of a girl named Ruth. She wasn't the stated leader of our young people's group. As a matter of fact, I was! But in terms of real influence, Ruth had the clout. She was attractive and vivacious, with a contagious enthusiasm for God. For most of us, high school is a time of cliques—trying to be part of the "in crowd," avoiding the outsiders. But Ruth moved from group to group with ease. To her, everyone was a neat friend.

I dated Ruth once or twice at the end of my junior year. It was all very casual, just some good times together. But I wanted it to be more. At the beginning of our senior year, she suggested we go together on a weekend retreat. "We'll have lots of time to do some serious talking," she suggested. My mind was flooded with images of us lying against a Lake Michigan sand dune gazing at the stars, our heads together in deep conversation. "I'm for it," I said.

Surprise! The serious talking we did was about Jesus Christ. Ruth assumed I was a Christian and wanted to help me draw closer to the Lord. She gave me the InterVarsity booklet *Quiet Time*. As we went through it together, she showed her excitement that God not only allows us to pray to him, but he actually desires it. She encouraged me to block out some time each morning to read the Bible and pray. So I did—just as simple as that. And I became a Christian in the process.

I obviously wasn't convinced so much by what Ruth said as by who she was. I was attracted to her and wanted to have a relationship that would go beyond the weekend. I hung on to her every word, the result being that I heard a lot about Jesus. Did I believe what I heard? Yes, but that wasn't the motive for entering the faith. The impetus came from my desire to be close to Ruth.

Now, identification isn't the most noble reason for changing your whole life around. And yet it's often where the action is. Not just in guy-gal relationships, but among friends of the same sex. Paul reminded the Thessalonians that they became followers of him, and through him, Jesus Christ.

A few things have to happen for identification to produce lasting change. You need a leader/persuader who's viewed as attractive and desirable. There's no absolute standard. It's all in the eye of the beholder. The more winsome the source, the greater the pull of identification. Second, the one to be influenced has to define himself in relationship to the attractive person. Sometimes it's a whole-hog desire to be just like his hero, like a star-struck Little Leaguer modeling his every action on Pete Rose, including the way he combs his hair. Other times it's a reciprocal role—lover, employee, disciple, daughter—in which the influenced party tries to live up to the other's expectations. Either way, he has to know what's wanted. Finally, the attractive source will hold sway only as long as the relationship is important to the admirer.

Note that Ruth didn't even know how greatly she affected me. It was only weeks later when I told her that she realized the impact she'd had. That's typical of change that occurs through a process of identification. It appears to happen in an offhand manner.

Identification poses two problems for a leader: the first is that people may have trouble getting past the person to the issue at hand. The man can get in the way of his message. Remember that the other person swallows the point of view whole because it was given by someone he admires. But opinions need to be chewed and digested if they're going to affect the body. Unless the leader makes a point of encouraging folks to question, probe, and even doubt his opinions, that vital nourishment may be lost.

The second problem is an ethical one. When the leader is irresistibly attractive, persuasion through identification is seductive. Søren Kierkegaard tells the parable of a prince who falls in love with a peasant maiden. First he thinks he will bring her to the castle so he can woo her. Plan B is to go to her humble cottage accompanied by his chariots, soldiers, and horses. But he realizes that neither course would be fair. How could she help but be dazzled by such princely splendor? So he resolves to cast off all royal advantage. He dons the garb of a poor woodsman and proceeds to her home to plead his cause.

Kierkegaard presents this story as an analogy of Christ stripping off his prerogatives as God and coming to earth as a mere mortal so men would not be roped into the kingdom of God without an honest chance to say no. But it is equally appropriate as a warning to the attractive leader. You may be held in such high esteem that your idle musing is instantly accepted as gospel truth. It's not a power most of us have, but I've seen it happen once or twice.

But if you avoid these two problems with identification, it can be useful. "If you love Me, keep My commandments," says our Lord (John 14:15 NKJV). That's a pure case of trying to persuade through identification. We've seen that it's a rather simple, straightforward approach to influence. It drew me into the kingdom, so I know it works.

Compliance

I wish I could say I remained constant in my prayer life after becoming a Christian. The first year, I faithfully blocked out fifteen minutes each morning to read Scripture and talk to God. But when I went away to college, I became much more sporadic. I was like the third kind of soil in the parable of the sower. The seed took root, but trouble and persecution choked it out.

I was still a firm believer; it was just that I was totally bankrupt in the spiritual disciplines of prayer, Bible reading, and witness. I came face to face with this problem at the end of my sophomore year.

I've always had a high need to exert influence. I decided I wanted to be president of the Michigan Christian Fellowship. I noticed that the two previous head officers had attended an InterVarsity camp in the summer, so I decided that I'd go to the

Campus-in-the-Woods, a remote camp on an island a few hours
north of Toronto. The camp schedule called for a forty-five-
minute quiet time every morning before breakfast. I thought I'd
go nuts.

I'm an activist. Given my spiritual state, there were a number of
things I'd rather have done than sit on a rock and pray: swim
around the island, play volleyball, repair the door on our cabin,
read a novel, write my girlfriend, talk with people, canoe—almost
anything was preferable to silent meditation. But I was out of
luck. There was a strong pietistic emphasis the whole month. The
main speaker stressed that God was more interested in who we
are than in what we do. While everyone else nodded solemnly,
my every nerve fiber shouted, "No!"

It soon became obvious that I wasn't playing the game. The
camp director took me aside and made the following offer: "Em, I
notice that you aren't taking advantage of our scheduled quiet
time. I'll make a deal with you. You want to speak when we go off
the island to conduct church services in Bracebridge. If you'll
settle down each morning like everyone else, I'll let you give the
children's sermon next week and the sermon the following Sunday."

I was hooked. I wanted to speak in those services so badly I
could taste it. I dutifully climbed up on a rock and read Scripture
for a half-hour. I then shut my eyes to pray for the final fifteen
minutes. Once or twice I'd hear the director tiptoe past.

Surprisingly, it turned out not to be an empty Pharisaical practice. Despite my poor initial attitude, what I read was helpful. I
began to study the life of Christ. I was intrigued by his encounters with people, his teachings, his miracles. My prayers became more balanced. Besides a lot of requests, I began to praise
God for who he was and to confess to him who I was. So all in all,
it worked. The director had what he wanted, and I complied with
his desire that I not disrupt others during the quiet time and that
I engage in prayer and Bible study. And I had what I wanted—I
spoke in the church services.

What I've described is a pure case of compliance. In order to
make it work, the leader has to have control over something the
group member wants. It can be a teacher with grades to give, an

employer with money, or a pastor with the promise of a church office. The desired reward is conditional on proper performance. It's really a "you scratch my back and I'll scratch yours" proposition.

Many of us are uncomfortable with this type of behavior exchange. We see this as nothing less than an overt bribe. But let's be honest about it. What really sticks in our craw is the blatant nature of the transaction. We wouldn't be so bothered if it were done in a more subtle manner.

Each term I ask students in my persuasion course to enlist a new donor to give a pint of blood. Ideally, a person could be recruited by an altruistic appeal: "Think of the life that might be saved by your contribution." As a practical matter, most students resort to compliance. All sorts of incentives are offered: chocolate chip cookies are high on the list, although back rubs, typing services, and cash are not unknown. I once overheard the conclusion of a successful transaction: "So it's agreed," a girl in my class said to a guy. "You give a pint of blood this afternoon, and I'll go out with you tonight." It's the blatant nature of the agreement that makes us squirm.

Personally, I don't have any trouble with compliance as a persuasive technique as long as the behaviors are ethical, both parties openly agree, and there's a parity of power between them. The last condition does not always hold. As leaders, we often operate from a position of privilege. Any time we make an offer that can't be refused, we've violated a person's freedom of choice. But barring this abuse, compliance seems ethically neutral.

There are problems with compliance, however, which trouble me. The first is that it may touch the body but not the soul. There were a number of days when I just pretended to read the Word. Once I even put my Bible cover around a paperback novel. I gave outward compliance to the director's will, but there was no inward conviction that this was really the way to go. Early missionaries to Asia found this compliance with the phenomenon of "rice Christians."

Surveillance is another problem. Persuasion lasts only as long as the guy with the goodies is monitoring our performance. "I have to watch him like a hawk" is the lament of many supervisors who operate by compliance.

I have a final hang-up with using compliance as a habitual style of influence: it can turn us into hypocrites. There's a place for merit badges, brownie points, and cash bonuses; but self-fulfilling prophecy holds sway. If you're convinced I'll only be moved by continually dangling baubles in front of my face, I'll be glad to oblige. I'll toss intrinsic motivation out the window. For the long haul, there has to be a better way. What we need is a way to have influence that will last—even after we're long gone. We want internal commitment that's not dependent on external props. There is such an animal, and it's called internalization.

Internalization

There's a twenty-year gap between my college experience with InterVarsity and the time when it would significantly touch my life again. In many ways I was the same person: an activist who continued to find it easier to talk to someone about Jesus than to get down on my knees and pray to him. There were some significant differences, however. I no longer wanted to get to the top of the organizational mountain just because it was there. People had become more important than programs or power. Close friendships had first call on my time.

I also had what I considered a second conversion experience, a new insight into the kingdom of God. I became convinced that our Lord had a special identification with the poor, the hungry, the oppressed, the hurting. It was this conviction that led me to attend Washington '80, an Urbana-type convention sponsored by InterVarsity. Instead of dealing with worldwide evangelism, the conference focused on the concerns of the city.

I came to Washington '80 with my own agenda. I knew God wanted me to get involved with the plight of the poor, but I was struggling to figure out how to serve without falling into the trap of paternalism. I had an even greater need. I was pretty well strung out in terms of energy. The demands of teaching, family life, friendships, writing, competitive sports, church responsibilities, and speaking had brought me to the point of emotional burnout. I wanted some relief. It was with these needs very much up-front in my life that I was influenced by Bill Leslie, pastor of LaSalle Street Church in Chicago. It's a church whose programs include evangelism, discipling, tutoring, an emergency food pantry, care for the shut-in elderly, job training and search, legal aid services, and aid for unwed mothers. All of these services are offered not only in the name of Jesus Christ, but in a spirit of love that has brought many to the Savior. This is why InterVarsity brought Bill to Washington to lead a seminar.

I sat in on Bill's session; it was good. Afterward I sought Bill out and said I'd like to get together and talk. We met twice within the next day and a half. The last morning, we had breakfast together. We sat at the table so long after eating that the waitress offered us a luncheon menu. Most of the time I talked and Bill listened.

I shared the changes that God had begun to work in me. Although I started with an account of my journey toward helping the poor and hurting, Bill's sensitive ear soon picked up the fact that I was hurting too. The continual hectic pace of life I had adopted was beginning to take its toll. Our second time together, Bill shared his own tendency to overschedule, overextend, and to be overwhelmed by the pressures on him. He suggested that the only way he could survive was through some periodic times of concentrated prayer and meditation. He stressed also that social action unaccompanied by an inner worship would quickly degenerate to an empty do-goodism. Times of contemplation were necessary as a wellspring of power.

I was impressed. But I figured this was a special gift he had. Different strokes for different folks, you know, and that was one ability that was far from me. We agreed we had the start of what could be a budding friendship, and vowed to get together along with our wives when we returned to Chicago.

The exhausting work pattern didn't let up. If anything, I was dashing from one thing to another more than ever. It was a month before the Leslies and the Griffins could mesh their schedules. During that time I thought a lot about what Bill had said. I picked up a book on the spiritual disciplines of prayer, meditation, and fasting. I was intrigued by the spiritual depths promised to the believer who pursued these means of grace. I was ready to give it a try.

When we finally met together as couples, I pumped Bill for advice on the specific route to go. He recommended blocking out a day or so for a personal retreat. While it would be possible to do this on my own, perhaps I'd find it helpful to have some direction. I agreed, not knowing exactly where he was going. Then he laid out a specific proposal.

He knew of a conference center where you could stay for various lengths of time. In fact, it was less than ten miles from my home. I could make a thirty-six-hour silent retreat without the interruptions of phones, upcoming appointments, or classroom responsibilities. He suggested the name of a person there whose vocation was spiritual direction. Bill didn't push it; he just gave me the center's phone number and suggested I consider the possibility. So that's what I did, and ended up taking his advice— length of time, place, spiritual director, and all.

It turned out to be a turning point in my prayer life. For the first time, I was able to meditate on a verse of Scripture and listen for that still, small voice of God. Instead of flooding heaven with a bunch of junk mail, I learned to concentrate on a single attribute of God and to taste that for a long period of time. I came away edified and refreshed. I will do it again without Bill's urging. More important, I've incorporated some of the meditation techniques into my daily quiet time. That's internalization.

The first thing to notice about the process is that it's made me a true believer. This is different from compliance, in which internal conviction doesn't match outward behavior. Or from identification, in which the belief is more in the person than the idea. Nor is continued belief or action dependent on Bill Leslie hovering over my shoulder to check up on me. Obviously, this is the kind of influence a leader would like to have.

In the pecking order of persuasion, compliance is at the bottom. It borders on the raw use of power and takes continual use of resources and energy to maintain. Identification is a good step up, but is dependent on the desire for a relationship. Internalization is the home run of influence. It's the ultimate aim of a sensitive Christian leader. The person really believes.

How does it work? In the first place, it takes a credible leader. He has to have some recognizable expertise so his words will have the ring of truth. That was Bill. He'd won my respect by the quality of his deeds. His actions spoke louder than words.

The next requirement is that the person being changed has to have some specific needs or desires that are up-front in his life. In my case, I desperately wanted to be effective over the long haul in serving the poor. Equally important, I wanted to get off my high-speed treadmill. Bill's suggestion tapped into these felt needs. It wasn't just a happy coincidence. By being a good listener, he was able to spot these desires. He then tied his advice into my over-riding values. Even though his solution was outside my previous experience, I was hooked.

Unless you see yourself as a mere coordinator, at least part of your job as a leader involves persuasion.

You have to select a strategy of influence. It is necessary for you to put yourself into the shoes of the persons you're trying to move. From their perspective, compliance doesn't look too great. Sure, they get something they want, but their actions are in no way linked to their conviction. They could easily turn bitter or cynical when they see themselves going through motions they don't believe in. It's not wrong per se to try to induce compliance. It may be the only option open to the leader who hasn't had the opportunity to develop a friendship with the group. But it would be wrong to stay there. Part of loving people is appealing to the highest, most noble thing that turns them on.

Can action taken through compliance turn into identification or internalization? Sure. This happened to me when I took a seminar in "Integration of Faith and Learning" at my college. The school decreed that it was a necessary part of getting tenure. So there I was—sheer compliance.

The leader of the seminar was an exciting scholar. I was attracted by his quest for learning, his encyclopedic knowledge, his ability to ask a penetrating question. I wanted to please him, to look good in his eyes. Compliance gave way to identification.

My topic was ethics of communication. As I got into the subject matter, I forged an ethical position that for me had the ring of truth. I felt a growing urge to translate this ivory-tower theory into a moral stance that would grab the man on the street. It became an obsession. The last two weeks of the seminar, I'd sit down to eat with a book in my lap. I'd wake up in the morning having dreamed about the stuff. Identification with the instructor was no longer the issue. I wanted to do it because I thought it was worth doing.

The conversion of my motivation to a higher plane happened because I had some freedom within the requirements of the seminar. Suppose the leader had put together a lockstep assignment that left no room for deviation. I would have done what was demanded in order to get tenure—but moaned and groaned every step of the way. I think my work would have been rather slipshod. But he gave me some room, and it made all the difference.

It doesn't take a son of a son of a prophet to conclude that effective ethical influence is best served by giving the group plenty of space. Freedom of choice—that's what Bill Leslie really gave me. It led to the most lasting results. It's okay to try to persuade. But never short-circuit the other's freedom to respond. Responsible means able-to-respond.

Too bad Angela Thompson didn't realize that when she stepped off the train.

12

Keeping Connected to the Power

*Spiritual power comes through experiencing God's presence, and
God's presence is found in sustained prayer.*

—JIM CYMBALA

One Sunday in our church services, a choir member—a former
drug addict who was HIV positive—told how she came to Christ.
She described in raw detail the horrors of her former life. A street
person named David stood in the back, listening closely.

The meeting ended, and I was exhausted. After giving and
giving, I had just started to unwind when I saw David coming my
way.

I'm so tired, I thought. *Now this guy's going to hit me up for
money.*

When David got close, the smell took my breath away—a mix-
ture of urine, sweat, garbage, and alcohol. After a few words, I
reached into my pocket and pulled out a couple of dollars for
him. I'm sure my posture communicated, *Here's some money. Now
get out of here.*

David looked at me intently, put his finger in my face, and
said, "Look, I don't want your money. I'm going to die out there. I
want the Jesus this girl talked about."

I paused, then looked up, closed my eyes, and said, "God,
forgive me." For a few moments, I stood with my eyes closed,
feeling soiled and cheap. Then a change came over me. I began to
feel his hurt, to see him as someone Christ had brought into the
church for that moment.

I spread out my arms, and we embraced. Holding his head to

my chest, I talked to him about his life and about Christ. But they weren't just words. I felt them. I loved him. That smell—I don't know how to explain it—it had almost made me sick before, but it became beautiful to me. I reveled in what had been repulsive.

I felt for him what Paul felt for the Thessalonians: "We were gentle among you, like a mother caring for her little children. We loved you so much that we were delighted to share with you not only the gospel of God but our lives as well, because you had become so dear to us" (1 Thess. 2:7–8 NIV). God put that kind of love in me.

The secret to Paul's ministry was what I felt that night. That divine love became supernatural power.

The minute my attitude changed, David knew it. He responded, and the gospel got through to David that night.

No matter where you serve or what challenges you face, no one can sustain a life-giving ministry without spiritual power. But how do we define spiritual power? What is it like to experience it? Can we do anything to seek more of God's power?

Baptism of love

When I think of spiritual power, I often think of a baptism of love. My wife and I have found that without the new baptisms of compassion and love God gives us, we would leave New York City and all its problems in a second.

Paul urged the Ephesians to be filled constantly with the Spirit. I have no desire to argue doctrinally about what that means; all I know is, if God doesn't do that for me, I stop caring. Often, when I hear about one more child molestation case, I want to say, "I don't want to deal with this anymore." Left to Jim Cymbala, I am not capable of continuing to care.

We deal with stuff that is so overwhelming. A guy said to me, "Pastor, what do I do? I killed this guy five months ago, and I don't know if the cops are looking for me or not."

"Killed a guy! What do you mean you killed a guy?"

"I shot him. You know, I needed money—the crack thing."

Hear enough of those stories, and you build a wall. You don't want to take the pain home because it will affect your wife and your children, but if you don't feel the pain, your ministry becomes mechanical.

When I'm looking at people through God's eyes and I'm feeling how Christ feels, then spiritual power can flow through me to them.

At the end of one church service, a fifty-year-old, three-decade alcoholic named Victor walked forward to the altar area. I knew him fairly well. He lived in the parks.

His hair was matted; he'd been drinking. He had been in a fight with a cop and gotten hurt. The gauze on his hand was so filthy he would have been better off with none.

It was the end of our third Sunday service, and I was seated on the platform. I didn't have the energy to get up to go to him, so I waved for him to come and sit beside me. As we were talking, I noticed a bulge in his ankle. I said, "Victor, what in the world . . ."

He pulled his pants leg higher, and his calf was so hideous I couldn't look at it. It was like elephantiasis.

"You're going to die," I said. "You're going to die, Victor. You're going to die."

Victor just nodded.

I didn't know what to do. So I held his hand and silently prayed, *God, what do I do? I don't even know how to pray.* As I waited on God, I began to experience what Paul described: "I am again in the pains of childbirth until Christ is formed in you" (Gal. 4:19 NIV).

I began to weep, and then so did Victor. After we sat holding hands and weeping for several minutes, I referred him to one of my associates. I never said a word in prayer.

But minutes later Victor committed his life to Christ, and he has never been the same. Somehow the truth we had told him so many times before about who Jesus was and what God could do finally got through. For the past three years, he has worked for the church in the maintenance department.

Power surge

When I came to Brooklyn Tabernacle at age twenty-eight, the church numbered under twenty people. The situation at first was so depressing, I didn't want to come to services, and I was in charge!

We struggled to make ends meet. The first Sunday offering was $85. I made $3,800 my first year here and $5,200 the second. I had a second job, and my wife had to find work.

After two years I got a cough in my chest I couldn't shake. For weeks I was spitting up phlegm, unable to go to a doctor because we didn't have money or health insurance. Finally I went to my in-laws' home in Florida to see if the sun and some rest would help me.

One day, sitting in a fishing boat, I prayed, "Lord, one book says buses are the key to building a church. Another book says cell groups meeting in homes is the key. Another, multiple elder-ship. Another, releasing people from demons.

"Lord, what do I do? I'm in New York City with people dying all around me. You couldn't have put Carol and me here to do nothing. But God, how can we get their attention? How can we get conviction of sin?"

Then God spoke to me in the closest thing to an audible voice I've ever experienced. The Lord told me if my wife and I would lead the people to pray and to wait on him, he would take care of every sermon I needed to preach (which I was very insecure about), he would supply all the money we needed, both person-ally and as a church, and no building we used would be large enough to contain all the people he would send in.

When I returned to New York, I told the congregation, "The barometer of our church is now going to be the prayer meeting. The key to our future as a church will be our calling on God to release his miraculous power among us."

We need continual outpourings of the Spirit. Jesus promises, "How much more will your Father in heaven give the Holy Spirit to those who ask him!" (Luke 11:13 NIV).

When God does pour out his Spirit, expect for him to also save souls. Acts 11:21 (NIV) says that when a group of Christians went to Antioch and preached the gospel, "The Lord's hand was with them." What was the sign that the Lord's hand was with them? It says "a great number of people believed and turned to the Lord." That's what we want to pray for.

At that time our prayer meeting had maybe fifteen people attending. In that weekly meeting, we began to wait on the Lord, and God gave us the gift of prayer. Worship and praise took hold. We saw that in direct proportion to the liberty God gave us in prayer, things happened: unsaved loved ones started getting converted. Other people came in—we didn't know from where.

Every Sunday since that day eighteen years ago, we have announced that on Tuesday evening the doors open for our most important service, the one we look forward to most, the prayer meeting.

Spiritual power comes through experiencing God's presence, and God's presence is found in sustained prayer.

Arrow to the heart

One misunderstanding about spiritual power is that grace comes to people primarily through the sermon or through understanding sound doctrine.

I talk to pastor after pastor who is sound in doctrine and teaches it well but who admits something is missing. Their churches are plagued by rampant divorce or young people slipping off into a worldly life style.

The spiritual power the church needs is not released primarily through the sermon but by coming to "the throne of grace" in prayer. Hebrews 4:16 says, "Let us then approach the throne of grace with confidence, so that we may receive mercy and find grace to help us in our time of need" (NIV). The sermon is supposed to be an arrow that directs the heart to God so he can minister fresh strength at the throne of grace.

I was at a meeting where the preacher gave an outstanding message. I could tell God had dealt with him through this passage. When he finished his sermon, the congregation applauded, and it was quickly announced that a special luncheon would immediately begin in another room.

What! I thought. *We're leaving? After that sermon we're going to go out and have a meal?*

I was thinking, *I would almost jump off this balcony in order to have somebody pray for me. Let me call out to God. Let me ask God to forgive me for what I've been convicted of. Let me get to the throne of grace.*

We truly lift up Jesus when our preaching leads people to call out to Jesus, when we point them to prayer and his personal dealing with their souls.

How can you have a New Testament meeting without a time for prayer after the sermon? Making the sermon the centerpiece of a service doesn't seem to fit with Jesus' words in Matthew 21:13: "My house will be called a house of prayer" (NIV). R. A. Torrey, former president of Moody Bible Institute, wrote that the Word of God alone will not break a self-righteous, proud person. You have to get him or her into the presence of God.

Too many church services have become a lecture series. The Christian church was born not in a clever sermon but in a prayer meeting. The difference between a lecture and a sermon is that the sermon calls for response, and the response must include prayer.

Irresistible force

Until age sixteen, my oldest daughter was a model child. But then she got away from the Lord and became involved with a godless young man. She eventually moved out of our house and later became pregnant.

We went through a dark tunnel for two and a half years. While wonderful things were happening at the church—we were renting Radio City Music Hall for large outreaches and starting other churches, and many were coming to Christ—no one knew I was hanging by a thread. I often cried from the minute I left my house till I got to the church door, thinking, *God, how can I get through three meetings today? My daughter . . .*

But I didn't want to make my need the focus. People are coming to the church because of *their* needs. Many live in ghettos, in violent, non-Christian homes.

During those years when Chrissy was away, the verse "My grace is sufficient for you, for my power is made perfect in weakness" (2 Cor. 12:9 NIV) became real to me, though I was weak emotionally.

My wife went through an especially dark time. The enemy attacked her with the thought, *So you're going to stay in New York City and influence a lot of people? Fine, but I'll have all your children. I've got one, and now I'm coming for the other two.*

Carol told me, "I can't take this sitting down. You can leave the church with me or stay, but I'm taking my other two kids. I've got to get out of this environment. I'm going to save our children. You can't do this to them."

I half agreed. But then I thought, *If I move, not knowing for certain that it's God's will, what will my next move be?* If you violate God's will, where does that end?

Carol's dad, a retired pastor, counseled her to stay: "Carol, it doesn't matter where you go. It won't change Chrissy." Somehow God held us there and overruled our weakness.

During those days, whenever the phone rang, my stomach tensed. I didn't approach the situation right with Carol most of the time, which made it worse. Many Sunday mornings I woke up feeling I couldn't go to church.

It's scary how many times while driving to the church I thought, *I'm making a U-turn, and I'm not coming back. I can't do this anymore.*

But when I got into the church building, a peace would hold me, and I could get through the day. Then Carol had to have a hysterectomy. There in the hospital at her lowest moment, God ministered to her, and she wrote a song called, "He's Been Faithful," which of all her songs has had the greatest impact on people.

That was a turning point for her.

After Chrissy had been away for two years, I again spent some time in Florida. I said to God, "I've been battling, crying, screaming, arguing, and maneuvering with Chrissy. No more arguing, no more talking. It's you and me. I'm just going to intercede for my daughter."

I told Carol to stay in touch with our daughter, because I was no longer going to talk to Chrissy; I would only pray.

I stayed in Florida until God brought me to a new realm of faith. When I returned to New York I stopped reacting as before to the discouraging things Chrissy did. I found I could praise God even though the news from her was getting worse. It wasn't positive thinking; it was faith.

Four months later, in February, we were in our Tuesday night prayer meeting (the choir and the church leadership now knew about Chrissy), when an usher passed a note to me. It was from a young woman in the church whom I felt was spiritual: "Pastor Cymbala, I feel deeply impressed that we are to stop the meeting and pray for your daughter."

Lord, is this really you? I prayed within myself. *I don't want to make myself the focus.*

At that moment Chrissy was at a friend's home somewhere in Brooklyn with her baby.

I interrupted the meeting and had everyone stand. "My daughter thinks up is down, white is black, and black is white," I said. "Someone has sent me a note saying that we are to pray for her, and I take this as being from the Lord."

Some of the leaders of the church joined me, and the church began to pray. The room soon felt like the labor room in a hospital. The people called out to God with incredible intensity.

When I got home later, I said to my wife, "It's over."

"What's over?" Carol said.

"It's over with Chrissy," I replied. "When we went to the throne of grace, something happened in the heavenly places."

Thirty-six hours later, I was standing in the bathroom shaving. My wife burst into the room. "Chrissy's here," she said. "You'd better go downstairs."

"I don't know . . ." I said, having intentionally kept my distance from Chrissy for four months.

"Trust me. Go downstairs," my wife replied.

I wiped off the shaving cream. I walked to the kitchen, and there was my daughter, nineteen years old, on her knees, weeping. She grabbed my leg and said, "Daddy, I've sinned against God. I've sinned against you. I've sinned against myself. Daddy, who was praying on Tuesday night?"

"What do you mean? What happened?" I said.

"I was sleeping," she said. "God woke me up in the middle of the night, and he showed me I was heading toward this pit, this chasm, and Daddy, I got so afraid. I saw myself for what I am. But then God showed me he hadn't given up on me."

I looked at my daughter and saw the face of the daughter we raised. Not the hardened face of the last few years. So Chrissy and our granddaughter moved back into our home.

That was several years ago. Today she's directing the music program at a Bible school and was married this past year to a man from our church.

If a church sincerely calls out to God week after week, "God, come and help us," is it possible, is it feasible, that God will ignore that plea? I don't think so. He's drawn by that. His ear is always open to our cry.

Our prayers are an irresistible force. I'm not what I ought to be, our church isn't all it should be, but there's something about calling on God that changes everything.

Section 2:
Deepening Your Ministry Through Personal Growth

People grow old only by deserting their ideals. Years may wrinkle the skin, but to give up interest wrinkles the soul. Worry, self-doubt, self-distrust, fear, and despair; these are the long, long years that bow the head and turn the growing spirit back to dust.

—Douglas MacArthur

PART 5

Evaluating Risk

13

Perils of the Professionally Holy

The call to pastoral holiness, then, is right. It's reasonable. It's also ridiculous.

—Mark Galli

Pick a century, any century, and you'll find lots of good advice given to pastors. In the sixth century, for instance, Pope Gregory, "the Great," wrote a whole book for pastors called *Pastoral Care,* in which he outlined the ideal pastoral life style, or what some might call pulpit-committee utopia.

The pastor, he wrote, "must devote himself entirely to setting an ideal of living. He must die to all passions of the flesh and . . . lead a spiritual life."

All well and good if you stick to generalities. Gregory doesn't.

"He must have put aside worldly prosperity; he must fear no adversity, desire only what is interior. . . . He is not led to covet the goods of others, but is bounteous in giving of his own."

Certainly. Well, most of the time, anyway.

"He is quickly moved by a compassionate heart to forgive, yet never so diverted from perfect rectitude as to forgive beyond what is proper."

Let's just say we manage this delicate balance, uh, every so often.

"He does no unlawful act himself while deploring those of others, as if they were his own. In the affection of his own heart he sympathizes with the frailties of others, and so rejoices in the good done by his neighbor, as though the progress made were his own."

No tasty resentment of spiteful elders? No gossip or jealousy of Pastor Homogeneous at Mega-Growth Community Church?

"In all that he does, he sets an example so inspiring to others, that in their regard he has no cause to be ashamed of his past. He so studies to live as to be able to water the dry hearts of others with the streams of instruction imparted."

Yeah, and the Pope is Protestant.

Yet Gregory is right. This is precisely what it means to be a pastor or Christian leader, because this is what it means to be a Christian. It's only reasonable to expect teachers of Christian virtues and leaders of Christian congregations to be first to model Christian behaviors.

The call to pastoral holiness, then, is right. It's reasonable. It's also ridiculous.

Not because Christian leaders are slothful, though sometimes we are. Not because we don't care, though sometimes we don't. No, most of the time, we fall short of holiness because we strive so diligently for holiness. Bonaventure, the great Franciscan leader, put it this way: "The devil is most eager to worm his way in where he recognizes that people are trying to live virtuously; he wants to seek out the innocent man and destroy him just where he was hoping to give himself to God's service."

This is especially true of those involved in "full-time Christian service." In his book *The Unpredictable Plant,* Eugene Peterson writes, "The moment any of us embarks on work that deals with our fellow humans at the core and depths of being where God and sin and holiness are at issue, we become at that same moment subject to countless dangers, interferences, pretenses, and errors that we would have been quite safe from otherwise. So-called 'spiritual work' exposes us to spiritual sins."

Spiritual sins

Christian leaders usually fret about the sins that stroll down the center of Soul Boulevard:

"I need to forgive the chairman for those remarks."

"If I were more disciplined during the week, I wouldn't have to come in on my day off."

"Can't I counsel an attractive woman without fantasizing about her?"

Fleshly sins—anger, sloth, lust—are at least obvious. No mistaking what's going on here. These are SINS.

Spiritual sins, though, come disguised as virtues—virtues we Christian leaders long to attain. But they are sins nonetheless. I'm talking about hypocrisy and pride.

Take hypocrisy, which comes in a variety of forms.

In some cases, for instance, we start calling evil *good*. Gregory the Great said that with pastors "vices commonly masquerade as virtues. Often, for instance, a niggard passes himself off as frugal, while one who is prodigal conceals his character when he calls himself open-handed. Often inordinate laxity is believed to be kindness, and unbridled anger passes as the virtue of spiritual zeal."

We've all seen "prophetic" preachers who are just angry young men. Some who dally at men's breakfasts and women's coffees ("I just love to be with my people") are merely procrastinating necessary paperwork. Others who lock themselves in their offices, scrutinizing commentaries ("Just honing my gift of teaching"), are simply avoiding hospital calls.

Euphemisms are another form of hypocrisy. Since real Christian leaders never get angry, we can go for months without calling it such. The chairman of the board has undermined my proposal for a new midweek youth program. Afterward, flushed with emotion, I say, "I'm not angry with the chairman, just concerned about the youth." Or "I'm just grieved for the chairman's attitude." Or "I'm burdened for the future of the church." Right.

Euphemisms quickly slide into lying. In a sermon, I say, "I just read *Prayer* by Richard Foster, and he says . . ."—in fact, I skimmed only the first and last chapter searching for a sermon quote.

I say, "I couldn't reach you today"—actually I never tried, so of course I couldn't.

I say, "I think you would make a wonderful fifth-grade Sunday school teacher"—I really mean, "You'd make a wonderful, warm-bodied baby-sitter for a class I'm desperate to staff."

The pressures to be holy, to lead righteously are so enormous that we sometimes start practicing a double standard—the ultimate form of hypocrisy.

One youth minister tells about hearing a speaker at a youth convention who gave a well-reasoned sermon arguing that the Bible is without error not only when it talks about faith, but also when it speaks about history, geography, science, or any subject. The speaker didn't qualify the statement; he allowed no exceptions.

Later in a small-group session with leaders of the conference, the speaker was asked if you could really claim the Bible is authoritative on all scientific matters. The speaker replied by talking about the parable of the mustard seed, which Jesus described as "the smallest seed you plant in the ground" (Mark 4:31 NIV).

"We know, of course," the speaker said, "that a mustard seed is not the smallest seed. The celery seed is smaller. We know that. You have to use common sense when you read the Bible. God is just saying in that parable that a very small thing becomes a very big thing."

The group sat in stunned silence, says the youth minister. The speaker didn't realize he had contradicted what he had argued in his sermon. Suddenly, there were qualifications and exceptions. When asked about the apparent contradiction, the speaker said, "You cannot tell the general population those kinds of things. If common people feel you have doubts about one part of the Bible, they might perceive the Bible is not accurate."

Many clergy feel that part of the "holy" side of their calling is to pose as an authority figure, to state things categorically even when they themselves have questions and doubts. Some proclaim a tithe and give only 5 percent ("But my whole life is given to God"). Others condemn gambling and then buy lottery tickets ("Well, it's not as if I'm poor and can't afford it; it's just a harmless diversion for me").

And so grows the spiritual sin of hypocrisy.

The other spiritual sin is pride. Like hypocrisy, pride often looks and feels like commitment, devotion, and sacrifice for the kingdom; like hypocrisy, self-righteousness takes many wily forms.

Holier than them

One October, our worship committee meeting began on a sour note: the senior pastor of our southern California church fumed while he waited for tardy committee members. The Los Angeles Dodgers were battling in the World Series, and the committee members were—he just knew it—catching the last few innings of game three.

"These people!" he sighed to me, an intern at the time. "I like baseball as well as the next guy, but if I can take the trouble to be here on time, they can too."

In a few minutes, the members drifted in, chattering about this hit and that catch. "Do you mind if we get started now?" the pastor snapped.

This incident and others convinced me this pastor thought himself superior to his parishioners. He tried to be patient with their interests in sports and crocheting and drag racing, but it was clear that since his priorities were kingdom priorities, he was more committed to Christ than they were.

I looked down on this pastor (snubbing the spiritual snob!) until I became a pastor. Members went skiing on winter weekends; they chose the garden club over prayer meetings; they thought themselves sacrificial when they tithed 2 percent of their income. Some days, I was furious.

Noticing the difference in commitment isn't the problem; it's getting angry about it that signals self-righteousness. Most pastors are, in fact, more committed than church members to the church, and for good reasons: one, they wouldn't have entered the pastorate otherwise; two, pastors get paid to eat, sleep, and breathe the church.

In the course of my ministry, then, I noticed people's lesser commitment, and my usual response was understanding ("These people have their own callings, and being on this committee is just one facet"), and compassion ("I'll bet after working a full day, it's no fun to come to a church meeting").

When I became angry about the difference, that should have signaled a problem in me, not them. And the problem more times than not was pride and self-righteousness.

I also noticed a holier-than-them attitude creeping within me when I thought about my colleagues in ministry.

In my first call, I served as an associate pastor of the largest Protestant church in the city. Without my knowing it, I began to equate the social dynamics of my setting (dynamic demographics, oodles of programs, sophisticated parishioners) with the spiritual dynamics of ministry.

I once took a drive to the country and passed through a small town with only one church. I was depressed as I left and tried to figure out why. I discovered I pitied the pastor of that church. He ministered to the same, simple people for years on end (no one was moving into this community!). He could offer few dynamic programs to his tiny congregation. He had no hope of church growth. *How does he keep himself motivated for ministry here?* I wondered. *Poor guy.*

It took me a few years—and a move to a small church—to realize how patronizing I had been. I couldn't imagine that ministry could be effective except based on my suburban assumptions. Unfortunately, I felt I was on the cutting edge of Jesus' work in the world. Pity the rest of the church.

Since then, I've become more sensitive to the patronizing comments of pastors of large churches: "Ah, yes. My favorite years in ministry were when I served that rural church in Sycamore, Illinois." (Then why didn't you stay in small-church ministry?)

"The pressures in the large church are so enormous. Sometimes I long for the simple days of pastoring a smaller church." (Ergo: "Now I'm sophisticated and adultlike, and someday you will be, too, if you work as hard as I do.")

"I admire those brothers and sisters who labor in the small vineyards without much recognition." (In other words, "You're good little pastors.")

I once interviewed a pastor of a large church whose view of

small-church pastors ("Bless their hearts. I love them," he said repeatedly) could be summarized in three words: *those poor jerks.*

After my move to a small church, though, I noticed the opposite self-righteous dynamic take effect. Suddenly, pastors of large churches were success driven; they were infatuated with numbers and graphs and indifferent to people and their spiritual needs; they strove to build organizations rather than kingdom communities. Et cetera, et cetera. I, of course, ministered out of purer motives.

Regardless of size of church, we're pretty good at finding ways to put ourselves above others. This is an especially strong temptation when we hear that another pastor has fallen morally, let's say, committing adultery. Our initial reaction is shock: "I can't believe it! How could he have done that? He seemed like a man of integrity."

For some, this is the healthy shock of recognition. Just as another's death suddenly reminds us of our mortality, another's adultery dramatizes our moral weakness. When a colleague falls, some of us fall to our knees, begging God to keep us from such sins.

For others, shock comes because a mentor has fallen. They may be saying, "I thought better of this colleague, whom I've always looked up to." This may lead to a new appreciation of the doctrine of sin. Or it may lead, as it did for me once, to despising the fallen mentor: "All these years I looked up to him while he was doing that. That fraud!" In my bitterness, I assumed I would never do such a thing.

For others still, shock is an act, especially if a prominent minister has fallen. Underneath the righteous facade runs a smug and triumphant jealousy, which somehow justifies our relative righteousness. I know whereof I speak. The old moral insight remains valid: hearing of others' more blatant evils tends to make us feel good. Unfortunately, this is especially true of those whose very identity and calling is tied to living holy lives.

Possessor of gnosis

Pastors spend a lot of time with knowledge, with truth. We read about the doctrine of God's sovereignty; we ponder biomedical ethics; we scrutinize God's revelation in holy Scripture. You would think that an intense acquaintance with truth would nurture humility. Sometimes it does; often it does not.

Helmut Thielicke, the great German theologian and pastor, spoke of the dark side of knowledge when he addressed students of theology:

> Truth seduces us very easily into a kind of joy of possession: I have comprehended this and that, learned it, understood it. Knowledge is power. I am therefore more than the other man who does not know this and that. I have greater possibilities and also greater temptations. Anyone who deals with truth—as we theologians certainly do—succumbs all too easily to the psychology of the possessor. But love is the opposite of the will to possess. It is self-giving. It boasteth not itself, but humbleth itself.

Though this temptation is stronger in the early years of ministry, I'm not convinced we're ever through with it. It doesn't help that church members defer to you when, in casual conversation, the subject concerns the Bible, morality, or theology: "Pastor, you're the expert. What do you think?" Nor does it help that, in fact, we know a lot more about these "sacred" subjects than do our people. We're acquainted with truths that should make living the Christian life easier.

It's not the fact of our greater knowledge that's the problem, but the posture we assume as a result. Take a related example: table manners. It bothers me to eat with a man who chews with his mouth open. If I'm loving, my attitude is, *He doesn't know what he's doing. I wonder how I can gently tell him.* If I'm haughty, I think, *Boy, is this guy ignorant. What a slob!* When it comes to spiritual knowledge, our congregations can become to us either lost sheep who need a gentle shepherd or just stupid goats.

Worse still is to use knowledge as a weapon to show people, especially opponents, their utter ignorance, at least compared to you. If someone tries to argue a fine point from Romans 9, I can trounce her with, "I see what you're saying. But C. K. Barrett wouldn't agree, nor would the great Ernst Kasemann. I will grant you that C. E. B. Cranfield is ambivalent here. But I think the most incisive argument comes from Karl Barth's classic theological commentary . . ." Game, set, match.

Thielicke notes:

> Truth is employed as a means to personal triumph and at the same time as a means to kill, which is in the starkest possible contrast with love. It produces a few years later that sort of minister who operates not to instruct but to destroy his church. And if the elders, the church, and the young people begin to groan, if they protest to the church authorities, and finally stay away from worship, this young man is still Pharisaical enough not to listen one bit.

The ground of all ministry

Perhaps the most subtle form of self-righteousness is described by Eugene Peterson in his book *The Unpredictable Plant:*

> In our ministerial vocation we embark on a career of creating, saving, and blessing on behalf of God. . . . It is compelling work: a world in need, a world in pain, friends and neighbors and strangers in trouble—and all of them in need of compassion and food, healing and witness, confrontation and consolation and redemption.

Because we are motivated by Christ, by his grace and forgiveness, because our goals are defined by kingdom values, it rarely occurs to us that in this spiritual work anything could go wrong. But something always does. For some reason, in our zeal to fulfill the agenda of our Savior, we forget our own need of daily salvation.

> At first it is nearly invisible, this split between our need of the Savior and our work for the Savior. We *feel* so good, so grateful, so *saved.* And these people around us are in such need. We throw ourselves recklessly into the fray.

Our ministries begin to deteriorate from there, says Peterson, so that it isn't long before we end up identifying our work with Christ's work, so much so

> that Christ himself recedes into the shadows and our work is spot-
> lighted at center stage. Because the work is so compelling, so en-
> gaging—so *right*—we work with what feels like divine energy. One
> day we find ourselves (or others find us) worked into the ground.
> The work may be wonderful, but we ourselves turn out to be not
> so wonderful, becoming cranky, exhausted, pushy, and patroniz-
> ing in the process.

In substituting our power for the power of the Holy Spirit, our goals for the goals of Christ, our all-too-human work for the work of God, we've succumbed to pride—at its most subtle, per-haps, but also in its most malevolent disguise.

Graceful attention

Hypocrisy and self-righteousness, then, are the special sins of ministry, so it shouldn't surprise us that these were the sins that most concerned Jesus. When he criticized religious leaders—really the only people he was severe with—he never chastised them for sloth or lust. Instead, he pointed to their hypocrisy and pride, the dangerous sins.

Part of the reason they're dangerous, of course, is that spiritual sins are not easy to defeat. They cannot be attacked directly. The more we make humility our aim, for instance, the more we're tempted to become proud of the humility we attain. One step forward, two steps back.

There is a more excellent way. The key, at least according to the church's best spiritual guides through the centuries, is grace-ful attention to our souls. Some have called it *spiritual direction,* others *contemplation.* In any case, as Eugene Peterson notes, it's the antidote to pride, and its cousin, hypocrisy: "The alternative to acting like gods who have no need of God is to become con-templative pastors."

Contemplation includes prayer and worship, but more centrally, it means taking time regularly to pay attention to what God is doing within and around us. To practice it effectively requires two things.

First, we need to find time to be alone, no small achievement for the modern pastor. Still, it is a minimum requirement. In his classic, *The Imitation of Christ,* Thomas à Kempis writes:

> Whoever intends to come to an inward fixing of his heart upon God and to have the grace of devotion must with our Saviour Christ withdraw from the world. No man can safely mingle among people save he who would gladly be solitary if he could.

Later he adds:

> Our Lord and his angels will draw near and abide with those who, for the love of virtue, withdraw themselves from their acquaintances and from their worldly friends. It is better that a man be solitary and take good heed of himself than that, forgetting himself, he perform miracles in the world.

Second, and even more critical, we need to practice a graceful contemplation. The spiritual sins are not conquered with gritted teeth. The harder we try to conquer them, in fact, the more we'll despair. A baseball player doesn't break out of a slump by swinging harder and harder.

Instead, contemplation, in the classic sense, is a *graceful* attention to our lives. For instance, let's say I've made a vow, as I often have, not to live a hurried life. I want to manage my days so I have time for prayer and for people, and for the many interruptions that may be divine opportunities.

A phone call one afternoon, though, leads me to teach my son's midweek Bible study class. Sunday, I agree to join a task force planning the new Christian education wing. The next week, I promise a friend I'll help him move.

Soon, I've packed my schedule as I always pack my schedule. I find myself rising early not to pray but to get to work. I don't chat with coworkers but stay huddled in my office. At home, I snap at my children and am cool with my wife.

Then I remember: *I wasn't going to do all this!* So I start brow-beating myself: *You idiot! How did you get talked into all these commitments? What were you thinking? Now you're hurried, you're impatient, and you're angry. Some Christian!*

I've become impatient with my impatience, and angry with my anger. I had somehow imagined that I could, by a mere act of the will and in a few weeks, conquer a lifelong pattern. That's pride multiplied.

Instead, graceful attention means gentle recognition. Gentle because we're noticing something that a gracious God knew all along. Since he didn't condemn us for it, neither do we need to condemn ourselves:

"Well, Lord, I see I've packed my schedule again, and there is hardly time for prayer anymore, let alone the important people of my life. This was certainly foolish. Forgive me. Help me to sort out exactly why I do this. Help me to accept my foolishness and your grace."

Only when *grace* is the first and last word of contemplation can the scars left by spiritual sins be healed. James I. Packer, in his book *Rediscovering Holiness,* writes:

> Pride blows us up like balloons, but grace punctures our conceit and lets the hot, proud air out of our system. The result . . . is that we shrink, and end up seeing ourselves as less—less nice, less able, less wise, less good, less strong, less steady, less committed, less of a piece—than ever we thought we were. We stop kidding ourselves that we are persons of great importance to the world and to God. . . . We bow to events that rub our noses in the reality of our own weaknesses, and we look to God for strength quietly to cope.

Two areas to contemplate

Everything is open for graceful contemplation, for the omni-present God can meet us anywhere in our lives. We can examine our motives and desires. We can reflect on the language we use to describe our ministry to others. But in particular, here are two areas worth examining regularly.

Pastoral activities. In *The Minister and His Own Soul,* Thomas Hamilton Lewis writes:

> The minister's daily routine, so comforting, so helpful, so blessed to his people, may be his own spiritual vampire. The surgeon becomes increasingly insensitive to suffering in his intentness upon removing it. And that is well for the surgeon and for us. But it is not well for a minister to become dulled in his spiritual sensibilities by ministering so constantly to keep alive the sensibilities of others.

The most troublesome state comes when a pastor,

> praying so much for others finds his prayers not moving his own soul, preaching so much to others and bringing no message to his own soul, serving constantly at the altar and failing to offer up sacrifices first for his own sins.

As a fresh graduate from seminary, having just arrived in the community I was to serve, I met the local Episcopal priest. I was taken aback.

He denigrated preaching: "Don't get your hopes up, young man. It doesn't make much difference."

He made fun of one of his parishioners in the hospital: "Maybe he'll learn a little humility."

He made jokes about Communion, which I won't repeat.

As I was to discover, he was a pastor who administered efficiently the many programs of his church. He visited his people regularly in the hospital. He was a fine preacher, but he had pastored so long, had done these holy tasks so often, he was oblivious to the sacredness of his calling.

Pastors spend a lot of time with the holy: reading the Bible, performing baptisms, serving Communion, praying here, there, and everywhere. The old adage applies: familiarity breeds contempt, more so when it comes to handling things holy.

The only way to throttle familiarity is to pay attention afresh to what has become familiar. Many pastors, therefore, periodically use their own messages to inventory their spiritual lives, or their denomination's prayer books and liturgies as devotional guides. Others meditate on the sacramental elements of water, or wine and bread. Others contemplate the mystery of words, how such intangible things can connect people and God.

God's presence.   When we start paying attention to what is going on in and around us, we start to become aware of God. All contemplation is, in the end, a fresh discovery of God's activity in one's life.

"Spiritual direction is the act of paying attention to God, calling attention to God, being attentive to God in a person or circumstance or situation," writes Eugene Peterson. "A prerequisite is standing back, doing nothing. It opens a quiet eye of adoration. It releases the energetic wonder of faith. It notices the Invisibilities in and beneath and around the Visibilities. It listens for the Silences between the spoken Sounds."

One warm summer night, I lay awake, restless, and lonely for my wife and children, who were away. Rather than picking up a book or writing or watching late-night TV, my first three lines of defense, I went outside and lay on our lawn. I started to pray but then decided just to pay attention to what was going on around me.

I decided to look up. I spend most of my day just looking at my level and below. I see doors and windows and people and cars and the bottom half of buildings. So I consciously tilted my head and looked up. I saw the branches of our maple tree swaying, swaying against a sky dotted with a thousand stars.

I decided to listen. I spend most of my day in my head, listening to my own agenda whirl away, or at best, hearing the words of others. Now I listened to the wind, to rustling leaves, swooshing, brushing, rushing here and there.

I decided to feel, which I rarely have time to do. The warm air glided over my skin. Grass tickled my neck. Firm ground pressed against my back.

Suddenly, and for no more than a few seconds, mystery and beauty were manifest. The universe seemed so fragile, like a glass ornament, yet so wonderful, like a best present of all. I felt insignificant. Yet love pulsed through me, around me. The glory of God. I lay there for many minutes, nearly in tears.

I relate this experience not because it's unusual, but precisely because it is so very usual. Not that it happens to us everyday, but most Christians have had these little epiphanies. The great spiritual teachers of the church tell us that though we cannot control such encounters, we can lead lives—of graceful attention—that can prepare us and make possible such epiphanies.

Paying attention is more than an exercise in moral vigilance. It is not the making of resolutions and willful activity. It is mostly making room for God, and making room for love. The first commandment is not to obey God or to be righteous. It is to love God, which means first to be loved by him.

Only then will we have the courage to contemplate our hypocrisy and gently probe the pride that snakes its way into our souls. Only then will we obtain eyes to see God in, with, and under us, even the ugly us. Only this love makes the moral demands of ministry bearable, even joyful.

"Love is a great and good thing," writes Thomas à Kempis, "and alone makes heavy burdens light and bears in equal balance things pleasing and displeasing. . . . The noble love of Jesus perfectly imprinted in man's soul makes a man do great things, and stirs him always to desire perfection and to grow more and more in grace and goodness."

In the end, the right, reasonable, and ridiculous call to pastoral holiness is mostly the call to know and share this love.

14

Pulling Weeds from Your
Field of Dreams

*Toxic weeds thrive in visions for ministry. A fertile spiritual
imagination is just as good at growing weeds as a crop.*

—DAVE HANSEN

In western Montana, a weed imported from France, spotted
knapweed, plagues some of our best agricultural areas and is
moving swiftly into wilderness areas. Only sheep will eat it. Cattle, deer, and elk won't touch it. A meadow of knapweed won't
support a cow. A hillside of it will not feed elk. An infestation of
knapweed can destroy a hay- or grainfield.

Beekeepers imported the plant for its purple blossoms that produce copious nectar even during drought years. The weed is un-
believably hardy, thriving in the driest of weather. It competes
unfairly with natural flora; it grows over three feet tall so it
shades shorter grasses. But if you clip it, knapweed will blossom
at two inches off the ground.

Its most pernicious characteristic, however, is that knapweed is
allelopathic. Knapweed's roots secrete a toxic substance that
stunts and even kills the plants in its vicinity.

Toxic weeds thrive in visions for ministry too. It is just as true
of spiritual tilth as it is of good dirt: "It will produce thorns and
thistles for you" (Gen. 3:18 NIV). A fertile spiritual imagination is
just as good at growing weeds as a crop. I've noticed at least three
weeds that can flourish in my pastoral visions.

The dream weed

I love being somewhere long enough to watch the kids grow up. I love preaching through whole books of the Bible. I love watching a church grow and change over time. I love presiding at funerals for people I've called on and loved for a long time.

But I really dislike receiving phone calls, back to back, one from Euodia telling me that we should have vacation Bible school in June because that's the only time we can get any teachers, and one from Syntyche saying that we should have VBS in August because three years ago at a Christian ed meeting, didn't we decide always to hold VBS in August to promote Sunday school?

What gripes me is that I know the real problem: these two don't like each other and are playing a game to see with whom I will side.

In such moments sprouts the dream weed, a mental flash, a phantasm from a subconscious reservoir of restlessness. It speaks to our disgust with the mess of the ministry. It shows us a place of benefits without blahs. It may be another church, another career, or just winning the lottery—my kingdom for a day without human foolishness! And of course, it can all be had in a moment, enjoyed in rush-hour traffic or in the middle of a fight at a council meeting.

The dream weed is only a dream away: "I gotta get outta here!"

I'm not naysaying daydreaming. Daydreaming can be an ally of ministry. Put to good use, the ability to live through experiences mentally is great for running through sermons, thinking through pastoral calls, and imagining what might be possible. God gave us the ability to "see" things in our minds.

However, I know this: the mental ability we use for daydreams, which God uses for visions, can be marshalled by our frustrations, our doubts, our anger, our self-pity, and our boredom. When these emotions control our mental scenery, our field of vision fills with dream weeds.

The dream weed is my weed of choice; I know it best. No other weed is this much fun. At Dream Weed University, I've gotten any number of Ph.D.s, been a professor at every seminary in the country, and published hundreds of books and articles.

I've pastored big churches, the mythical kind where all you have to do is hang around with a totally cool staff who do the down-and-dirty work with all the messed-up people. I've had offices where I didn't have to answer the phone, and where three receptionists stood between me and Mr. McBlab, the parishioner with the personality disorder of critiqueophilia.

How do you subdue such weeds?

The best way is through confession and repentance. Confession is simply recognizing a false vision for what it is and speaking to God about it: "Here it is again, Lord; the old dream weed is back." Repentance is simply returning to prayer for the right thing: for people, for the church, for stamina and joy.

Other strategies help. Dream weeds are intolerant of contact with anything specific. Jesus tells us to wash one another's feet. There's nothing dreamy about that. So I call a grump. I go out and bless a curmudgeon. I immerse myself in the details of church work. I fix the leaky toilet in the men's room. I pick the popcorn off the floor from the Wednesday night program. We have a custodian for that. But sometimes I *need* to do it.

Every Sunday morning before people arrive, I sweep the outside walks as metaphoric prayer. God talks to us in parables and metaphors, so I return the favor. I talk to him in a metaphor: "Lord, as I sweep this morning, help me commit myself to washing the feet of this church." Then I take the broom and go up and down the concrete walks, brushing away the gravel, dirt, and bird droppings. I'm sweeping away daydreams. As I sweep, I am parabolically committing myself before God to care for this particular church and these particular people.

With the dream weed gone, I find a reappreciation for my church. With my field of vision cleared, I can see that God has truly been in this place, and that he calls me to work here.

The greed weed

My fifteen-year-old son and I were hunting white-tailed deer on a local cattle ranch. Evan was sitting quietly on a knoll overlooking a hayfield, waiting for game to appear. I sneaked around a section of cottonwood trees, willows, and brambles adjacent to the hayfield and walked through it, hoping to flush a nice buck into the field.

I didn't disturb an animal, but I got covered with burrs. I don't remember seeing the burr-bearing weeds, but when I emerged, my hunter's-orange sweatshirt was covered with spiky burrs the size of Ping-Pong balls. Sharp-pointed foxtails coated my socks; they lost no time working through my cotton socks into the flesh of my ankle.

Rambling through a river bottom, praying for my congregation, I hope to flush out a vision for our corporate life. I never stumble upon a burning bush. I see cottonwood trees and a red-tailed hawk. I hear wind, rushing water, and a Clark's nutcracker.

Visions come like Elijah's still small voice—gentle-whisper visions, unobtrusive projections upon my imagination. They present themselves with the utmost modesty. They don't demand faith; they inspire it. I don't propel them; they propel me. I don't need to flesh them out; they flesh themselves out in me and in my congregation.

When I pray for a parishioner, often I "see" the person in my mind. As I pray for people, often I see them not as they are, but as they could be. I see possibilities for them. I see what their life might become under the lordship of Christ. These little visions don't intrude or demand; they suggest and propose. They are the working capital of my pastoral calling.

Such visions are good, but opportunism clings to them like burrs. In the middle of "seeing" the building made new, the pews full, and our Sunday school bursting at the seams, I also see a mental image of a new fly rod that I could purchase with the raise I'd get if my ministry thrived. It sickens me.

When my spiritual imagination is at its best, I am also at my worst. Hedonism works its way into the fabric of my visions like foxtails into socks.

Too often greed sprouts are treated like playthings, harmless plants. They are not harmless. Greed was the sin of Hophni and Phinehas, the sons of Eli. They looked with "greedy eye" at the sacrifices and offerings of the people of Israel, "fattening themselves" on the choicest parts of the offering. Their sins brought down the house of Eli and destroyed their own lives.

Calling on a ninety-six-year-old blind woman who lives in a tarpaper shack doesn't present a conflict of interest. But put the same woman in a richly decorated home three times bigger than she needs, and visions of discipleship can become stuck with burrs and foxtail visions of big donations.

If the power of ministry is the love of God working in and through us, what happens to our power for ministry when we cast a greedy eye on the sacrifices and offerings? We stop seeing the person; all we see is her money.

Before I make a pastoral call on people with financial resources, I pray through my motivations vigorously and relentlessly. I have to pull the greed weeds. When my mental landscape is congested with greed weeds, I try resetting my timetable for the things I want. Greed has a crude intolerance for delayed gratification. Greed wants it now. I want a new fly rod (they aren't cheap). So I reset my goal for getting a new fly rod by a year. We want to put new windows in the church. Not this year. We must wait. A new computer! Wait. A nice fat raise? Let the little ones build up over time.

Patience pulls greed weeds, and a patient heart is an inhospitable environment for greed weeds. Funny thing is, once the greed weeds are cleared away, love appears. The fruit of the Spirit grows best in a well-cleared field of vision.

The hero weed

An older lady stuffed a note into my hand as she greeted me in line after church. She winked at me. Five years later, serving a different church, I have that note taped to the window in front of my office desk. It reads: "There is no limit to the good you can do, if you don't care who gets the credit."

I don't keep that note for sentimental reasons. It's there because, like most of us, I like being a hero. I like getting credit when things go right. Maybe my sagacious friend knew it.

When we desire hero status in our churches, we become allelopathic to the people who serve with us. Like that toxic weed from France, we may come off as sweet as honey, but we stunt the growth of those around us. The poison of our pride places a limit on the good that we can do, and the good that those around us can do.

My visions are saturated with my face. It is repelling and embarrassing, but I must admit it: I can take a wonderful vision and muddy it with a mental image of my getting credit. What a glorious vision to see a little country church on the brink of closing its doors come to life! What a sad splotch of spilled ink to see myself in front of packed pews basking in the glory of being the one the people came to hear. It's repulsive. But I can't seem to eradicate the problem. Is the answer throwing out vision? If a vision is spoiled by an ego spill, must the picture be thrown out? Can any part of a vision in which I project myself as the hero ever be from God?

It's not a matter of throwing out visions, however. It is a matter of extracting our egos from them. What pulls the hero weed is private prayer.

A parishioner was going through an especially acrimonious divorce. Of course, there were darling children involved. Of course, the couple fought over everything, including the Jimi Hendrix albums. I prayed for all parties involved, but one of them attended church regularly, so I felt for him a special pastoral responsibility.

I wanted to save the day. I felt like it was my job to go in and make a difference. I knew well how my pastoral capital would go up if I had a profound impact on this person's life and he shared it with people. I could "see" their accolades. I became more concerned with the glory for being a good pastor than being filled with love and pity for my suffering friend. That's hard to admit.

A couple of times, I decided to give an afternoon of prayer to the guy. I can't sit still and pray, so I walk. Well, when I took a long walk and prayed for him, I saw myself staying away from him. The vision was odd, unusual. My impression, though vague, was that my whole responsibility was to pray and stay away. Over and over I asked, "Is this right? Am I just supposed to stay away?"

I didn't hear a voice; I just saw myself staying away. "But what if I get called on the carpet for not reaching out to him? Staying away makes me look uncaring." Fear entered in. Ultimately I obeyed the quieter picture of my staying away and just praying for the person. My interest piqued when, after his divorce, his church attendance picked up. A year after the dust settled, I visited the gentleman. We talked about his divorce. As he began, a deep confidence filled his eyes. The bitterness was gone. I knew he'd lived through hell. He recalled the difficult times. He did not dismiss the pain. But he went on to tell me that whenever he was at his lowest point, for some unexplainable reason, God had always shown up.

"When I was all used up and had nothing left, God was just there. He comforted me in my very darkest hours. God has been so good to me!"

This man, who few would have mistaken for a mystic, had learned to pray. He could hardly contain himself.

I could hardly contain myself. I wanted desperately to shout out "I prayed for you! I prayed for you!" Thankfully, I held my tongue and smiled.

Private prayer is therapy for allelopaths.

A cleared field of vision

As we pull the dream weeds, greed weeds, and hero weeds, we find a cleared field ready to produce a crop. True vision for ministry can grow.

In my mind, I can still see nails protruding from badly weathered siding. If you pounded them in, they popped back out. The eighty-year-old wood wasn't worth another coat of white paint. The sanctuary was so poorly insulated that the water in the Christmas tree stand froze every December. Of course, the water pipes froze every winter too. The windows were cracked. The ceiling tiles bore yellow-veined stains from the leaky roof. The concrete steps and sidewalks were decomposing.

I did not pray for the renovation of the sanctuary. Frozen pipes and peeling paint were the least of our problems. But as I walked through the woods praying for the church, in my mind I saw not a broken-down church building, but a clean, white renovated sanctuary. I did not realize it then, but "seeing" the renewed sanctuary was a vision. It was so modest a spiritual phenomenon that I barely took it into account.

These little visions never came as announcements, prophecies, or revelations. At no time did I feel a message had arrived from God to oversee the renewal of the sanctuary. I never thought that seeing a pretty building in my mind constituted a vision. But that gentle, unobtrusive Spirit-whisper became a focus for my ministry at that church.

So I never announced to the church council, "I have had a vision: our sanctuary is going to be made brand new, and we need to start working on it right away." Fixing up the place never became an intentional goal, but for whatever reason, at council we began to talk not about my vision or anybody else's vision; we just started working away at fixing up the building.

Over nine years, little project by little project, the church was made new. We got a new roof. We applied new siding, insulated the walls, installed new exterior doors and double-paned windows. We added handicapped access. We poured concrete sidewalks and steps and painted the sanctuary walls and ceiling. We relandscaped the front yard, planted a new sign, and even insulated the crawlspace under the building so the pipes wouldn't freeze. The sanctuary is now the brilliant white building I saw in my vision. Actually it is prettier than I thought it would be. The fulfillment exceeded the vision in beauty.

No aspect of church life is too spiritual or too material for visions. We need visions for deeper spirituality, more functional buildings, greater passion for God, steadier finances, and more effective Christian education. Seeing these ahead of time (even if not recognized as visions from God) constitutes the pastor's spiritual field of vision. We simply need to clear that field of its weeds.

15

The Approval Addiction

Most of us in ministry have the same set of ego issues as people in any other profession. We just have a different way of keeping score.

—JOHN ORTBERG

Mayor Richard J. Daley, who was as celebrated in Chicago for his malaprops as for his ability to get votes out of corpses, once said of his opponents, "They have vilified me, they have crucified me, yes, they have even criticized me."

Mayor Daley could have been speaking for those of us in ministry. Whether it's politics or the pastorate, not everyone will believe we're wonderful. Criticism, especially "friendly fire," can pull the plug on our motivation and energy. Generally we pastors have a fairly high need to be liked. While not a bad thing, the need for strokes can set us up to have difficulty dealing with criticism.

But if the actions of Jesus and the prophets are any indication, then giving effective spiritual leadership will surely mean doing things that displease the very people whose approval we desire. For most of us, it's only a matter of time (and usually not very much time) before the people we're supposed to serve have vilified, crucified, or even criticized us.

Our strong reaction to such criticism reveals, I believe, a serious addiction problem. It has nothing to do with substance abuse or chemical dependency. It is, rather, a craving for approval. Its primary symptom: the tendency to confuse my "performance in ministry" with my worth as a person; to seek the kind of approval from people that can only satisfy when it comes to God.

This addiction has been around at least as long as the church. Paul thunders against it to the Galatians: "Am I now trying to win the approval of men, or of God? . . . If I were still trying to please men, I would not be a servant of Christ" (1:10 NIV). Even more disturbing is the diagnosis from John about people who were blocked from faith because of this addiction: "They loved praise from men more than praise from God" (12:43 NIV).

Addiction shows up in odd ways and at unwelcome times.

It's four o'clock in the morning. I am awake. Recently I left a secure job with a real church to plant a new one, with no buildings, no offices, no secretaries, no handbell choirs, no professional scaffolding at all, and only six weeks' worth of expenses (including my salary) in the bank. I do some of my best worrying at 4:00 A.M.

Something disturbs me about this particular concern, however. It occurs to me that a good chunk of my apprehension over this venture is not just that if we don't succeed, many people will not meet God, although that's part of it. My anxiety is not just over the financial needs of a family with three small, ravenous children; if worse comes to worst I can fall back on a degree in psychology. (There will always be enough rich, neurotic people to counsel.)

Part of the fear nagging at my heart—a bigger part than I want to admit—is that if we don't succeed, I won't look successful. Recognition, paradoxically, is the first step toward liberation. At least when I become aware of my need to appear successful, I can say, "I refuse to make decisions or hold back on risks based on something as stupid as my need to impress people who most likely are not even thinking about me anyway. I refuse to allow the approval or disapproval of others to determine my worth as a person."

But recognition doesn't make it go away.

The voice within

When I get up to speak on Sunday morning, the congregation hears my voice, but I hear another, more confusing voice in my head. It's also my voice. Sometimes it shouts, *Thus saith the Lord.* But at other times, more often than I care to admit, the voice is less prophetic.

What will they think of me? the voice wonders.

Sometimes I feel less like the prophet Amos and more like Sally Field at the Academy Awards. I find myself desperate to be able to say as she did when she'd won her second Oscar: "You like me! You really like me!" I do not like this Sally Field voice. I wish I had more of a Rhett Butler voice and could greet evaluations at the door with, "Frankly, my dear, I don't give a . . . rip."

When Jesus spoke, he was free from the need to create an impression, free to speak the truth in love. But the voice within me is not free. It is driven by ego and pride. It is ugly to me, and I'd turn it off if I could, but turning it off proves not to be so simple. Where does this voice come from?

In *Lake Wobegon Days,* Garrison Keillor writes about growing up without praise under the theory that compliments cause swelled heads. But the years of emotional malnourishment, far from weaning him away from the need for approval, instead created an insatiable appetite for it:

> Under this thin veneer of modesty lies a monster of greed. I drive away from faint praise, beating my little chest, waiting to be named Sun-God, King of America, Idol of Millions, Bringer of Fire, The Great Haji, Thun-Dar the Boy Giant. I don't want to say, "Thanks, glad you liked it." I want to say, "Rise, my people. Remove your faces from the carpet, stand, look me in the face."

This would make for a rather awkward benediction, however.

Approval and anger

Sociologist George Herbert Meade wrote about the "generalized other," the mental representation we carry inside ourselves of that group of people in whose judgment we measure our success or failure. Our sense of esteem and worth is largely wrapped up in their appraisal of our work.

Your generalized other is a composite of all the Siskels and

Eberts in your life whose thumbs up or thumbs down carries, for you, emotional weight. This may include parents, seminary professors, key lay leaders, or other pastors. My guess is that most of us in ministry have the same set of ego issues as people in any other profession. We just have a different way of keeping score.

When my identity is wrapped up in whether I am perceived as successful, I am set up for the approval addiction, for it is my very sense of self that is on the line.

"Who am I?" Henri Nouwen asks. "I am the one who is liked, praised, admired, disliked, hated, or despised. Whether I am a pianist, a businessman, or a minister, what matters is how I am perceived by my world."

And when my drug of choice is withheld, I respond with the same anger as any other addict: *Don't these people know I have the best interests of the church at heart? Don't they know I could have gone into some other profession and made lots more money?* It's as if I'm entitled to universal trust and consideration.

Nouwen goes on to write:

> Anger in particular seems close to a professional vice in the contemporary ministry. Pastors are angry at their leaders for not leading and at their followers for not following. They are angry at those who do not come to church, and angry at those who do come for coming without enthusiasm.
>
> They are angry at their families, who make them feel guilty, and angry at themselves for not being who they want to be. This is not an open, blatant, roaring anger, but an anger hidden behind the smooth word, the smiling face, and the polite handshake. It is a frozen anger, an anger which settles into a biting resentment and slowly paralyzes a generous heart.
>
> If there is anything that makes the ministry look grim and dull, it is this dark, insidious anger in the servants of Christ.

Wherever it comes from, whenever my craving for approval makes itself known, I'd better pay attention.

One Sunday morning, as I was greeting people at the door, a visitor handed me his card.

"I usually attend Hollywood Presbyterian," he said. "But we're visiting here today. Give me a call sometime."

I looked down at his card—"Speech Instructor."

Hollywood Presbyterian is the home of Lloyd Ogilvie. Lloyd Ogilvie is perfect. His hair is perfect, his robe is perfect, his smile is perfect, but above all, his voice is perfect. Deep as the ocean, rich and resonant, Lloyd Ogilvie sounds like what I expect God will sound like on a really good day. Next to his voice, mine sounds like I'm in perpetual adolescence. It's difficult to feel prophetic when you hear yourself chirping like Mickey Mouse: "Okay, now, let's repent."

When I catch myself comparing myself to others or thinking, *I could be happy if only I had what they have,* then I know I need to withdraw for a while and listen for another voice. Away from the winds, earthquakes, and fires of human recognition, I can again hear the still, small voice, posing the question it always asks of self-absorbed ministers: *What are you doing here?*

I reply by whining about some of my own Ahabs and Jezebels. And the voice gently reminds me, as it has reminded thousands of Elijahs before me, that I am only a small part of a much larger movement, and at the end of the day there is only one King whose approval will matter.

The voice also whispers, *Do not despise your place, your gifts, your voice, for you cannot have another's, and it would not fulfill you if you could.*

Celebrating solitude

To truly care *for* people requires not caring too much *about* their approval or disapproval. Otherwise the temptation to give their preferences too much emotional weight is almost inevitable. To effectively lead people—without being damaged in the process—requires regular withdrawal from the very people I'm trying to lead.

Thomas Merton wrote that the desert fathers considered society to be a shipwreck from which all individuals must swim for their lives. The very pecking orders and ladders of success that I naturally find myself climbing, they fled in horror. In solitude I see the career successes and failures—which look so huge in my day-to-day life—take on a much smaller look from an eternal perspective. ("If you can meet with triumph and disaster," Kipling wrote, "treat those two imposters just the same.") And the development of my soul, which I can lose sight of altogether in my routine strivings, is revealed as the one great task of my life.

Approval addiction involves some irrational thought processes, which solitude helps clear. Psychiatrist David Burns notes it is not another person's approval or compliment that makes me feel good, it is *my belief* that there is validity to the compliment. Suppose you were to visit a psychiatric ward, he imagines, and a patient approaches you: "You are wonderful. I had a vision from God. He told me the thirteenth person to walk through the door would be the Special Messenger. You are the thirteenth, so I know you are God's Chosen One, the Prince of Peace, the Holy of Holies. Let me kiss your shoe."

Most likely your self-esteem-o-meter would not rise. Why not? Because between other people's approval and your pleasure in it is your assessment of the validity of their approval. You are not the passive victim of others' opinions. In fact, their opinions are powerless until you validate them. No one's approval will affect me unless I grant it credibility and status. The same holds true for disapproval.

Several years back, at a previous church, I used to get regular complaints from a parishioner about all aspects of the service, mostly that the music was too loud. When he couldn't get satisfaction from me, he hounded other staff and board members. One afternoon my secretary informed me that I had a visitor from OSHA, the federal watchdog agency. It turned out this same parishioner, as a last resort, asked for government assistance to get the sound system turned down on Sunday mornings. By law, OSHA was required to send someone out.

"Can you imagine the kind of ridicule I've taken all week," the OSHA representative said apologetically, "with people knowing I'm going out to bust a church?"

Though dramatically stated and strongly disapproving, these

complaints didn't bother me at all. They originated from a character who lived on the fringe, as far as I was concerned. I realized from this incident that no one's disapproval can emotionally affect me without my authorization. For me to allow disapproval to subtract from my sense of worth as a human being is both irrational and destructive.

Getting guidance

In addition to solitude, I find it helpful to have another person or two to whom I regularly go for guidance on these issues.

Some time ago I heard from an attender that our church doesn't talk enough about sin.

"Can you imagine that?" I said later to one of my spiritual guides in my nondefensive, emotionally open way. "What he really wants is a sermon series promoting the legalistic, superficial, developmentally arrested approach to morality that will condemn outsiders and reinforce his own self-righteous spiritual smugness."

I waited for my friend to agree with me that this guy had obviously fixated at Kohlberg's lowest stage of moral development (preconventional level—heteronomous morality).

Instead he asked me two pointed questions:

"Well, *do* you preach about sin enough?"

Then, after I had squirmed, he added, "And what is this need you have for everybody to agree with everything you do?"

He forced me to reexamine my own understanding of sin and to proclaim it in a clearer way. He also reminded me that ministry is not about getting people to like me.

A certain amount of discontent is inevitable, and probably even healthy, in any group of people. Not every infection calls for a massive dose of penicillin. Many of the personal hits a pastor takes will be absorbed in the natural flow of events. But at least two types of situations call for criticism to be confronted and refuted.

One is if the criticism affects the health of the body.

I have a friend who pastors with as much sensitivity and integrity as anyone I know. Because of several changes going on in the church, however, he was accused of (among other things) being a megalomaniac. This has about as much validity as charging Mr. Rogers with inciting violence. This criticism, however, went far beyond what his psyche could tolerate. It struck directly at his ability to serve effectively and at the church's trust in its own leadership process. Because it affected the health of the body, this attack had to be handled head-on.

The other time I probably need to respond directly to criticism is—unfortunately—when I don't want to. Recent studies on self-esteem suggest that most issues involving our sense of worth revolve around approach/avoidance tendencies.

That is, when we sense ourselves avoiding something out of fear, we interpret ourselves as wimping out, and our self-esteem drops proportionately. On the other hand, when we approach directly a situation we'd rather avoid (even if we're not particu-larly effective in it), our sense of esteem rises because we did the difficult thing.

At one point early in my ministry, we had a particularly diffi-cult EGR ("extra-grace required," as Carl George calls them) per-son on the governing board. When his term finally expired, I breathed a prayer of thanks. Sometime later I was engaged in what was supposed to be an extended time of prayer, when I realized I was deep into an anger fantasy involving this former board member.

In my anger fantasies, I never torture my opponents too bru-tally, because then I would feel guilty (and that would rob my sense of revenge of its purity). Usually in my fantasies, whomever I'm angry at suddenly realizes with painful, shame-ridden clarity the massive, unfair hurt they've inflicted on me and my family.

"I hope you're satisfied with what you've done," I always say, pouring hot coals upon their too-late repentant heads until they feel like scum.

"I hope when you go home and look in the mirror tonight you can live with what you see."

It occurred to me that I might still be angry with this guy. I realized then I needed to meet with him and discuss it, even if all issues didn't get resolved (they didn't). Otherwise, there would always be that suspicion lurking in the back of my mind that I had avoided a confrontation I needed to have.

The discipline of secrecy

We have yet another weapon in the battle against the approval addiction: the discipline of secrecy.

"Be careful not to do your 'acts of righteousness' before men, to be seen by them," Jesus warned. "If you do, you will have no reward from your Father in heaven" (Matt. 6:1 NIV).

His particular examples relate to financial contributions, fasting, and prayer, but they reflect a deep insight into all of human nature. I used to think Jesus meant God had a reward stored up for me in heaven, but if my motives were self-serving, I would lose it. What he's really talking about, however, is losing the intrinsic power that these good deeds have of helping me enter the life of the kingdom. He was talking to people who were addicted to having their righteousness admired—so addicted, it was impossible for them to enjoy righteousness for its own sake.

If I give my money away, I have less opportunity to become a slave to it, and I can experience true freedom and joy. If I choose to impress people by making sure they know about my generosity, however, the nature of my action changes. I settle for the narcotic of approval, and instead of becoming a little more free, I become a little more enslaved.

On one particularly busy morning at our house, I voluntarily emptied the dishwasher before my wife got up, even though it wasn't in *my* job description. That evening, when she still hadn't commented on it, I tactfully mentioned how fortunate she was to have such a thoughtful husband. At this point, the fundamental character of what I had done was altered. Instead of one tiny action helping me become more like Christ, more like a servant without feeling I had done something extraordinary, it became one more item on a quid pro quo checklist.

Jesus says to do good things without telling anybody about it. Eventually you'll find you lose the need to let people know. And you'll also find you can do good because it really is the most liberating, joyful way to live.

I try to implement this discipline of secrecy regularly in my own life. If I'm going to a meeting where there will be people I perceive as important (my "generalized others"), I try ahead of time to identify the things I'll be tempted to say to impress them, and declare those topics off limits. (I don't get carried away with it, though. You'll notice this chapter didn't get published anonymously.)

Weaning myself from the approval of others is a lifetime project. Its viselike grip on my soul can be broken, however, enabling me, when vilified, crucified, and even criticized, to rest in the approval of the One I serve.

16

Big Shoes to Fill

I want the Lord to burn my mouth. If my mouth is burned with a heaven-sent fire, then the result will be the work of God.

—GARY V. SIMPSON

When I became pastor of Concord Baptist Church, in the heart of Brooklyn, I had an idea of what would be expected of me.

I was not coming as a stranger. I had served as associate pastor there for five years before taking a senior pastorate in New Jersey.

For 149 years, Concord Baptist has had a vibrant community-centered ministry. It has enjoyed a long tradition of positive pastor-congregation relationships. I am only the tenth pastor in the church's history.

Recent history is most impressive. Concord has had as many pastors in its first fifteen years as it has had in the 132 years since. Since 1863, I am the fifth pastor. In all these years, thanks be to God, there have also been no splits nor schisms.

Most of my predecessors enjoyed recognition and accomplishment during their pastorates. My immediate predecessor, Gardner C. Taylor, served for forty-two years, instilling a vision for the church and community from the Concord pulpit. He is a master preacher, an effective leader, my former boss, a friend, and a second father.

Each of these identities presented me both a blessing and burden. I could not help but feel the pressure to live up to such a record.

When I first came to this historic pulpit, I wanted to live up to the legacy of eloquence and profundity that emanated from this station. For five years, I had heard Dr. Taylor preach Sunday after Sunday. I studied him closely. He preached with grandeur and power, eloquent beyond words, and the most awesome part of it was that it appeared almost effortless.

I knew, at least I thought I knew, that this was what the church wanted and needed each Sunday. During my first two years, I worked hard to make my preaching profound. People quoted Dr. Taylor. I wanted to be quotable. I figured that's what it meant to be pastor of Concord Church.

I worked so hard to say something memorable every week that I almost forgot the central focus of the gospel—to say something salvific. But another sermon haunted me, one I heard my father— another great preacher—preach during my youth. It was based on 1 Samuel 17, where Saul gave David his armor and the shepherd boy was dwarfed by the king's equipment that did not fit.

My father's point: "You've got to wear your own armor." That sermon stayed with me as I struggled to make the transition into this historic parish.

Then something happened that redefined my preaching course. For our Watch Meeting on the last night of 1992, I planned to preach from Psalm 51: "Renew a Right Spirit Within Me." I had been very ill over the Christmas holiday. In fact, I had lost my voice after preaching the Sunday before Christmas, and I was not even sure I was going to be able to preach at all for our Watch Meeting.

Besides my feeling physically subpar, I also began to question the message I was going to deliver. Somehow I felt an unction to return to Isaiah 6. I changed the message to "My Prayer for the Church."

In this sermon, I conveyed my earnest sentiments as a pastor— What was it I saw and believed the church should become? When I got to the verse referring to the angels placing the live coals on Isaiah's mouth, the Scripture seemed to be speaking directly to me. That's it! That's what I want. I want the Lord to burn my mouth. Never mind profundity for profundity's sake. If my mouth is burned with a heaven-sent fire, then the result will be the work of God.

Since then I have been preaching more freely from the fire in

my soul, using the gifts—music and a peculiar sense of humor—
that are unique to me.

The wall of the church lounge displays pictures memorializing
each of my pastoral predecessors. Underneath the commissioned
oil portrait of Dr. Taylor is a frame containing a well-worn piece
of the carpet from right behind the pulpit where he stood for
thirty-five years.

Before anchoring in and beginning to speak, he had a habit of
moving his left foot over the carpet. Many a legend began from
this small movement. Some said he was making the sign of the
cross with his foot and thereby standing in the power of the
crucified Lord. Others said he, like a batter, was clearing his own
place and digging in to take his best swing.

On the framed carpet, you can clearly see where his feet made
their impression in the fabric. The engraved label reads: FOOT-
PRINTS OF THE PREACHER, 1955–1990.

Looking at my own size 9s, I am humbled by the reminder of
Dr. Taylor's size 12s that stood firm and strong for so long.

Shortly after I assumed this charge, I walked through the sanctuary and saw one of our custodians behind the pulpit. The scent
of freshly cut carpet filled the air, and there was a new red carpet
where the framed carpet had been. The custodian looked up and
said, "Reverend, it's your carpet now!"

Now, as I step up to that historic pulpit, I have to dig in too. I
know that I'll have some misses and a few hits. But I am firmly
planted and I know I must take my own swings.

PART 6

Taking Measures

17

Reading Your Gauges

*The spiritual and physical aspects of life were important,
but I had failed to consider another area essential to healthy
ministry—emotional strength. I needed a third gauge on the
dashboard of my life.*

—Bill Hybels

For many of the years I've served in ministry, I monitored myself closely in two areas, continually checking two gauges on the
dashboard of my life.

I thought that was enough.

First, I kept an eye on the spiritual gauge, asking myself, *How
am I doing spiritually?* Apart from Christ I can do nothing. I know
that. I don't want my life's efforts to be burned up because they
were done merely through human effort, clever tactics, or gim-
mickry. I am gripped by the fact that I must operate in the power
of the Holy Spirit.

To keep my spiritual gauge where it needs to be, I have committed myself to the spiritual disciplines: journaling, fasting, solitude, sacrifice, study, and others. Like many Christians before
me, I have discovered that these disciplines clarify spiritual issues
and pump a high-octane fuel, providing intensity and strength for
ministry.

Even though the pace of ministry has dramatically quickened
in the past few years, I honestly don't think I often misread my
spiritual gauges. Looking at my life's dashboard, I can tell when I
am spiritually half-full, three-quarters full, or, sometimes, full.

When I'm full spiritually, I can look at my life and honestly say
I love Jesus Christ and I'm attending to my spiritual disciplines
and keeping myself open to the leading of Christ. When I'm spiri-

tually full, I don't need to apologize for my motives. I can truly
say: "I'm not in ministry because it gives me strokes. I'm excited
about the fruit being borne through the ministry of Willow
Creek."

Second, I have monitored the physical gauge—How am I doing
physically? I know that if I push my body too hard, over time I
will experience a physical breakdown or psychosomatic complications associated with high stress.

If I don't exercise, eat properly, and rest, I will offer the Lord
only about two-thirds of the energy I have the potential of giving.
The Holy Spirit tugs at me to be wholly available—mind, soul,
and body—for the work to which he has called me.

Consequently, I have committed myself to the physical disciplines of running and weight lifting. I closely watch what I eat.
And I receive regular medical checkups.

Near crash

Since these spiritual and physical gauges—the only two on my
dashboard—have consistently signaled "go," I have pushed myself as hard and fast as possible. But then a different part of my
engine began to misfire.

While preparing for a particularly difficult series of sermons,
the message that week wouldn't come together. No matter how
hard I tried, no ideas seemed worth saying. Suddenly I found
myself sobbing with my head on my desk.

I've always been more analytic than emotional, so when I
stopped crying, I said to myself, *I don't think that was natural.*
People who know my rational bent laugh when I tell them that.
Individuals more aware of their feelings might have known what
was wrong, but I didn't.

All I knew was, *Something's not right with me, and I don't even
have time now to think about it. I'll have to journal about this tomorrow.* I forced my thoughts back to the sermon and managed to
put something together for the service.

But the next morning as I wrote in my journal I considered, *Am
I falling apart in some area spiritually?* My gauges said no. My

practice of the disciplines seemed regular, and I didn't sense a spiritual malaise. *Physically, am I weak or tired?* No, I felt fit.

I concluded that maybe this was my midlife crisis, a phase I would simply have to endure. But four or five similar incidents in the next few weeks continued signaling that my anxiety and frustration could not be ignored.

Then I noticed I was feeling vulnerable—extremely temptable—in areas where I hadn't felt vulnerable for a long time. And the idea of continuing on in ministry seemed nothing but a tremendous burden. Where had the joy gone? I couldn't bear the thought of twenty more years of this.

Maybe God is calling me to a different kind of work, I thought. *Maybe he's getting my attention by these breakdowns in order to lead me to a different ministry. Maybe I should start another church or go back into a career in the marketplace.*

At that time, the church was deciding whether to take on a major building expansion, which intensified my feelings. I knew that if we moved ahead, it would be unconscionable for me to leave the senior pastorate until the expansion was complete. Yet when I looked honestly at whether I wanted to sign up for another three or four years, the answer scared me. It was a big fat no.

You don't feel like it anymore? I asked myself in disbelief. *You want to bail out? What is happening to you?* Maybe I did need a change of calling.

Whatever it was, I was astounded that I could be coming apart, because I put so much stock in the spiritual and physical gauges, and neither of them was indicating any problem.

Overlooked gauge

After a Christmas vacation that didn't change my feelings, I began to seriously inspect my life. After talking with some respected people, I learned that I had overlooked an important gauge. The spiritual and physical aspects of life were important, but I had failed to consider another area essential to healthy ministry—emotional strength.

I was so emotionally depleted I couldn't even discern the activity or the call of God on my life. I needed a third gauge on the dashboard of my life.

Throughout a given week of ministry, I slowly began to realize, certain activities drain my emotional reservoir. I now call these experiences IMAs—Intensive Ministry Activities.

An IMA may be a confrontation, an intense counseling session, an exhausting teaching session, or a board meeting about significant financial decisions. Preparing and delivering a message on a sensitive topic, which requires extensive research and thought, for instance, wear me down.

The common denominator of these activities is that they sap me, even in only a few hours.

Every leader constantly takes on IMAs. I didn't realize, however, that I could gauge the degree of their impact on me. As a result, I was oblivious to the intense drain I was experiencing.

For example, many times while driving home from church, I would feel thin in my spirit. Sensing something wrong, I would examine my two trusted gauges.

In the spiritual area, I'd scrutinize myself: *Did you give out the Word of God as best you knew how? Did you pray? Did you fast? Did you prepare? Were you accurate? Did the elders affirm the message?* If that gauge read normal, I would proceed to the physical area: *Have you kept to your diet? Yes. Have you been working out? Yes. I must be okay. Buck up, Bill.*

But something was wrong. I needed that third gauge—an emotional monitor—to determine my ministry fitness.

Often we attribute our discouragement to spiritual weakness. We berate ourselves: "I'm a bad Christian," or "I'm a lousy disciple." And sometimes our problem does signal that we are not rightly connected to Christ. Yet some problems in ministry stem not from spiritual lapses but from emotional emptiness.

Gauge reading

I have now committed myself to installing an emotional gauge in the center of my dashboard and learning how to read it. I take responsibility to manage the emotional reservoir in my life.

When my crisis hit, I didn't realize my reservoir was depleted until I (1) began to feel vulnerable morally, (2) found myself getting short and testy with people, and (3) felt a desire to get out of God's work. Suddenly I knew the tank was nearly dry.

Now my goal is to monitor my emotional resources so I don't reach that point. What signals do I look for?

If I drive away from a ministry activity and say, "It would be fine if I never did that again," that's a warning signal. Something is wrong when I look at people as interruptions or see ministry as a chore.

Another indicator: On the way home, do I consciously hope Lynne isn't having a problem and my kids don't want anything from me? That's a sign I don't have enough left to give. When I hope that the precious people in my life can exist without me, that's a sign of real trouble.

A third check for me is how I approach the spiritual disciplines. I journal and write my prayers. For months I found myself saying, day after day, "I don't have the energy to do this." I journaled anyway, but more mechanically than authentically. I dislike myself when my Christianity is on autopilot.

Each person has to find the warning signals for his or her own life. But after an intense ministry activity, it helps to ask some questions of yourself: Am I out of gas emotionally? Can I not stand the thought of relating to people right now? Do I feel the urge to take a long walk with no destination in mind? Am I feeling the need to go home, put on music, and let the Lord recharge my emotional batteries?

Reserve recharge

My next discovery was humiliating: I found that when my emotional fuel was low, I couldn't do an Indy pit stop and get a fast refill. Replenishing emotional strength takes time—usually more time than it took to drain.

The best analogy I can offer is a car battery. If you sit in a parking lot and run all your car's accessories—radio, headlights, heater, horn, rear defogger, power windows—you can sap that battery in ten minutes. After that massive drain, suppose you then take the battery to a service station and say, "I'd like this battery charged. I'll be back to pick it up in ten minutes."

What would they tell you? "No, we're going to put the battery on our overnight charger. It's going to take seven or eight hours to bring it all the way back up." It has to be recharged slowly or else the battery will be damaged.

A slow, consistent charge is the best way to bring a battery back to full power. Likewise, to properly recuperate from an emotionally draining activity takes time.

When I first learned I couldn't get a quick emotional recharge, I shared my frustration about that with another pastor friend. He said, "Bill, you have found a rule you're not an exception to. You can fast and study the Scriptures and lift weights and do whatever you want, but there's no shortcut to rebuilding yourself emotionally. A massive drain requires a slow and steady recharge."

That discouraged me. I looked at my average week, and almost every day had an intense ministry activity—preparing a message, delivering a message, meeting with elders, or making some tough decision. I would find little snatches of refreshment during the week, but I finished most weeks with an emotional deficit. Then my family wanted me to have some fun and exciting things planned for them, but I was totally depleted.

I'm going to overload the circuitry, I said to myself. *One day I'm going to find myself in the proverbial fetal position.*

It has been humbling to take an accurate, honest reading of my emotional gauges. When I see my emotional gauge is reading low, I take time to recharge. Some people recharge by running, others by taking a bath, others by reading, others by listening to music. Usually it means doing something totally unrelated to ministry— golfing, motorcycling, woodcarving. The important thing is to build a ministry schedule that allows adequate time for emotional recharging.

Gifting priority

I've learned a second thing about maintaining emotional resources for ministry. The use of your major spiritual gift breathes life back into you. When you have identified your spiritual gifts and use them under the direction of Jesus Christ, you make a difference. You feel the affirmation of God, and many times you feel more energized after service than before.

I think of when Jesus had that important conversation with the woman at the well. The Twelve came back from buying food and said: "Jesus, you must be famished. We had lunch, and you've just worked through your lunch hour."

Jesus responded: "I've had a meal. I had food you're not aware of. I was used by my Father to connect with a woman who was in trouble." Jesus found that doing what the Father had called him to do was utterly fulfilling.

Conversely, serving outside your gift area tends to drain you. If I were asked to sing or assist with accounting, it would be a long hike uphill. I wouldn't feel the affirmation of the Spirit, because I wouldn't be serving as I have been gifted and called to serve. This is why many people bail out of various types of Christian service: they aren't in the right yoke.

The principle is self-evident, but unwittingly I had allowed myself to be pulled away from using my strongest gifts.

About the time Willow Creek was founded, I conducted an honest analysis of my spiritual gifts. My top gift was leadership. My second gift was evangelism. Down the list were teaching and administration. I immediately asked two people with well-developed teaching gifts to be primary teachers for the new congregation. God had given me a teaching gift, but it was far enough down the list that I had to work very hard at teaching—harder than a gifted teacher does. Both people declined to teach, however, and we had already set our starting date. I remember thinking, *Okay, God, I'll start as primary teacher, but I'm doing it reluctantly. Please bring a teacher and let me lead and evangelize as you have gifted and called me to do.*

Recently, when I hit emotional bottom, I decided to do another gift analysis. The results were exactly the same as before: leadership and evangelism above teaching and administration. But as I thought about my weekly responsibilities, I realized I was using teaching as though it were my top gift. Seldom was I devoting time to leadership or evangelism.

I have talked with well-respected teachers across the country, and I have never had one tell me that it takes him more than five to ten hours to prepare a sermon. They have strong teaching gifts, so it comes naturally and quickly to them. If I, on the other hand, don't devote twenty hours to a message, I'm embarrassed by the result. I was willing to put in those hours, but slowly and surely, the time demand squeezed out opportunities to use my gifts in leadership and evangelism.

In order to adequately prepare my messages, I had delegated away almost all leadership responsibilities. And too often in elder or staff meetings, I was mentally preoccupied with my next message. My life became consumed by the use of my teaching gift, which wasn't my most fruitful or fulfilling ministry. Yet people kept saying, "Great message, Bill," and I wrongfully allowed their affirmation to thwart my better judgment.

As a result, we implemented a team-teaching approach at Willow Creek. It has been well received by the congregation and has allowed me to provide stronger leadership in several areas. It would be difficult for me to describe how much more fulfilled I'm feeling these days.

I have also found new opportunities for evangelism. Recently I met with three guys at an airport. One is a Christian, and the other two are his best friends, whom he is trying to lead to Christ. As we talked, I could feel the Holy Spirit at work. After our conversation ended, I ran to my gate, and I almost started crying.

I love doing this, I thought. *This is such a big part of who I am. I used to lead people to Christ, but I've been preparing so many messages in the past five years that I've forgotten how thrilling it is to share Christ informally with lost people.*

If I'm using a third- or fourth-level gift a lot, I shouldn't be surprised if I don't feel emotional energy for ministry. We operate with more energy when we're able to exercise our primary gifts. God knew what he was doing as he distributed gifts for service.

As we minister in a way that is consistent with the way God made us, we will find new passion for ministry.

Eternal and earthly balance

Finally, becoming emotionally depleted retaught me a lesson I had learned but forgotten. I learned the hard way that a Christian leader has to strike a delicate balance between involvement in the eternal and involvement in the mundane. The daily things of life provide needed counterweight to timeless truths.

When we started the church in 1975, I had discretionary time that I used to race motorcycles, fly a plane, golf, and ski. I had relationships outside the congregation and interests other than the church.

Since that time, the needs of the church inexorably squeezed out these earthly pursuits. I became consumed with the eternal. I'm an early riser, so from 5:30 in the morning until I crash at 10:30 at night, barely one moment of time is not related to something eternal. I don't exercise at the YMCA anymore; I work out on equipment in my basement. While I'm cycling I read theological journals. When I pump weights, I listen to tapes or think of illustrations for a message. The eternal co-opted the daily routines.

In Jesus' day, people approached life differently. In the Bible, after Jesus ministers or delivers an important discourse, usually you'll find a phrase like this: "Then Jesus and the disciples went from Judea into Galilee." Those small phrases are highly significant. Such journeys were usually many miles long, and most of the time Jesus and his disciples walked. You don't take a multi-mile walk over a lunch break.

What happens on a long walk? Guys tell a few jokes, stop and rest a while, pick some fruit and drink some water, take a siesta in the afternoon, and then keep going. All this time, emotional reserves are being replenished, and the delicate balance between the eternal and the mundane is being restored.

It's a different world today, and I wasn't properly aware of the changes. Put car phones and fax machines and jet airplanes into the system, and suddenly the naturally forced times for the mundane disappear.

Once I made a commitment to speak in northern Michigan. Later the person who invited me called back and asked, "Can you give two talks while you're here?" I agreed. He called back several weeks later and said, "Bill, we need you to give three talks while you're here, and if you could meet with some of our people for breakfast, that would be great too."

"How am I going to get there in time?" I asked.

"We'll send a plane for you."

Not too long after that call, another person called me from Texas.

"Bill," he said, "I'm in deep weeds. I've got a thousand college kids coming, and the speaker we had lined up bailed out. Most of these kids have read your book *Too Busy Not to Pray,* and we built the whole thing around your book. Could you help us out?"

"When is it?" I asked. He told me, and I said, "I don't think that's going to work, because I'm going to be in northern Michigan that morning."

He asked, "How are you getting there?"

"This guy's sending a plane," I said.

He said, "Well, could you call the guy and see if the plane could bring you down here?"

The result was that I got on a plane at 7:00 on a Friday morning and flew to northern Michigan, met with the leaders, gave three talks, and had a meeting over lunch. Then I got back in the plane and flew all the way to southern Texas, with a person pumping me for information most of the time. I met with another set of leaders over dinner, gave two talks, got back on the plane, and arrived home at 1 A.M. Saturday morning. Then I preached Saturday evening and twice on Sunday morning.

The point is that spiritually, I was fine—I had maintained my disciplines and was striving to obey Christ. Physically, I held up fine—it wasn't like running a marathon. But I was totally depleted emotionally. I was filling my life chock full of eternal opportunities.

What's wrong with that? Besides the emotional drain, I realized two other hidden costs of such a ministry-centered life style.

First, if you are concerned only with spiritual activities, you tend to lose sight of the hopelessness of people apart from Christ. You're never in their world.

Second, you lose your wonder of the church, of salvation, and of being part of the work of God. You can overload on eternal tasks to the point that you no longer appreciate their glories.

I should have known this, because what has saved my ministry are my summer study breaks. During those weeks away, in between studying, I jog or sail, often with nonbelievers. That's when I feel a renewed compassion for them, for I see afresh the hopelessness and self-destructiveness of life outside of Christ. During these breaks I also start missing worship at our church, and I begin craving relationships with the staff and elders.

Having enough of the mundane in my life makes me see the futility of the world and the wonder and delights of the Christian life. I cannot continue to work seventy- and eighty-hour weeks for many reasons, not the least of which is that they don't allow enough time to be away from the church so that I love it when I come to it.

Knowing this, I have renewed my commitment to integrate into my life more activities that are not church related. I'm golfing more. I recently enrolled in a formula-racing school and learned to drive race cars. This past summer I learned how to barefoot ski. I want to fly airplanes. If I don't schedule these things—if I wait till my calendar opens up—they don't happen. In Christian ministry the needs of people are endless.

At a certain point I have to tell myself, *Bill, you had better wake up to the fact that you're not going to get all your work done. It will be there tomorrow.* I'm determining to live a healthy life so that I can offer more than a few short years of frenzied activity.

My goal is to monitor my spiritual, physical, and emotional resources so that I can minister, by God's grace, for a lifetime. I often think of Billy Graham, who has been a high-integrity leader for the cause of Jesus Christ for more than fifty years. He's humble, pure-hearted, and self-effacing, and every day he draws on the sufficiency of Christ.

It was a penetrating thought for me to think, *What if God wants*

*to elongate my ministry? If God doesn't change his call in my life,
can I continue to live at my current pace for another twenty years?*

I knew I couldn't.

I'm convinced God wants us to live so as to finish the race
we've started. That's the challenge of every Christian leader. And
monitoring all three gauges—spiritual, physical, and emotional—
plays an important part in our longevity.

18

Finding a Spiritual Director

It is not wise to treat lightly what most generations of Christians have agreed is essential.

—Eugene H. Peterson

Many years ago in Baltimore I heard Pete Seeger play the five-string banjo. I was seized with the conviction that I must do it too. I was in graduate school at Johns Hopkins University at the time and had little money, but poverty was no deterrent in the rush of such urgencies: I went to the pawnshops on East Baltimore Street the next morning and bought a banjo for eleven dollars.

I found an instruction manual in a used-book store for fifty cents. I was on my way. I applied myself to strumming and frailing and three-finger picking. I had neither the time nor the money for formal instruction, but in odd moments between seminars and papers, I worked at making the sounds and singing the songs Seeger had introduced into my life.

In the years following, the impetus of the first enthusiasm slackened. I repeated myself a lot. From time to time I would pick up another instruction book, another songbook.

Occasionally someone would be in our home who played the banjo, and I would pick up a new technique. At such moments I became fleetingly aware of a great pool of lore that banjo players took for granted. I recognized some of the items from the footnotes and appendixes in my instruction books. Eventually I realized if I was going to advance, I would have to get a teacher. It wasn't that I lacked knowledge—my stack of instruction books was now quite high. It wasn't that I lacked material—there were already far more songs in my books than I could ever learn well. But I didn't seem to be able to get the hang of some things just by reading about them.

I have not yet gotten a teacher. It was never the right time. I procrastinated. I am still picking and singing the same songs I learned in the first few years. My crisp, glittering banjo sound that used to set feet tapping and laughter rippling now bores my wife and children to tears. I am not a little bored myself. I still intend to find a teacher.

Soul instinct

A desire for prayer was kindled in my early life. When the embers cooled, as they did from time to time, I applied the bellows of a lecture or a book or a workshop or a conference. The evangelical movement, in which I grew up, gave frequent exhortations to pray. I was told in many and various ways that prayer was urgent. There was also a great quantity of didactic material on prayer, most of it in books. I responded to the exhortations and read the books. But useful as these resources were to get me started and established, there came a time when I felt the need for something else—something more personal, more intimate.

But what? As I groped for clarity, I found out what I did not want. I didn't want a counselor or therapist. I was not conscious of any incapacitating neurosis that needed fixing. I did not want information; I already knew far more than I practiced. It was not for lack of knowledge that I was unsettled. And it wasn't exactly a friend I wanted, a person with whom I could unburden my inner hopes and fears when I felt like it.

My sense of need was vague and unfocused. It had, though, to do with my development in prayer and my growth in faith—I knew that much. But I didn't know how to get it. I began to pray for someone who would guide me in the essential, formative parts of my life: my sense of God, my practice of prayer, my understanding of grace.

I knew from my books that in previous centuries, spiritual

directors were a regular part of the life of faith. I also knew that in other traditions it was unthinkable for persons with any kind of leadership responsibilities to proceed without a spiritual director. Spiritual intensities were dangerous and the heart desperately wicked: anyone entering the lion's cage of prayer required regular, personal guidance. But this knowledge, like the footnotes and appendixes in my banjo books, was outside the orbit of my associations.

Besides, I like doing things on my own. Figuring them out. Mastering skills. Fasting. Frailing. Double-thumbing. Meditating. I was all right for a person who was uninstructed or unmotivated to get help, but I was neither. It was better to strike out through virgin territory on my own. "Just Jesus and me" was deeply embedded in my understanding of the mature Christian life. The goal was independence from every human relationship and intimacy with Christ alone.

All the same, going against the grain of training and inclination, I found myself with a focus prayer: "Lead me to a spiritual director."

I considered various friends and acquaintances. Somehow no one seemed right. I sensed they would not understand my needs. I may have been wrong in this—in one instance, I know now that I was. But no one seemed to be the answer to my prayer for a spiritual director.

I was in no real hurry. I kept alert. In the course of this waiting and watching, I met a man whom I gradually came to feel was the right person. The more I knew him, the more confident I became that he would understand me and guide me wisely.

At this point I greatly surprised myself: I didn't ask him. I was convinced I needed a spiritual director. I was reasonably sure this person would help me. And suddenly I felt this great reluctance to approach him. We were together quite regularly, and so I had frequent opportunities to approach him. I procrastinated.

It didn't take me long to get to the root of my reluctance: I didn't want to share what was most essential to me. I wanted to keep control. I wanted to be boss. I had often felt and sometimes complained of the loneliness of prayer, but now I found cherished pleasures I was loathe to give up—a kind of elitist spirituality fed by the incomprehension or misunderstanding of outsiders but which would vanish the moment even one other comprehended and understood. I wanted to be in charge of my inner life. I wanted to have the final say-so in my relationship with God.

I had no idea I had those feelings. I was genuinely surprised at their intensity. I tried the route of theological rationalization: that Christ was my mediator, that the Spirit was praying deeply within me, beyond words, and that a spiritual director would interfere in these primary relationships. But while the theology was sound, the relevance to my condition was not. What I detected in myself was not a fight for theological integrity but a battle with spiritual pride.

It took me exactly one year to ask John to be my spiritual director. But it was not a wasted year. Now I knew at least one of the reasons the old masters recommended a spiritual director and why they insisted that we never grow out of the need for one. It was because of pride, this incredibly devious, alarmingly insidious evil that is so difficult to detect in myself but so obvious to a discerning friend. At the same time, I understood one component of my spiritual loneliness, of not having anyone appreciate the intensity of spiritual struggles and disciplines.

Again, pride: pride isolates.

Soul benefits

In our first meeting, John asked what my expectations were. I didn't have any. I had never done this before and didn't know what to expect. I only knew I wanted to explore the personal dimensions of faith and prayer with a guide instead of working by trial and error as I had been.

In reflecting on what has developed in these monthly conversations, three things stand out.

1. My spontaneity has increased. Since this person has agreed to pay attention to my spiritual condition with me, I no longer feel solely responsible for watching over it. Now that someone experienced in assessing health and pathology in the life of faith is there to tell me if I am coming off the wall, I have quit weighing and evaluating every nuance of attitude and behavior. I have always had a tendency to compulsiveness in spiritual disciplines and would often persist in certain practices whether I felt like it or not, year in and year out, in a stubborn determination to be ready for whatever the Spirit had for me. I knew the dangers of obsessive rigidity and tried to guard against it. But that was just the problem. I was the disciplinarian of my inner life, the one being disciplined, and the supervisor of my disciplinarian. A lot of roles to be shifting in and out of through the day.

I immediately gave up being "supervisor" and shared "disciplinarian" with my director as well. The psychic load was reduced markedly. I relaxed. I was no longer afraid that if I diverged from my rule, I would be subject to creeping self-indulgence, quite sure it would now be spotted in short order by my director. I trusted my intuitions more, knowing that self-deceit would be called to account sooner or later. The line that divided my structured time of prayer and meditation from the rest of my life blurred. I no longer had the entire responsibility for deciding how to shape the disciplines. I found myself more spontaneous, more free to innovate, more at ease in being nonproductive and playful.

2. I have become aware of subjects I rarely, if ever, discuss with other people in my life that I regularly bring to my director. These are not shameful things, nor are they flattering things about which I am modest. They are the mundane, the ordinary things in my life. I don't bring them up in everyday conversation because I don't want to bore my family and friends. I don't want people to lose interest in me and look for a more exciting conversationalist in the same way they have gone looking for a better banjo player. But these matters take up a great deal of my life. My director expressing interest in who I *am* (not what I do) and directing attention to what *is* (not what ought to be or what I want things to be) makes conversational reflection possible in these areas.

I am used to looking for signs of God's presence in crisis and in blessing. I must be forced to look to God when I have failed or sinned. I am already motivated to look to God when everything comes together in an experience of wholeness and arrival. But the random ordinary? That is when I am getting ready for the next triumph. Or drifting into the next disaster.

My director keeps exploring everyday ordinariness for the presence of God and the workings of grace. When "nothing is going on," is there, perhaps, something going on? The flat times, the in-between times, the routine behaviors are also charged with the grandeur of God. I have always known that but have been fitful and sporadic in exploring the territory.

Now, because there is this person with whom I don't have to hold up my end of the conversation, I have space and leisure to take expeditions into the ordinary. I remembered James Joyce's insistence that "literature deals with the ordinary; the unusual and extraordinary belongs to journalism," and saw the analogy to what was going on in these conversations.

3. I have been struck by the difference of being in touch with an oral tradition as compared to a written one. I discovered prayer masters of the church at an early age and subsequently immersed myself in their writings. Their experience and analysis are familiar to me. I profit from reading them. Some of them seem very alive and contemporary. For a long time that seemed to suffice. But there is a radical difference between a book and a person. A book tells me about the dark night; the person who comments on *my* dark night, even though the words are the same, is different. I can read with detachment; I cannot listen with detachment. The immediacy and intimacy of conversation turn knowledge into wisdom.

There is also the matter of timing. Out of the scores of writers on prayer, the hundreds of truths about faith, and the myriad penetrating truths of the spiritual life, which one is appropriate right now? Searching through indexes to find the page where a certain subject is presented is not the same as having a person notice and name the truth I am grappling with right now in my own life.

In meetings with my spiritual director, I have often had the sense of being drawn into a living, oral tradition. I am in touch with a pool of wisdom and insight in a way different from when I am alone in my study. It is not unlike the experience I have in worship as I participate in Scripture readings, preaching, hymn singing, and sacraments. These are not so much subjects you know *about* as an organic life you enter *into*. In spiritual direction I am guided to attend to my uniqueness and discern more precisely where my faith development fits on the horizon of judgment and grace.

Quite obviously none of these experiences depends on having a spiritual director. None of them was new to me in kind but only in degree. I do not want to claim more for the practice than it warrants. Some people develop marvelously in these areas without ever having so much as heard of a spiritual director.

Still, for most of the history of the Christian faith, it was expected that a person should have a spiritual director. It was not an exceptional practice. It was not for those who were gifted in prayer or more highly motivated than the rest. In fact, as responsibility and maturity increase in the life of faith, the urgency of having a spiritual director increases.

Søren Kierkegaard wrote in his *Concluding Unscientific Postscript* that spiritual direction "must explore every path, must know where the errors lurk, where the moods have their hiding places, how the passions understand themselves in solitude (and every man who has passion is always to some degree solitary, it is only the slobberers who wear their hearts wholly on their sleeves); it must know where the illusions spread their temptations, where the bypaths slink away." The greatest errors in the spiritual life are not committed by the novices but by the adepts. The greatest capacity for self-deceit in prayer comes not in the early years but in the middle and late years.

It strikes me that it is not wise to treat lightly what most generations of Christians have agreed is essential.

19

Getting Good Advice

The first step in getting good advice is deciding to seek it.

—FRED SMITH SR.

Years ago I remember listening to Arthur Godfrey do a radio ad for a cure-all medicine. The ad went, "At last, hope for middle age." Godfrey paused and said, "Hope? I've got hope. What I need is help."

At times, most of us could echo Godfrey's words. We need help. Especially in the complex situations we encounter in church life, we often need wise counsel. There's never any shortage of opinions, but how do we get *good* advice?

Here are the principles I've discovered.

Becoming a seeker

Some time ago I had an experience that let me know, particularly in the business world, how difficult it is for some people to seek advice. I was with executives from a major oil company, discussing a troubling problem the company faced. I remembered a friend of mine had faced a similar problem, and so I called him.

Within fifteen minutes, he told me exactly what I needed to know. After I hung up the phone, one of the executives turned to me and said, "Fred, you just did something I could never do."

"What do you mean?" I asked.

"I couldn't have asked for help like that," he admitted. "My ego wouldn't let me."

"Getting advice is a way of life with me," I said. "It never occurs to me not to ask for it."

The first step in getting good advice is deciding to seek it. This, of course, is very scriptural. The Bible is full of words about how one's strength can be multiplied with the advice of others. I especially think of the proverb that says, "But in the multitude of counselors there is safety" (Prov. 8:14 NKJV)

But you must differentiate between asking for advice and asking other people to make your decisions. I will never let anybody else take the responsibility of making my decisions. I am asking their advice, not delegating the decision to them.

Figuring out your need

The second step is to decide what specific help you need. The president of a company came to me the other day and said, "I'm in my early forties, and I've done well in my business, but now I'm thinking about changing careers. Tell me, how do you see me?"

"In relation to what?" I said. His question was so general, it was impossible to answer with any substance. Before asking for advice, you need to do your homework, getting your questions as specific as possible. The question I test myself with is, *If these questions were answered, would my problem be solved?* Then, when you've focused your questions, you need to know when to ask them. Timing is crucial. There's no reason to ask how to close the barn door after the horses are out. Many people who are afraid of asking for advice tend to procrastinate.

Also, to get good advice, you've got to give the one you ask some lead time. The person may need to think about the answer for a while. Rarely will spur-of-the-moment advice be good advice on big decisions. I had just completed my talk at a church and was beginning to greet the people when a man came up and asked, "My brother and I are in business together, but we're not getting along. Should we continue our business or separate?"

He was asking a life-changing question in the midst of hi-how-are-yous. If he was serious about getting advice, his timing was poor. I told him I couldn't give that question its due. I didn't want to shoot from the hip. And if he was serious, he wouldn't have wanted any advice I could have given him in that setting. Unfortunately some people want a guru, not thoughtful advice.

Validating the adviser

A woman came up to a pastor friend of mine and said, "I have the gift of correction." I run from people like that. Unsolicited advice is usually criticism, not advice. This woman is just couching a critical spirit as a spiritual gift. Since good advice seldom comes unsolicited, whom do we ask?

In seeking someone for advice, one of the biggest temptations is to assume that a person who verbalizes well also analyzes well. It's not true. Good talkers aren't always good thinkers. When I evaluate my advisers, I ask myself several questions.

Is the person technically qualified? If I go to a doctor, I want to make sure he or she is licensed in the specialty. If I go to a lawyer, I want to see a diploma. I want evidence that the person is technically qualified.

Does this person have a good track record in handling the type of problem I'm asking about? For example, if I ask a man about an investment, I want to be sure he's been successful in his own investments. If I ask about personal relations, I want to be sure he is not in divorce proceedings with his spouse.

Some people assume that because I'm a businessman, I fully understand international trade or leveraged buyouts. I don't. That's not my specialty. I can give an opinion in those areas, but it wouldn't be good advice. Good advice is specific, informed advice. In this day of specialization, I want to know whether the person is competent in the area I'm talking about.

Next, I have found that those who give the best advice have a personal empathy for me. So before seeking advice, I ask myself, *Does this person care about me or the cause I represent?* If he does, he will listen well. One way to tell if someone is being empathetic is to mention a problem. If the person asks a question that helps me to express the problem more clearly, I begin to sense empathy, and I'm more likely to seek and to trust this person's understanding of my question.

Does the adviser take his responsibility seriously? I've been involved on some organizations' boards on which board members don't do their homework. They come without thinking through the issues before the meeting. They don't take responsibility seriously. Not only does that lack integrity, in my opinion, but it invalidates the reliability of their advice.

On the other hand, I was working on a corporate matter with the chief loan officer of a bank, and he said, "Fred, I hope you don't think my questions are too nitpicky. I really want to understand this thing, and you need to know I don't plan to help the company halfway across the river. I want to be in the boat with you all the way across."

I appreciated his sense of responsibility. I was much more likely to accept his advice because he took his charge seriously.

Then, I want to know if the person has the time to do what I'm asking him to do. I often will ask, **Do you think this is going to take more time than you can commit?** I realize I'm asking the person for a favor, and I want to give a graceful out if he's too busy. If a person says, "No, I'm interested and willing to commit whatever time is required," I am much more willing to bare my problem.

Building your bench strength

One of the more important ways to make the foundation of your life secure is to build your list of advisers before you need them. I call it "building my bench strength."

Wherever I go I meet interesting people. If I meet someone who is an expert in some area, I'll write down his or her name and file it. If I ever need to talk to somebody about that area, I want to remember that person. But not all good advice comes from outside experts. Don't overlook the advice that can come from your own family. I'm at the wonderful time in life when my children are old enough to become my mentors and advisers.

Perhaps the first time I realized this was many years ago when I was getting ready to speak to a few thousand students at a denominational university chapel program. My oldest daughter, still in her teens, was with me. Just before my talk, she said, "Dad, I hope you're not going to tell them the world is waiting for them."

Well, that was basically what I had intended to say. Her comments shook me so much that I quickly altered my talk. The result was perhaps the best talk to a student body I've ever given. My wife and our children have been extremely helpful advisers. I often ask their opinions on books, people, causes, and ideas. We exchange all types of information.

Besides my family, I have a few trusted friends to whom I'll go for their intellectual, emotional, and spiritual synopsis of a given situation. I stay in close contact with these people because I want them to be current with where I am in life.

For example, I have several categories or areas in which I have one or more advisers: theology, business, investments, relations (family/social), speaking, writing, legal, tax, and humor. I include humor separately because it's so essential to my emotional well-being.

Jack Modesett, president of Cornerstone Investments, and I feel responsible for each other's humor quotient. Once I sent him a humorous critique of an item he had sent me. His reply was simply a Bible reference: Psalm 50:9a. I looked it up and laughed—"I will accept no bull from your house."

For theology, one of my mainstay advisers was Ray Stedman. For business, Harry Peckheiser, former executive vice president of Mobil. For speaking, there are several, but I was greatly encouraged and enlightened by Oswald Hoffmann. I've benefited from my advisers in all these areas of my life.

Timing for advice

There are several situations that may suggest it's time to seek advice. Among them:

When you face a problem you've seen others experience. There's no point in learning something the hard way if someone else has already been through it. Of course, you want to be sure that the other person truly dealt with the problem. That doesn't mean he came out of it as success personified. It means the person saw the situation through to a reasonable conclusion, and he understands the principles involved, not just the technology.

When you fear a negative pattern might be developing in your life. If you have three or four failures in a row and you don't know why, there's probably a poor pattern developing. A friend could advise you on how to break the pattern and get back on the right track.

Russell Newport, one of my favorite Christian singers, once told me how he regularly seeks out his voice coach to make sure his vocal reflexes are correct. He doesn't want careless habits to creep in.

When you've been on a plateau too long. Nothing is changing in your life. Everything is status quo. You may be comfortable, but you might be in a gradual deterioration.

If you feel a loss of confidence. A good adviser can probably see the bigger picture better than you.

When you have a change in personal relationships. You're having too many confrontations, you begin to become estranged from friends, and you don't know why. It may be time for a good conversation with a trusted adviser.

When you realize you're rationalizing. Sometimes it's difficult to spot your own rationalizing. For example, I asked a pastor friend whose church wasn't doing well, "Why do you think people aren't coming to hear you preach?"

"People will not stand sound doctrine," he replied.

He was rationalizing his poor preaching. People were going to other churches where sound doctrine was preached. He needed somebody to help break his rationalizing. If you find yourself rationalizing, it's good to talk it over.

When you're ready for a candid answer. Candor is a compliment, but we're not always ready for it. Sometimes hearing the truth is painful. Sometimes we're not ready to act on the advice even if we know it's true. But when you're ready to face the issues, then you're ready to accept good advice.

Maximizing the advice

How do you help your advisers give you their best advice? In addition to giving them sufficient time, I follow these ground rules:

1. *Let the person know what you want.* Don't ask for advice if you just want somebody to listen. Often I've gone to a friend and said, "Look, I need to hear what I'm thinking about. Can I use your ears to practice on?" And I'll refine my thoughts simply by expressing them. But I'm right up front with him. I'm not looking for advice or correction; I'm just practicing my material. I want him to know he's doing me a favor by listening.

Other times, however, I want advice. I'll tell my advisers, "Your responsibility is to evaluate my opinions," or "I'd like you to evaluate my situation and identify my options." Advisers are useful in increasing options.

A physician once told me that great diagnosticians know more symptoms and so can more correctly diagnose. Similarly, experienced advisers know more options, so when we're under the gun and fail to see alternatives, they can help us.

For example, people in grief need advisers to help them think through what they must do. Likewise, in periods of success we sometimes need someone who can point out the dangers success brings. So many young businessmen in Dallas have crashed because they couldn't foresee the dangers in success. One of our most successful Christian organizations recently asked several "older heads" to help think through the dangers it would face in success. It was a wise move.

2. *Never argue with your adviser.* When you argue with advice, a contest starts. When advisers sense resistance, they'll tend to back off. They may agree with me just to avoid conflict, and that isn't the reason I asked their opinion.

We should examine the advice we're given. We can ask some questions. But we should never ask in an argumentative way. I also try not to lead the adviser—subtly tipping off what I want him to say. An adviser who is empathetic can be vulnerable to saying what you want to hear. I don't want to be caught leading the witness.

My friend Steve Brown, president of Key Life and a marvelous speaker, had the opportunity to do professional inspirational speaking for a large fee. He asked my advice. He could have said, "I'm sensing God's call to do this. What do you think?" He would have been leading me to an affirmative answer.

But he asked, "Do you think a preacher should do inspirational speaking?" I suggested that inspirational speaking, in which everything rides on audience approval, and Bible teaching, which may or may not win audience approval, can conflict. He agreed and passed up the money such speaking would have brought him.

3. Don't ask for advice just to compliment someone. Many people will ask for advice when they really mean, *I'd like your support*. That, of course, lacks integrity and plays the person for a sucker. If I want to make someone feel good, it's better to compliment his tie or his suit than ask his advice.

4. Don't be casual in asking for advice. I find it's important in serious matters to write out my thoughts and questions rather than to verbalize them in an impromptu manner. One friend wrote me for advice, and at the end of his letter he summarized, "It's been helpful just writing you this letter. Writing sure burns the fuzz off your ideas."

5. Shun quick fixes. The temptation is to seek some bit of advice that will solve the problem immediately. Many creative people can come up with cute answers. But the long-term effect isn't valuable. Quick fixes are seductive but ultimately damaging. Good advice usually points you in a direction. It demands time, a process, a commitment.

A bright young executive called from Michigan and said, "I'm addicted to my work. I can't let go. It has me."

I've known enough workaholics that I asked a few simple questions such as, "Following an accomplishment, no matter how large, do you feel depressed?" He gave an emphatic yes. After a few more questions, I suggested he might be adrenaline addicted, a fairly common condition in high accomplishers.

I suggested a good book and a few experiments he could try, and passed on the name of two or three individuals who have come through the problem. Even though I didn't solve his problem, he was relieved to have a start toward a solution.

Advice, I've discovered, is mutual. Those who learn to seek good advice will be better able to give it to others. Perhaps you've heard the old saying, "It's better to borrow advice than money. Advice you don't have to pay back; money you do." Yes, you can keep advice, but those who are recipients of good advice are obligated to pass on good advice when asked.

Good advice, unlike Arthur Godfrey's tonic, can provide both hope and help.

PART 7

Managing Time

20

Slaying the Sly Saboteur

Procrastination is easy to rationalize, and tough to overcome.

—JOHN MAXWELL

We pastors are tempted to put off tough but necessary tasks. We need to confront a member about gossiping, but that could get ugly, so we visit someone in the hospital.

We need to propose some cuts to balance the budget, but the trade-offs will be painful, so we read a book.

We need to clarify the church's ministry philosophy, but the more specific we get, the greater the risks appear, so we return phone calls and visit with staff members.

We're working, but we're letting important, difficult priorities slide. That's procrastination, and the cost is high. Procrastination is easy to rationalize, and tough to overcome.

Why we do it

Reasons to procrastinate abound, some obvious, others subconscious. The more we uncover and understand them, the better we can develop a game plan to defeat the delay habit. Here are four of the more common causes.

Poor self-confidence. When we know we can do a good job, we can't wait to do it; when we feel inadequate, we procrastinate.

We're poor, say, in administration, so we avoid it every way possible, neglecting even fundamental planning. Or a past failure paralyzes us. Mark Twain said that once a cat sits on a hot stove, it won't sit on a hot stove again. Of course, he said, it won't sit on a cold stove either.

Our failures are the hot stove. You squared off with a stubborn board member at your last church and lost your temper. You forgave him superficially, but bitterness settled in, poisoning your ministry there. Now you're gun-shy of confronting strong personalities. The stakes are too high, the emotions too volatile.

After too many failures, a person won't attempt anything, like the Little Leaguer who has struck out again and again. Now he just keeps the bat on his shoulder and hopes for a walk. The kid who has belted some home runs can't wait to get to the plate and take his cuts. When the game is on the line, he wants to be the hitter.

Success breeds confidence and aggressiveness.

New situations can also intimidate us—a new church, a building project, a novel program, a counselee with a problem never encountered before. When I face things not routine, not habitual, I have to fight consciously the tendency to hold back.

Lack of problem-solving skills. Many pastors who don't normally procrastinate do so in the face of problems. They don't know how to work through problems systematically: how to ask key questions, accumulate pertinent information, create and explore and weigh options, move forward even when the options aren't perfect, and make midcourse corrections.

Building limitations, for example, are one of the most common and intractable problems we face. So naturally, we're inclined to drag our feet rather than begin dealing with the countless details that a building project entails. Since the problem usually doesn't become a crisis, people drift away because of overcrowding or substandard conditions—or they never come back once they've visited.

Problem-solving skills, though, can be learned, and such skills are one of the surest ways to liberate a pastor from procrastination.

Distaste for certain tasks. The big three sour balls are confrontation, money, and vision. Often our distaste causes us to delay important action.

No one enjoys confronting others, yet from time to time the church's health depends on it. When I speak at pastors' conferences, pastors regularly say, "I've got a troublemaker in the church. What should I do?"

My first response is "Have you sat with this person one-to-one and talked through the issues?"

Ninety-five percent of the time the answer is no. By avoiding the problem we aggravate it, allowing bitterness to fester, misunderstandings to occur, and falsehoods to spread.

Subject to emotions. We're tempted to follow feelings rather than priorities. If I wake up asking myself, "Okay, John, how ya' doing, buddy? You ready for the day? What do you think you can handle?" I'll put off many essential tasks, because many days I don't feel like getting much done.

Strong leaders are priority based rather than feeling based.

Unresolved emotions like anger and guilt also weaken us to the point where we drag our feet. Soon after arriving at my first church, I had a run-in with Joe, a church leader. Joe's mother painted a picture that hung in the foyer for years. The first time I laid eyes on it, I decided it had to go. I took it down and put it in a closet. Joe didn't say a word. He just retrieved it from the closet and rehung it.

When I noticed it the following Sunday, I asked various people, "Who put the picture back up?" Joe admitted, unapologetically, he'd done it.

I stewed for two months about what to do. I knew I had to confront him, but because I was new, I felt insecure in the church. My feelings not only inhibited my dealings with Joe, they had me so tied in knots I put off other important tasks. Eventually I went to Joe's work and confronted him about it. I didn't convince him of my views, but from then on I was free from anger.

What it steals

Someone has called procrastination the thief of time. That's certainly true, but procrastination also steals things far more dear to a pastor.

Putting off ministry tasks is like neglecting maintenance on a new car. If you don't change your oil every 3,000 miles, your car will still start and run. The doors will still open, and the brakes will work. You're getting away with it!

But after 8,000 or 10,000 miles, the engine oil has been saturated with dirt. Those particles are now grinding like liquid sandpaper at the lining of the cylinders, pistons, and rings. Eventually the metal wears away to the point that the car burns oil, the engine knocks. Left unattended, an engine designed to run over 130,000 miles is ready for the junkyard at 80,000 miles.

The cumulative effects of procrastination in ministry are similar. For quite a while, you don't see what's happening. But eventually a blue cloud starts billowing behind you. Here are a few of the costs of doing first things last.

We lose productive people. One pastor I know is an effective preacher but a weak administrator. He has pastored small churches that can't afford secretaries. Although he prepares his sermons well, he usually doesn't get around to organizing announcements or planning worship services until Sunday morning. His pulpit ministry attracts some sharp people. But when they start working in the church, many grow frustrated with the disorganization and eventually leave.

If we procrastinate, we immediately lose respect from our leaders and activists. Such people are not leaders by accident. They succeed in work and life because they have seized opportunities; they see openings and run for daylight; they size up situations quickly.

When leaders try to work with laissez-faire pastors, they go nuts. They're thinking, *We could have done this. We should have done that.* Eventually they decide the pastor is not going anywhere, so they go elsewhere. The people a procrastinating pastor first loses are the ones he needs most.

We squander opportunities. Opportunities abound for those who do the right thing at the right time. Alfredo Pareto, an Italian economist, first espoused the 80/20 principle of effectiveness. Eighty percent of your productivity, he said, comes from doing well the top 20 percent of your priorities, while only 20 percent of productivity comes from doing the bottom 80 percent of priorities.

Based on this principle, Pareto said to work smarter, not harder. Those who work the bottom 80 percent of their priorities but neglect the top 20 percent can work four times harder but only be one-fourth as productive as those who work the top 20 percent.

It follows, then, that if we procrastinate on our top 20 percent, we squander our biggest opportunities. It's not only that we procrastinate, but what we procrastinate. Some pastors pay a much higher price for dallying because of what they dally.

Preparing the Sunday bulletin, for instance, is busywork with little return for a pastor. I have never met anyone who attends a church because of the bulletin, yet every week pastors spend important hours doing something that could be delegated.

We lose momentum. Momentum is one of a pastor's best friends, easily worth five staff members. With it, you're bigger than life. You walk up to the pulpit and say, "Good morning," and everyone says, "He's deep." Without momentum, or when you experience downward momentum, you're swimming against the current. You say, "Good morning," and people say, "He's shallow."

Procrastination murders momentum. If we drag our feet, we slow the wagon. People excited about starting a new program quickly lose interest if we procrastinate getting them a budget. They may decide never again to take initiative. If we don't get around to calling (or getting someone else to call) the couple that visited last Sunday, they'll likely go elsewhere next Sunday, taking their network of unchurched friends, spiritual gifts, tithes, and winsome personalities with them.

Much of that inaction and the wagon stops, and it's a lot harder to start again.

Decisiveness and prompt action are like the solid fuel boosters that propel the space shuttle into orbit. Doing first things first energizes a church. People sense the can-do faith, the let's-roll-up-our-sleeves-and-go enthusiasm.

We lose self-respect. Pastors can only lose so many productive people, so many opportunities, and so much momentum before they lose their sense of worth.

On the other hand, even if results don't flower immediately, self-regard takes strong root when we do what's difficult, face daunting challenges, smooth rocky relationships, begin solving thorny problems, organize work, and plan a significant future.

How to break it

Procrastination is a habit, but we can break it. The first step is listing your priorities. This keeps us from procrastinating where it costs most. Prioritize based on the three R's.

The first R is requirements. Ask, What is required of me? What must I do whether I like it or not? What tasks, if neglected, will cost me leadership, credibility, even my job?

A pastor decides that visiting members in the hospital isn't bearing much fruit. So instead of visiting members every other day, as he has customarily done and as the previous pastor did, he visits them only once a week, without ensuring that someone else in the church visits them at other times. Before long, people complain, "Pastor Robinson doesn't care about us. He's too busy trying to build himself a big church to take time with the hurting."

So I encourage leaders to sit down with their staff and ask, "What must I do that no one else in the church can do? When is it critical that you see my face and touch my hand?"

When the search committee of Skyline Wesleyan Church interviewed me for the senior pastor position, I asked them what I had to do as senior pastor of Skyline that they would not be willing to have anyone else do.

After much discussion we concluded that only I could (1) cast the vision, (2) be the primary preaching pastor, (3) take responsibility for the progress of the church, (4) live a life of integrity as senior pastor, and (5) teach leadership to the pastoral staff.

The second R is return. What brings the greatest return to the church? What do I do better than anyone else that helps the church? I'm not talking about just what you do well. You may file better than anyone in church. You may coach basketball better than anyone. But those jobs pay low dividends. What do you do well that significantly benefits the congregation?

My church gets the greatest return when I (1) communicate the vision and direction for the church, and (2) equip key people for leadership and strategic planning.

If our first and second Rs clash severely, we'll suffer. For example, if the church requires us to begin and maintain an abundance of programs, but we're weak in administration, both we and the church will be unhappy. Unless we resolve the tension through give-and-take, negotiation, and education, such a problem will continue to plague us.

The third R is personal reward. We need jobs that we look forward to, that rejuvenate us, that we thank God someone actually pays us to do. Usually these jobs we're good at.

I get the greatest reward from watching people grow, sensing God's presence when I communicate, sharing Christ with others, and developing and equipping people to lead.

After listing your three Rs, take all factors into account, weigh the trade-offs, and prioritize your pastoral tasks.

By the way, procrastination isn't all bad. It's healthy to leave lower priorities undone to ensure we're covering what's most important. Rather than trying to fix everything at once, overcome procrastination in the top 20 percent of priorities and then move down from there.

The second step is to develop accountability. When I pastored in Lancaster, Ohio, I decided one of my highest priorities was to model an evangelistic life style for the church. Given my other pastoral responsibilities, that wouldn't be easy, so one December I told the congregation, "Next year I'm going to lead 200 people to Christ. I want you to hold me to that."

A few weeks later on a Saturday night, I went to the church to study and pray for the next morning's service. In the lobby, I met one of our members. "Pastor, I've been praying for you every day," he said, "that God will help you win people to Christ. And every time I pray I wonder how you're doing."

Good night! I thought. *I'm done for.* "Well," I said, "I haven't won anyone yet this week, but there's still time."

Instead of going into my study, I turned around and went to the car. I had one prospect card, Larry and Sue, living on Fair Avenue. I drove to their home, introduced myself, sat down in their living room, and before the night was over they prayed to ask Christ into the center of their lives. They attended church the next day and walked the aisle in a public dedication.

Accountability changes behavior. In the case above, of course, God was gracious enough to allow my effort to be fruitful. In any event, if I had a serious problem with procrastination, I would sit with trusted church leaders and admit my struggle. I would show them my list of priorities and ask if they agreed that those priorities were best for the church. Then I would ask them to hold me accountable for my top priorities.

Often these leaders sense that if you are to handle the top priorities, you will need someone to handle lower priorities. They may, in fact, volunteer to help.

The third step is to do things that develop confidence. As a boy I wrestled almost daily with my brother Larry. He always pinned me. He was two years older, strong and husky, and at that time I was literally anemic.

My dad watched Larry pin me over and over, and he saw what it was doing to my confidence. One night he told Larry, "You can't wrestle with John this week. I'm going to wrestle him."

My dad let me win every match. Then he would wrestle Larry and beat him. As I got wins under my belt and saw that Larry was beatable, I gained confidence. After a week he turned us loose to wrestle again. This time we wrestled to a draw. My brother never pinned me again.

Did I gain strength in one week? No, I gained confidence. And we can gain confidence the same way: by getting small wins under our belts. We can find things (no matter how small) we can succeed at, stay with them long enough for confidence to grow, and then build from there.

Another way to develop confidence is by learning from others. Almost everything I know I learned from somebody. At my second church, we grew beyond anything I had experienced before.

We were seating people in the aisles, and frankly, I didn't know what to do. I called up Bob Grey, pastor of a large church in Jacksonville, Florida. "My name is John Maxwell," I said. "You don't know me. I'm a pastor, and I'm coming to Jacksonville on vacation. I need to talk to you. I'll give you a hundred dollars for an hour of your time."

Bob agreed to see me. Several weeks later I walked into his office with a tape recorder, a yellow legal pad, and a list of questions. I punched the recorder and fired away for an hour, asking him about the aspects of ministry that puzzled me most. To correct our overcrowding, the problem I was most concerned about, he suggested two Sunday morning services, a novel idea at that time. When we were finished, I reached into my pocket and pulled out the check, but he refused it. In fact, he took me out to lunch, and we became good friends. That went so well, I did the same with other prominent pastors. These sessions developed my confidence. Not only did I take home pages of great insights that boosted my know-how, their faith-filled attitude rubbed off on me.

The fourth step is to develop a problem-solving mind-set. Along with developing the problem-solving skills mentioned earlier, we need continually to nurture a creative attitude. The more creative we are, the more we'll find solutions.

We can learn to be creative. Creativity isn't anatomically fixed in our brains, solely dependent on whether we're dominantly left- or right-brained. It's a way of thinking, an outlook, a habit. We find creative solutions to problems when we (1) think outside of the rigid boxes we're accustomed to, (2) step out of our security zone, and (3) sometimes move forward before we completely figure everything out.

The piano player in a small church moved out of town, leaving the congregation without a replacement. For a few weeks, the congregation sang a cappella, but people began complaining. "The worship just isn't the same. One off-key person throws everyone off."

The pastor thought about hiring a pianist, but the budget was too tight. So they did nothing, and attendance slowly declined.

How did one Chicago church solve that problem? With a boom

box and worship cassettes available in any Christian bookstore. No one had heard of a church worshiping along with a tape, but they tried it. The church grew, and eventually another pianist began attending.

We can't wait till we have all the answers before we start moving. After we take the first creative step—even though we don't know what the second will be—we often get new insights and answers.

The fifth step is to break large projects into small steps. The toughest part of tackling elephant-sized projects is getting started. Facing the entire task before us, we're intimidated and overwhelmed. The key is to break the project into small pieces and start with what you can do best. Doing the small job you feel most able to conquer may not be the project's logical first step, but it's the emotional first step. Getting that done encourages you to start the next most doable step. After that, you've got momentum, and before long you're a few steps from the finish.

For example, you may see the need to develop a written statement of your church's vision and goals. Setting ten-year goals and settling on an overarching theme for your vision can't be done in a snap. But sitting down and listing needs doesn't take deep thought. Once that's out of the way, thinking about your strengths is encouraging. Then the pieces of the vision start to fall in place naturally.

The sixth and final step is this: work in imperfect situations. On a flight with a staff member, I opened my briefcase and starting working. I noticed he read the newspaper the entire flight. I thought, *We may have a problem here.* I didn't say anything; I wanted to see if that was an exception. It wasn't. On the next flight, he did the same thing. An hour or two into the flight, we began to discuss things to be done, and I asked him to call someone in the church. He wrote it in his calendar to do when he returned home. I asked, "Dick, when are you going to call him?"

"Well, you know, we'll be back in the office in two days," he answered. "I'll call him then."

"Dick, why don't you call him from the airport when we land?" I said. "We've got an hour layover. You can handle it in five minutes."

Dick got the point quickly. He was used to working in an ideal setting.

As pastors, we wait for uninterrupted time to do our sermon preparation, and it never comes. We intend to work on the church's vision when we can get away for a few days at a cabin, but those days never become available. Looking for the perfect setting to do a task usually leads to procrastination.

The best time to arrest procrastination is now.

21

Feeling Good About
the Non-Urgent

*There is a balance, a happy medium between wearing out and
rusting out. Embracing the work ethic need not mean we never do
anything but work.*

—STEVEN L. MCKINLEY

It was a Friday night, 6:15 P.M. I sat in my car waiting for the
green arrow so I could turn left into the church parking lot.

A stream of cars heading north paraded past me, away from the
city. Many were pulling boats, a clear sign they were headed for a
weekend at "the lake." The golf clubs in the backseats of others
suggested they were heading for the Friday night league at a
nearby golf course. Still other cars were driven by commuters
whose faces showed relief. The busy work-week was over. The
weekend was here.

Or so I fantasized.

I was heading for a wedding rehearsal, then a rehearsal dinner.
I knew I wouldn't see home before 10:00 P.M. Most of my Saturday would be tied up with the wedding and reception. Sunday
morning there would be the usual three worship services, then
worship at two local nursing homes in the afternoon, and an
orientation session for new church members that evening.

As I waited for the light to turn, watching the cars passing me,
I felt envious, depressed, maybe even bitter. Everyone else had
the weekend free (at least, that's how I imagined it); I had a full
weekend of work ahead. I do not hate my work—far from it. The
folks getting married were perfectly pleasant; the reception would
be at one of our favorite places; Sunday morning worship is a joy;
there is satisfaction in worship at the nursing homes; it is always

exciting to welcome new members. But it was still work, and I was more in the mood for kicking back. I had already put in a solid week of work, without a day off. And when the next Monday morning rolled around, I would be at my desk.

Why the urgent tyrannizes

What is it that keeps us pastors so earnestly plugging along? Why do we live urgently, ignoring our own bodies, spirits, families, and relationships—all for the sake of our work (or so we say)? After I reflected on my own drivenness, I came up with several reasons.

1. What will "they" think? I assume they would think less of me if they found out I wasn't at my desk. Avoiding that feeling is difficult. I feel uncomfortable when I bump into a member of my congregation at the golf course at two o'clock on a weekday afternoon—even if I had worked twelve hours the day before, spent 8:00 A.M. to 1:00 P.M. earlier that day on church business, and planned to be back at church for an evening meeting.

But would they really think less of me? Some might. Some might not. After all, "they" are something I sometimes create in my own mind. When I ask myself, *What would they think?* what I am often asking is, *What would I think?* I take my expectations of myself and project them onto the people I serve.

Over the years, when I've dared to raise this with members of my congregations, I've found invariably they're not nearly as demanding of me as I am of myself. They really don't care if I take time off. In fact, they expect it. They might not stand over me weekly, insisting I take one day of rest each week, but they do expect me to be responsible enough to do that on my own.

And if they did get irritated with me for taking an afternoon on the golf course, so what? Every congregation has a few people who will never be satisfied with the pastor. Saint Paul has a few not-so-nice words for those trying to be "people pleasers," rather than "God pleasers."

2. The work ethic. Our teenage daughter, Meg, is mentally handicapped. One afternoon I wanted her to help me prepare a congregational mailing, the kind of work she can do well. When I raised the topic with her at lunch, however, Meg said she didn't want to work that afternoon.

Then I did a terrible thing about which I still feel guilty. I asked her to bring me her Bible. When she did, we looked up 2 Thessalonians 3:10: "While we were with you, we used to tell you, 'Whoever refuses to work is not allowed to eat' " (TEV).

Meg takes her Bible seriously; she also takes eating seriously. No more argument. She worked that afternoon. And ever since, when she or some other family member tries to avoid work, she occasionally refers to that verse. This makes Meg a typical American Christian. We take that verse so seriously that it becomes in our minds an admonition to work all the time.

I subjected Meg to what is sometimes my underlying philosophy of work: I'd rather wear out than rust out. I've come to see this motto for what it is: self-righteous. Why? Either way, I'm out! It's like saying, "I'd rather drive my car 100 MPH than 10 MPH." Neither one is a particularly good choice—and they are not the only choices. It is possible to drive my car 50 MPH. A car at 50 MPH will both get farther than the car at 10 MPH and outlast the 100-MPH car.

There is a balance, a happy medium between wearing out and rusting out. Embracing the work ethic need not mean we never do anything but work.

3. The myth of indispensability. You've probably heard the story of the small-town pastor who regularly walked away from his work to watch the trains that passed through his town. When asked why the trains fascinated him so, he answered, "I love to see something that moves without my pushing it!"

Often it seems as though things happen in the church only when we prod and provoke and push them along—and maybe wind up doing the work ourselves. Always there are church people who need us to help them make their way across life's battlefields. Convincing ourselves we are indispensable is not difficult.

We are not. The time will come when I'll no longer serve my current congregation. It will survive my departure. The life of the church is carried along by the power of the Holy Spirit, not the skills and personality of any one pastor.

Saw sharpening

Once we have broken the shackles of "their" expectations, the relentless work ethic, and the myth of indispensability, we're ready not only to grant ourselves time off but to start feeling good about doing the non-urgent: prayer, reading, putting up our feet and dreaming, recreation, rest.

Indeed, because doing important-but-not-urgent things can make us better pastors and better persons, we can feel good about indulging in the non-urgent.

For several years, I've given myself permission to spend time on the non-urgent. Recently I read a book that helped crystallize and clarify for me its importance: Stephen R. Covey's bestseller, *The Seven Habits of Highly Effective People*. Many of the ideas in the balance of this chapter are derived from Covey's book.

Covey tells this story:

> Suppose you were to come upon someone in the woods working feverishly to saw down a tree.
>
> "What are you doing?" you ask.
>
> "Can't you see?" comes the impatient reply. "I'm sawing down this tree."
>
> "You look exhausted!" you exclaim. "How long have you been at it?"
>
> "Over five hours," he returns, "and I'm beat! This is hard work."
>
> "Well, why don't you take a break for a few minutes and sharpen that saw?" you inquire. "I'm sure it would go a lot faster."
>
> "I don't have time to sharpen the saw," the man says emphatically. "I'm too busy sawing!"

This man's foolishness is apparent. But when the man with the saw is me, when I'm hip deep in work, claiming I'm too busy to sharpen the saw, it isn't so apparent to me.

Covey proposes that saw sharpening has four dimensions: mental, spiritual, physical, and social/emotional. Reading, prayer, exercise, being with friends, rest—these are ways of sharpening the saw. They are as essential as the work we do. They are, as a matter of fact, what makes it possible for us to do what we do. (I can't help remembering the famous quote of Martin Luther: "I'm so busy today that I don't have time not to pray.")

Taking time for saw sharpening is how we maintain what Covey refers to as the P/PC balance. P stands for production. As pastors, we are responsible for producing certain things: sermons, lessons, programs, the newsletter, spiritual direction, pastoral counseling, worship leadership.

PC, on the other hand, stands for production capability, the ability to produce those things. In the story, the man in the woods is so geared to his production—cutting down the tree rather than taking the time to sharpen his saw—he is neglecting his production capability.

I can certainly identify with that. There have been times in my ministry (and probably will be again) when I have been so caught up in my production that I have ignored my production capability. You know the scenario: one or two sermons a week, two or three adult classes, confirmation classes, four meetings; a funeral, a wedding, a cancer surgery, a fragile newborn; a weekend retreat, a newsletter to get out, a worship service to plan, that "must-go-to" denominational meeting, a few counseling appointments; start the day early, end it late, too busy for a day off—everybody has a week like that now and then.

But sometimes a week like that is followed by another like that, and another, and another. I find myself snapping at my family, flinching when the telephone rings, laboring to produce a sermon that does not have my heart in it, wondering if I really have anything to offer the people I meet. When that happens, I've ignored my production capability. As a result, I am working harder and harder, producing less and less.

P/PC restructure

Covey proposes looking at the organization of our time via a "Time Management Matrix." This matrix is divided into four quadrants on the basis of urgency and importance.

Something that is urgent requires our immediate attention. If I'm in the office by myself, for example, and the telephone rings, it is urgent. Something that is important, on the other hand, might not require my immediate attention, but it does contribute substantially to my priorities.

In quadrant I, Covey places that which is both urgent and important. If the church custodian informs me that the sanctuary is on fire, that is both urgent and important! If the hospital calls to tell me that a child from the congregation was just struck by a car and is in critical condition—that is both urgent and important.

In quadrant II, Covey places that which is not urgent but is important. The care of my own spiritual life, for example, may not be urgent, but it is important. Sitting down with the rest of the church staff to plan a special series of Lenten services may not be urgent (as long as I do it, say, before February 1), but it is important. Much of the professional reading we do is not urgent, but it is important.

In quadrant III, Covey places that which is urgent but not important. If I'm alone in the office and the telephone rings, it is urgent. But if the call is from a firm trying to interest me in doing a new church pictorial directory and my church just finished doing a church directory, it is not important. Often telephone calls, visitors, mail, and other requests make themselves sound urgent without being important.

It was Good Friday at 11:00 A.M. We were winding down from the celebration of Holy Communion on Maundy Thursday, taking care of the last-minute details for the Good Friday service, and making certain everything was ready for Easter Sunday. I was polishing the Easter sermon and anticipating home services of Holy Communion with several of our shut-ins that day. All of a sudden, my office doorway darkened, and Randy emerged.

"Pastor," he said, "I need to talk to you right now."

"Fine, Randy, come on in. What's up?"

"We'll, I've been thinking about the congregational golf tournament we have every August. I think we should have trophies this year, and my wife and I would be willing to donate them. But I'd like to know what you think of the idea and what we should put on the trophies. I have the day off today, and I'd like to get everything taken care of."

Randy's appearance in my office was urgent. He wanted attention right away. But ordering trophies for an August golf tournament is definitely not an important part of my April priorities— definitely a quadrant moment! But I must tell the truth. I did, in fact, plan the trophies that day. I'm not proud of it, but I did it.

Even when that urgency does not correspond to importance, it is hard for us not to respond to urgency. Since urgency has a way of getting our adrenaline pumping, many of us thrive on emergencies and feed on urgency. But feeding on urgency can make us neglect the more significant nutrition of importance.

In quadrant IV, Covey places that which is neither urgent nor important. We call it trivia. The trivial can become alluring, an escape from the day's pressures. Few of us avoid quadrant IV totally. I confess to having a quadrant-IV machine in the family room of our house. It is called a television set. Of course, there are times when the television set brings me something urgent (a tornado warning) and/or important (a debate between presidential candidates). But most television programming is neither urgent nor important. It might be entertaining, and there is nothing wrong with entertainment as such, but it is not important.

A few years ago, I had lunch with a pastor named Earl. Those of us who were his neighbors heard rumors that things were not going well for Earl in his congregation, that his church members were unhappy with him. During lunch, I began to sense the reason. Earl's conversation was packed with reports on the guests Phil Donahue had on his program last week and the incredible plots of some of the daytime soap operas. It became clear that Earl was spending an inordinate amount of time in front of his TV set!

We all visit quadrant IV from time to time. But when we start to live there, we've got problems.

Quadrant II living

In keeping with Covey's advice, I've made it my goal to spend as much time in quadrant I—the urgent and important—as I have to, and as much time in quadrant II—the non-urgent but important—as I can.

I try to be discerning about quadrant III—the urgent but not important; mistaking urgency for importance can be tempting. I do visit quadrant IV—neither the urgent nor important (as when one of my favorite teams is playing a crucial game)—but I refuse to live there.

Spending time in quadrant II—the important but not necessarily urgent—can make me a better preacher. I've always admired those preachers who have a keen insight into a complex portion of Scripture, a good quote, an illumining story. But powerful sermons don't happen by accident.

I've been playing golf since I was a teenager. I love the game, but I've never gotten very good at it. I admire those golf professionals who play the game close to par. Each year the LPGA—Ladies Professional Golf Association—plays a tournament in our area. One summer I went to one of their practice rounds.

When I arrived early in the morning, some of our nation's finest women golfers were on the practice tee. I watched a while then walked over to the practice green to watch others putt. Then I headed onto the course and followed a group around the first nine holes. When I returned to the clubhouse, I checked the practice tee again, and some of the same women were still there—three hours later.

Then I walked the second nine holes. After those nine holes, I found that many of the women who had been on the practice tee earlier in the day were now working on their putting, and vice versa. They weren't playing that day, but they were practicing—for hours!

Practicing was not an urgent task for them that day, but it was an important task. This experience made clear to me why they are great golfers and I am a duffer: practice. They work at it, constantly. I just step up to the first tee and assume that I should be able to play as well as they do.

Much of the difference between the great preachers and average preachers may be the time taken for study, reflection, prayer, and reading. This is not time spent grinding out the sermon for next Sunday, but rather it is time spent sharpening the saw, a quadrant-II activity. When the time comes for actual sermon preparation, they are sharp.

Sharpening the saw—spending time in quadrant II—includes the kind of mental and spiritual sharpening described above. It also includes the social/emotional and the physical. Recent ministry studies have highlighted the tendency of some pastors to be "Lone Ranger" types, seeking to carry out their work in isolation from partners and colleagues. That often leads the Lone Ranger to get saddle sore, to run down and burn out.

When I spend time with those whose professional adventures are similar to mine, we are each sharpened. Once a month I attend a lunch with pastors whose congregations are like my own. Many of them are facing the same issues I'm facing. Some months my urgent pressures make me wonder if I can afford taking the time to attend this meeting. But I do attend most months. I find that when I do, I am encouraged, even if it's only because I've shared my frustrations with others who understand them perfectly well.

Likewise, I am more effective when I care for myself physically. Some months ago, my energy on the wane, I could tell I was being less effective than I wanted. My wife suggested that perhaps arriving at the church office before seven every morning was not essential. I took her advice. I began sleeping one hour later each day and discovered I was getting more done than I had before.

When I shove a daily walk or ride on the exercise bicycle off the schedule, I lose my sharpness. When I never step away from work to play golf or go bowling or see a movie or go to a concert, I get "flat."

The call that never came

When a few years ago I decided to wean myself from the tyranny of the supposedly urgent to practice what I've just described, I braced myself for the fallout. I expected that at least some of my church members would be unhappy with me, that I'd hear complaints about what was not getting done. I wondered how long it would take to get the first phone call of complaint.

I'm still waiting. That phone call has never come. My annual performance evaluation that year from the church council, in fact, was the best I'd ever received. Apparently my people affirmed Covey's principle. Sharpening the saw and spending time in quadrant II can make you a more effective pastor.

22

Renewing Your Strength
Without a Sabbatical

*Instead of taking off on a three-month getaway, I embarked on a
day-to-day hike through the wilderness of weariness.*

—GREG ASIMAKOUPOULOS

Twelve years of task-oriented ministry had taken its toll. I was
battling pastoral burnout, and I was losing. The very week the
Allied Forces were claiming victory in the Persian Gulf War, my
own spirit was surrendering to battle fatigue. Emotional exhaustion. Physical weariness. Spiritual anorexia.

In a conversation with my superintendent, I confessed despair.
He suggested a four-syllable remedy: sabbatical.

An extended time away from the never-ending responsibilities
of the church (with full pay) was not a foreign concept to me.
Two of my closest colleagues had been granted twelve-week sabbaticals the previous summer. For both, the experience was one
of travel, rest, family reunions, and solitude. No degree was pursued. No article published. No manuscript written. Yet each returned home focused, fresh, and infused with a renewed desire to
preach.

The thought of "getting away from it all" had presented itself as
a welcome hope even before the superintendent's call. His endorsement fanned my flickering fantasy into a burning desire. I
approached members of the congregation whom I was close to. I
confessed my hopes that the church leadership might endorse a
sabbatical leave.

Their responses were less than encouraging.

"A sabbati—what?"

"For how long?"

"You'd still collect a check?"

"You're kidding, right?"

Although mentally I had begun packing my bags, their negative reactions stalled my sabbatical flight on the runway. The
word *sabbatical* did not translate into the vocabulary of my congregation, who were largely blue-collar workers and middle-
management lifers. The concept was utterly foreign.

Even the one person with whom I had attended college (whose
father was a university professor) protested the proposal.

"I know all about sabbaticals for educators," he said. "But I've
never heard of it in the ministry. Besides, if you take off for three
months, the church's finances will plummet."

His words characterized the feelings of those I approached. My
superintendent's prescription for emotional survival was viewed
as an unjustified vacation.

I felt betrayed. I thought my church cared for me. Resentment
stirred the waters of my already troubled spirit. Once the anger
dissipated, I devised an itinerary for survival. Instead of taking off
on a three-month getaway, I embarked on a day-to-day hike
through the wilderness of weariness. I developed what turned out
to be twelve ways to take a sabbatical in the midst of work.

Pack only the essentials

A wilderness hike is a survival course. It demands living lean.

Christian management consultant Fred Smith learned firsthand
what it takes to survive: "I ought to be able to write down the
two, three, or four major things I simply cannot slight and be
sure only to work on them. These are my current majors, the
items of greatest importance today. Everything else has to be
pushed aside."

Realizing a sabbatical would not be forthcoming, yet realizing
my need for refreshment, I took the initiative and informed the
pastoral relations committee what areas I would attend to for
three months (and what areas I planned to neglect). They agreed.

The essentials in my backpack included worship planning, preaching, writing, and emergency pastoral care.

Office mail that I normally would have dealt with, I stuck, unopened, in the boxes of board members. When a couple phoned late one day and asked if they could meet me that night to discuss their marriage problems, I made a judgment call. I decided their problem was not an emergency and said we could schedule an appointment (normally I would have forgone my planned family time and counseled them that night). It turned out that the problem was a temporary flareup that passed, and we never needed to meet.

The weight of my pack proved just right.

Secure a reliable guide

I sensed that I should avoid solitary climbing along the edges of burnout at all costs. Emotional exhaustion can disorient us. We need others to point us in the right direction.

I took the advice I had given to scores of hurting people and sought out a reputable Christian therapist. His penetrating questions and tested observations provided weekly guidance as I kept trudging the seemingly insurmountable mountains of ministry. I had the security that, no matter how lost I felt, he would help me stay on the trail.

Guides come in all shapes and sizes. Whereas a therapist helped me, so did my wife, a colleague across town, even my church chairman. The only prerequisite for trustworthy guides: they need to provide unconditional acceptance that allows you to climb out of your pit at your own pace.

I had to struggle against false guilt during this time of healing. For instance, though I feel called to write and find it fulfilling and therapeutic, I felt guilty about taking time away from church-related ministry. My guide assured me that writing was part of my calling, part of what my church supported me to do in its outreach not only to our local area but to the larger world. Talking this through gave me a whole new sense of assurance and peace.

Take along binoculars

It's so easy to fix my focus on the trail that I forget the song-birds overhead that originally called me to ministry. I found it essential to take my eyes off my desk to daydream or drink in the beauty of God's creation at least once a day.

For six weeks I limited the length of my daily to-do list. Not everyone in the hospital got visited. Letters remained unwritten. Some phone calls weren't returned. And I recycled a newsletter devotional from two years ago instead of writing a new one.

As a result, I recaptured enough time to reflect on what I had done and to enjoy the good feelings that accompanied these ac-complishments. The field glasses of discretionary time allowed me to see the world that existed apart from next week's sermon.

Pitch your tent nightly

I gave myself permission to sleep in for a week or two. Adrena-line can camouflage how tired we really are. I figured that if I felt the need for a sabbatical, I most likely needed to catch up on my sleep.

Archibald Hart from Fuller Seminary's School of Psychology suggests a way to determine how much sleep your body de-mands: if you hide your alarm clock in your nightstand for a week, your body will wake up on its own without artificial stimu-lation. When I followed his advice, I discovered how weary I really was. Much of my depression was actually my body's muf-fled cry for rest.

At first I felt guilty for sleeping in and watching the *Today Show* while sipping coffee (or catching a few warm rays of sunshine while reading the paper on the deck). But after two weeks of not meeting anybody for early morning meetings or worrying about what time I clocked in at the office, I got rid of both my guilt and the accumulating luggage under my eyelids.

Grab your walking stick

I also needed to establish a realistic exercise routine. My therapist suggested that my life was in need of balance. For me that meant incorporating an aerobic workout into my daily regimen. I'm not an athlete by profession (or life style), and my body gave ready witness to the flabby truth. I began to walk briskly for an hour a day. (I could afford an hour because of my scaled-down demands.)

Ironically, that hour away from my desk was most productive. It gave me time to pray, which I hadn't been doing much of in my depressed state. Walking also gave me time to reacquaint myself with the exhilaration of muscle fatigue, to be alone with my thoughts, or to catch up on the news. I'd often wear my Walkman. After two months of power walking, I began jogging. (I'm up to four miles a day and actually enjoying it!)

I've discovered there is something refreshing about achieving personal goals (like exercise) that don't have to pass by the board first. Of all the steps I've taken to survive without a sabbatical, regular exercise was the most immediate salvation. At the end of the first week, I was sleeping better and awaking rested. After two months my head cleared considerably, and I felt more optimistic.

Remember your whittling knife

What do you mean you don't know where your knife is? That's just the point. Your whittling knife (or whatever your forgotten knife is) most likely hasn't been handled for far too long. But making it through ministry requires making time for *you.*

Organize an expedition to find your buried golf clubs. Dig out that ol' fishin' pole. Invest in a new tennis racket. Start a stamp collection. I chose to pursue a latent interest in photography, which developed into a meaningful expression of my captive emotions.

With the pressures of people's problems, pessimistic pew sitters, and sermon preparation, factoring joy into a pastor's journey makes perfect sense. Call it a hobby. Call it a divine diversion.

Just call it fun, and call it often. But don't give up because of a busy signal.

There will always be a legitimate excuse for not relaxing and having fun. But such excuses are no excuse. Recreation by definition is a means of being recreated from within. Besides, who ever heard of a hiker who didn't pack a knife, harmonica, or camera?

Carry along a hiker's log

Journal your journey. When emotions and thoughts held me hostage, I learned that a pen and notebook are a way of escape. Getting my feelings onto paper relaxed their strangulating grip and let me look at the invisible.

I've heard it said, "Thoughts untangle and make more sense when they pass through articulating fingertips."

In addition, documenting the difficulty of present circumstances became a valuable testimony to my tendencies and God's faithfulness. My journal from seminary days reminded me that discouragement and drivenness have shared my berth before. As I reread my restless seminary journal, I found reason to believe God would rescue me once again.

I didn't follow a schedule or place demands on myself to journal. When needed, I used it as an emotional catharsis, not a diary, usually for about fifteen minutes at a time.

Look out for the lookouts

Take time to pause in the midst of the climb.

Howard Thurman from Harvard Divinity School first introduced me to the concept of "minute vacations" in his book *The Inward Journey*. There's something to be said for a wee pause for our network of nerves to identify themselves and relax. Reclining in a chair. Feet on the desk. Eyes closed. Meditation. (Almost sounds spiritual, doesn't it?) Three or four times a day, such an inner panorama can recalibrate one's perspective.

But minute vacations can be enlarged to include an afternoon of antiquing with your wife, a day at an art museum with your son, going away on a solitary retreat for a night or two to read and pray, or religiously taking a minivacation from work once a week. Some call it a day off—now there's a novel idea!

Listen to the waterfalls

Emotional exhaustion is often accompanied by apathy and dulled feelings; life loses its song. If music could make a difference for someone as tormented as King Saul, how much more for a pastor.

I incorporated my car stereo and boom box into my daily grind, turning on the music that fueled my feelings. I discovered my Walkman to be more than a source of news. It was my emotional jumper cable. Praise music and classical masterpieces, even the big band sounds of the '40s lifted my spirits.

I cranked up the volume and luxuriated in melodies that ministered to my shriveled heart. The sounds of these alpine waterfalls helped keep this hiker on the hoof.

Pull the snapshots out of your pack

Update the photos on your desk. Those framed faces remind me whom I'm providing for, and that my provision is more than just bringing home the bacon; my wife and kids want the whole hog. They need someone to hug and spend time with.

An occasional glimpse at those we love helps us focus on what ultimately matters most (and it's not Sister Jones's hernia). Remembering my identity as a husband and father keeps me from being too compulsive about my role as pastor.

One night, when we were sitting around the dining room table together, out of nowhere my seven-year-old daughter said, "I'm so happy when we're all together as a family."

Now there's positive reinforcement!

Collect firewood

In other words, build altars of praise. I practiced the discipline of personal worship even when the desire to do so was absent. If ever an awareness of God is needed, it is in the blindness of burnout.

On the mountain trail in the withering midday heat, the need for firewood is not as obvious as it will be come nightfall. It means doing what we don't feel like doing at the time.

When I annually explain the process of confirmation to our sixth-grade parents, I suggest that in confirmation we are laying the logs of truth in the fireplace of Christian community, so that when the Holy Spirit ignites a flame of faith, there is something to sustain a fire. That is similar to what I experienced in my times of quiet before the Lord. Upon the cold hearth of my cold heart, I placed the logs found in poetry, music, silence, Scripture.

At first I was tempted to go through the motions of a routine quiet time. But my ability to fake it soon faded. I resisted benign devotions in favor of honest communication with God. No regimented Bible study. No protracted periods of prayer. At times just thoughtful sighs and audible groans in an empty sanctuary were the only twigs I could find. But God was there.

He also found me in King David's diary of depressions, the Psalms. He even spoke to me through a couple of those radio Bible teachers our congregations compare us to. Through simple and sincere expressions of friendship with the Father, I collected a pile of logs for when the flame of passion would return.

As of now, those spiritual flames are still in the process of returning. It's been a slow recovery, with emotional restoration coming far more easily than spiritual. I feel more loved and accepted by God, though, than at any time in my ministry.

Keep in contact with the lodge

When paraplegic park ranger Mark Wellman climbed Half Dome in Yosemite National Park, he maintained regular contact with the lodge. His supporters anxiously waited on the valley floor because of the precarious challenge facing their friend. Mark complied with their need to know how he was doing and used his walkie-talkie often.

I chose to share with my board my ups and downs. I disclosed my own need for pastoral care from a therapist. I distributed articles on the phenomena of pastoral burnout and ministerial stress. Their willingness to believe the despair to which pastors are prone was not only enhanced by the articles, it was strengthened by my willingness to be up-front about myself. The trust that emerged from my continual communication actually quieted most of my insensitive critics.

Still, a few critics pointed to my nonsabbatical as evidence of my shortcomings. Our church had been going through a conflict of sorts before and after this period. My candid approach of dealing with my needs lost me a few more credibility points with them.

But for most in our church, I gained credibility. Many people repeatedly thanked me for handling the situation as I did, and they were more open about their own struggles as a result. If I were to do it all over again, I wouldn't change a thing.

Well there you have it, a hiker's handbook to which I'll probably refer again. Following these guidelines gave me a refreshed spirit apart from a sabbatical. If I turn to this survival handbook again in the future, I will probably never *need* a sabbatical—while my church leaders might see the value of giving me one!

PART 8

Building Character

23

Going to Your Left

Strengths alone do not a ministry make.

—KENT HUGHES

Most basketball players are right-handed. They find it easier to dribble to the right than to the left. Going to the left requires them to use their other hand, which isn't natural. Only the best players are ambidextrous, able to play well with either hand.

Sometimes even pastors have to go to their left.

Soon after I became a Christian in high school, I was certain God wanted me to preach. But I had a problem: shyness. Even today, when I'm with new acquaintances, I'm not the type to assert myself. I'm perfectly happy to sit at the back and follow other people's leads.

Since I had been called to preach, though, I knew I would have to deal with this weakness. So as a teenager, I intentionally took leadership positions: I was a student body officer in high school and a leader in my church youth group. In front of such groups, I felt terrified. At times I achieved the illusion of being a confident, articulate leader, but I wasn't. Nothing I did was spontaneous. Even with announcements, I'd prepare a script.

As a seminarian, I remained nervous when up front. When I led devotions, I made sure not to look at my wife, because if I caught her eye I would be distracted by how I was doing. At times I'd get twitches in my cheek, my eyes would water, and I'd blush. Yet I still felt called to public ministry. Today people tell me I'm an accomplished preacher, and I've been a pastor so long they think I naturally fit the role. Many in my congregation would never suspect my basic shyness.

All this convinces me that pastoral ministry means more than using one's strengths for Christ. In fact, I've come to believe that Christ uses our weaknesses in ministry as much as our strengths.

Some people wonder, *Isn't it poor stewardship to work on a weakness? Doesn't God create us with strengths so we can major on them, and by doing so, work most efficiently and fruitfully for him?* Others think, *Doesn't God want us to enjoy ministry? And won't we receive the most joy in ministry when we go with the things we naturally do well?*

These questions contain a kernel of truth, of course. But I've found that strengths are only part of the pastoral picture. To be effective, I've had to work out of my weaknesses too. Here's what I've noticed along the way.

Strength's downside

It's fun to work in areas of strength. I find ministry less toilsome and more enjoyable when I do. But strengths have a downside.

I've seen many gifted high school athletes, for example, who quarterback the football team, pitch and hit superbly in baseball, or score high in basketball. Then they go to college, and I never hear of them again. Why? The gifted young athlete had become uncoachable. He was so confident in his abilities, he didn't relish advice or practice. Soon he was passed by less gifted, more coachable athletes.

I've also known some gifted preachers who didn't go far. It was apparent that even in seminary they knew how to use language. Their timing was superb, and there was a magnetism about their physique and bearing. But because they met so much early success, they stopped honing their preaching skills. They stopped studying. They wouldn't take seriously others' comments. Instead of relying on the Lord in prayer and working hard, they began to rely on clichés and technique. They calcified. Giftedness doesn't last without effort.

We don't have much problem giving our weaknesses to God. Since we don't think we have much choice, it's easy to tell God, "I'm not good in administration. Lord, help me." The problem is giving him our strengths. Oswald Chambers says, "God can achieve his purpose either through the absence of human power and resources, or the abandonment of reliance on them. All through history God has chosen and used nobodies, because the unusual dependence on him made possible the unique display of his power and grace. He chose and used somebodies only when they renounced dependence on their natural abilities and resources."

Of course, God has also chosen to use people with great gifts—Augustine and his intellect, Spurgeon and his eloquence—but only when they renounced dependence on their natural abilities and resources.

But strengths don't lend themselves to such humility. In some ways, they make godly ministry more difficult. Up to this point I've used strengths and gifts as synonyms. Ultimately I know they are not. Some people are strong communicators but not gifted by the Spirit to preach. Others are efficient administrators, but they don't have the gift of godly administration. The difference is simply this: a strength is something we do well or easily and enjoy doing. A gift is a skill, strong or weak, that God uses for bearing spiritual fruit.

I'm a good administrator, but I'm not naturally gifted in or motivated to do administration. I don't find it enjoyable. The constant drudgery of the task makes it difficult to face. However, the daily discipline of intelligently attacking a task I naturally dislike has made me a competent administrator. In fact, my staff says I run a "tight ship," and by God's grace, lives have been blessed. I've overseen programs and guided staff people well enough to minister indirectly to others—many more than I could have through my direct contact.

But if early on I had determined that because of my lack of interest in administration I shouldn't spend much time at it, I would have missed this God-given opportunity to minister.

Another danger of focusing on strengths is procrastination, personal and corporate. I often hear that a church should wait for the gifted, meaning those with natural talent, to come forth before it undertakes a ministry. Again, there's a measure of truth in that logic, but it can be turned the wrong way: if such-and-such isn't my gift, then I have no responsibility to get involved. I've been in too many situations, however, where waiting for talented people to come forth led to procrastination of obedience to Christ.

There are too many needful things to be done to wait around for someone to feel gifted. In fact, I've noticed that when some things need doing—like cleaning up after Sunday school or doing dishes after a church dinner or putting away chairs or repainting the choir room—there is an acute shortage of people who feel gifted! Nonetheless such things need to be done.

Strengths alone, then, do not a ministry make.

Needs first

I've found it much more helpful first to determine not my strengths but rather the areas of greatest need in the church and community. When I do that, I've noticed that much more of Christ's work gets done.

The most obvious case in point is the need for people to hear about Christ. Evangelism has never come easily for me. But in each of my ministry settings, I've made it a point to evangelize and to train others to do it.

When I was a youth pastor, I'd take my kids with me when I would preach on the streets. Such preaching was hard for me, but I knew I was called to do it. In my last church, I taught Evangelism Explosion and then regularly went calling with people. In homes I would sit, sometimes so nervous I'd be sick to my stomach, and talk to people about their souls.

In both cases, evangelism needed to be done. I didn't feel I could wait until people who thought they had the gift of evangelism came along to lead us. I was the pastor, so I was responsible for leading in evangelism.

Now if it's not my strength, I may not make a lifetime commitment to train people in Evangelism Explosion. But strength or not, I may have to commit three, four, or five years of time and energy to get the ministry started. In this context, I often think of Mother Teresa. I doubt if she thinks of herself as gifted at changing bedpans. I doubt she finds that fun, but she's called to meet the needs of the dying, so she does what needs to be done.

Ministry is like war, and ministers like platoon leaders. Sometimes platoon leaders give orders; sometimes they fire on the enemy; sometimes they clear minefields; sometimes they carry the wounded; sometimes they bolster the frightened with horseplay. Platoon leaders don't spend a lot of time deciding if they're talented at shooting or good at carrying the wounded or gifted at finding mines. Likewise, when you're fighting principalities and powers in high places, it's usually more productive for the kingdom to do things that need doing when they need doing, regardless of one's strengths.

Renaissance pastor

Almost all pastors have to give leadership in more areas than they can possibly have strengths. To be an effective pastor, then, I must be a Renaissance pastor: I have to be an administrator, managing well the life and business of the church; a communicator, teaching my people the good news; a visionary, leading people to new vistas; a contemplative, listening to the voice of God; a compassionate person, hearing the hurts of people; a decision maker, making the many hard choices of church life.

If I were to concentrate my ministry in one or two areas of strength, I think my ministry would become flat. I've known ministers who think of themselves as primarily communicators. The problem is, when they are away from a pulpit or lectern, they are not very interesting people. They are even less effective pastors. Because ministry for me is an occupation that demands my attention in many areas, it stretches me—about as much as I can be stretched!

In addition, I've found that working on one skill often improves another. For example, I wouldn't say I have the gift of mercy. I don't enjoy, as some do, going from room to room in a hospital, ministering to the ill. But I regularly do hospital visitation, though I could easily delegate the entire task to the rest of my staff.

And I've never regretted going. First, I get to know my people. And second, by knowing my people, I've become a better preacher, one who can connect with their real struggles.

A Renaissance pastor is not only a more interesting person, but a better pastor.

Weakness strengthening

If needs come before strengths for the Renaissance pastor, it means weaknesses need to be attended to. But how do we improve our inadequacies? Here's what I've done.

Solicit honest feedback. A turning point in my ministry occurred one Sunday afternoon when I was in my early thirties. I wasn't feeling good about my sermon. So I asked my wife, "What did you think of the sermon?"

She began to tell me, and I didn't like what I was hearing. So I started arguing with her. She was small of stature but forceful in her response: "If you want my opinion, don't argue with me when I give it. If you don't want it, please don't ask me."

I was steamed. It took me half a week to come to grips with what she said. I finally told her I did indeed want her feedback. Since then my wife tells me the absolute truth, both good and bad, about how I do in the pulpit and in the ministry. By God's grace she's not a critical person, and we know not to discuss the bad report when I'm already feeling down!

But her honest feedback has remarkably improved my ministry, especially my preaching. Consequently, I've expanded my feedback pool over the years. Our staff now evaluates weekly the Sunday morning service. I encourage new staff members to question why we do what we do in the service so we won't fall into empty worship routines. And I try to foster an atmosphere where we can freely say when we think an idea won't work. Sometimes the atmosphere gets thick with disagreement, but that's okay.

On occasion I also solicit feedback from my staff about the

sermon. I know they are careful about what they say, so I have to read more between the lines, but they too have helped me learn and grow.

Getting feedback isn't always pleasant, especially when I'm seeking to improve a weakness—after all, it's going to be weak, especially at the beginning of the process. But it's never going to improve if I don't know the truth.

Delegate and train. I was a youth pastor for nine years, and if you can't do funny things with a banana, there's little hope for you in youth ministry. But I'm not a funny person. I don't know how to make people laugh spontaneously, which may explain why I like zany people and comedians like John Cleese. (Maybe I'm gifted at laughing.)

So what did I do? I began developing some of the high schoolers who were funny. I'd also find other adults who could do the zany stuff well and simply delegate that part of the meeting. Naturally, there were many other factors in the success of the youth ministry, but if we hadn't been able to make youth laugh part of the night, I don't think ninety to one hundred kids would have kept coming every Wednesday night for years.

Use strong resources. Today entertainment so pervades our culture, sermons must not only be interesting but captivating. Consequently, stories and humor are essential. At a minimum, they keep people interested, and at their best, they drive home serious points. But I'm not a natural storyteller. So I compensate by drawing on strong resources—that is, material that is genuinely engaging.

After I was in youth ministry for about five years, I began receiving invitations to speak at youth conferences. That didn't happen because I had suddenly been transformed into a funny person; I had simply learned to make use of good material. I used to tell the story about Jonah getting spit out on the seashore, and I'd tie in the kids' beach experiences (getting greased up with cocoa butter, having sand stick to your body), and allude to Jonah's likely aroma, texture, and appearance. No wonder people repented! Not a lot of that shtick was original—most of it was material I'd heard here and there and pieced together. But it worked to make youth groups laugh.

For my sermons, I memorize good stories, knowing that otherwise I'll forget key parts. In fact, if you ask me to relate the humor
or story I told in a sermon from two days earlier, I can't remember it. But, when practiced for timing and delivery, stories work
beautifully in a sermon when the material itself is good.

Deal quickly with what you hate. I hate confronting people.
While some people thrive on that sort of encounter, exhortation
is plainly not my strength. Nonetheless, when I must confront, I
find it best to attend to the matter as soon as possible. If I procrastinate, the situation only becomes worse, and since I'm not
particularly gifted at it, the encounter also becomes worse.

A couple of times in the past, I've delayed confronting staff
members who weren't performing well. For instance, once I failed
to convey adequately to a staff person the intensity of what was
being said about him—how much people were dissatisfied with
his inability to follow through on assignments.

Because I let my dislike for confrontation dictate relative inaction, it became worse for everybody. A little dissatisfaction slowly
grew into a mushroom cloud of frustration for many people—
members became more angry, and I finally had to let the staff
member go—which was utterly distasteful to me. Had I confronted my colleague with more specifics, he would have had a
chance to improve or bow out before the situation became so
painful. Not only that, our relationship would not have under-
gone increasing strain.

Now when a small concern presents itself, I immediately see
the person in question. That way little things don't build and
become even harder to deal with.

Practice makes much better. If a man of moderate athletic ability shot five hundred free throws every lunch hour, he'd get better
at free throws. If he hired a coach to critique his technique, he'd
get even better. Because this hypothetical man is not particularly
gifted, he will never be as proficient as Michael Jordan, but he'll
be very good.

I know lots of pastors who are effective communicators.
They're not particularly gifted—not in the same league as Billy
Graham or Chuck Swindoll—but they have exercised a profound
dependence on God. In addition, they've asked for critiques of

their preaching; they've written out their sermons to avoid clichés; they've memorized their transitions; they've attended preaching clinics. As a result, they're able to engage their listeners and drive home the Christian message.

Practice may never make us perfect, but it certainly makes us much, much better.

Certainly there is a place to talk about the effective use of our God-given strengths. But in my ministry, it's been equally vital to work on my weaknesses. When Paul talked about God using our weaknesses, I'm sure he meant that in our weaknesses we tend to depend more on God, allowing God to work more through us. Without denying that, I would also add that by God's grace, our weaknesses can be improved and be used effectively by him.

24

Developing a Christian
Mean Streak

*One of the hardest lessons I ever learned was that I can't please
everyone. I want to; I desire to be what everyone wants me to be. I
want everyone to love me. The problem is, I simply can't do it.
And until I understand that, I will never be effective.*

—STEVE BROWN

A number of years ago, a pulpit committee representative from a
large southern church took me to lunch and asked if I would
consider becoming their pastor.

"Tell me about the church," I said, and after touching on a
number of points, he squared with me: "Steve, our church has a
serious problem because it is controlled by one man. He gives
a lot of money and has probably been there longer than anyone
else. Because of who he is, he pretty much gets his way. The last
three pastors have left because of him. But we believe we have a
majority and we can take him."

"You're not looking for a pastor," I commented. "You're looking
for a drill sergeant."

"Well," he replied, "I wouldn't put it that way, but yes, that's
probably it, and you're the only one we know who is mean
enough to clean up the mess."

I quickly told him I didn't feel led to become their pastor, but I
did have a hit list of fellow clergy I'd be glad to submit for the
committee's consideration.

As I thought about that incident later, I was horrified at the
reputation I had somehow developed. How could I have become
known as a drill sergeant when all I wanted to be was a faithful
and godly man? That incident happened a long time ago. Now I
am a lot older and a little wiser, and I have come to value my

drill-sergeant reputation. In fact, I have begun to see it as a mani-
festation of faithfulness and godliness.

No more mister nice guy

I spend a portion of my time teaching seminary students, and
one of the pastoral traits I urge my students to develop is, for lack
of a better term, a "mean streak." All too often in American
churches, pastors have become sitting ducks for neurotic church
members (and they are a small minority). If people don't like the
way a pastor parts his hair or ties his tie, they feel free to tell him.
If they don't like his wife's dress because it clashes with the cur-
tains in the church, they tell him. You wouldn't believe the comments on my beard I have received over the years! Some people
feel free to criticize and correct pastors on things for which they'd
never think of criticizing anyone else.

Not long ago I was talking with a pastor in serious trouble with
his congregation. He was being second-guessed and ridiculed in a
shameful way. As we talked, it became apparent this young man
needed to develop a mean streak to survive. He told me he felt he
had been called to love his people, to understand them even
when they were cruel and abusive.

"While you should be loving and kind," I said, "it's equally
important to be honest and strong. Why don't you bring the
people making those comments before the ruling body of the
church and have them justify their disturbance of the peace and
unity of the church, or leave."

The young pastor's reply was interesting: "Steve, I know that's
what I *should* do, but I'm just not made that way. I feel my
ministry is to pour oil on troubled waters, not put a match to it."
Needless to say, that young man is no longer in the ministry. He
didn't have enough oil for all the troubled waters, so he is now
selling insurance.

Former professional football player Norm Evans told me once
about a massive freshman lineman—six foot five—with whom he
played. In the lineman's first game, the opposing lineman kept
pulling this man's helmet down over his eyes. The young lineman

went up to the coach and said, "Coach, he keeps pulling my helmet down. What should I do?"

The coach smiled and said, "Son, don't let him do it."

Urge to please

One of the hardest lessons I ever learned was that I can't please everyone. I want to; I desire to be what everyone wants me to be. I want everyone to love me. The problem is, I simply can't do it. And until I understand that, I will never be effective.

I've noticed the problem isn't confined to clergy. Many Christians share it with us. We swallow spurious doctrines, refuse to ask questions, avoid confrontation, stifle protests, keep quiet when we ought to speak, allow ourselves to be manipulated—all because we're afraid people won't love us if we don't please them.

In an insightful essay entitled "The Inner Ring," C. S. Lewis wrote:

> I believe that in all men's lives at certain periods, and in many men's lives at all periods between infancy and extreme old age, one of the most dominant elements is the desire to be inside the local Ring and the terror of being left outside. . . . Of all passions the passion for the Inner Ring is most skillful in making a man who is not yet a very bad man do very bad things.

I can understand that need to be in the inner circle, to be liked, because it is one of my problems. Have you ever noticed the Christian liturgy that takes place not during the worship service but after it? The pastor goes to the door, and everyone files past. As they pass, the liturgy requires them to say, "Pastor, that was a wonderful sermon." Then, according to liturgy, the pastor responds by saying, "Thank you, I'm pleased God used it."

This practice works fine except on those occasions when I have preached a bomb. I know it, and the congregation knows it. During the sermon, people were checking their watches, and then they were shaking them to make sure they weren't broken. Everybody was bored, and the sermon died before it got to the first pew.

Never mind. The Christian liturgy is chiseled in stone: I must still go to the door, and the people still have to file past me mumbling the same comment and receiving the same response. I'm sure you've had those days too.

The problem comes, however, when we decide we have to avoid those days more than anything in the world. So we pen sermons to please the congregation. We know there is truth to be said, but we don't say it because it might offend someone. We know we need to be strong, but if we are too strong, people might be upset, so we pass out pious pabulum that doesn't offend anyone.

Because our self-identity as pastors is so caught up in what we do in the pulpit, the distance soon narrows between being kind, sweet, and insipid in the pulpit and being kind, sweet, and inspired in every area of life.

Courage to offend

I used to have a book in my library (since borrowed and never returned) with a great title. I don't remember who wrote it, but it was titled *Bible in Pocket; Gun in Hand.* It was about the frontier preachers in America and their determination to preach the gospel whether or not anybody wanted to listen. They would have been uncomfortable in many contemporary churches. In fact, most of our churches would have been uncomfortable with them. Those gun-totin' parsons simply would not have been able to play the game.

If we examine the biblical record without bringing preconceived ideas, we become acutely aware that *most* of the men and women of the Bible and church history would also be uncomfortable in many churches today. Moses might get angry enough to find some stone tablets to break. Joshua might call out his fearless troops and fight to give the land back to the pagans. Gideon, Deborah, and Samson would probably wonder who's leading, and the prophets would laugh. John the Baptist would never get invited to dinner—and be glad.

Somehow many have translated leadership into terms of

servanthood and love that are divorced from the biblical sense of the words. As a result, a mild style of leadership has made them targets for every upset church member with a theological or cultural gun. Such pastors could benefit from a Christian mean streak.

We've got people thinking pastors are supposed to be nice people whose calling is to tell other people to be nice. Then they talk of "a crisis in pastoral leadership." I believe the crisis has more to do with the inability to develop toughness than it does with burnout or lack of money or training.

If every media representation of a pastor paints a smiling, harmless wimp, and if we begin to interpret the Scriptures from that cultural perspective, after a while we start becoming what everybody thinks we are. Much of the anger directed at outspoken Christian leaders, I believe, is not from what they say but because they aren't supposed to say anything at all. They break the established tradition of niceness, and that simply is not done.

Tough love

I'm no expert, but I am a survivor. I have isolated four principles that I violate only at my own peril. And, preacher that I am, the principles are in the form of an acrostic spelling out WIMP. Let me share them with you.

First is the principle of **waves:** any time you refuse to make waves when you ought to, you will face greater waves later.

Almost every time I have tried to avoid a problem by looking the other way or by covering it with sweetness and light, what could have been handled with honest and loving confrontation at the beginning has become so monstrous it requires a major shooting match at the end. By waiting, I needlessly hurt others, the church, and myself.

Elijah's question to the people, "How long will you falter between two opinions?" (1 Kings 18:21 NKJV) is an appropriate admonishment to those of us who try to put off dealing with problems. I served a church once where the clerk of the Session (the leading lay office) was constantly resigning when he didn't

Steve Brown

get his way. I tried to be nice, to understand and soothe him, but it didn't work. I finally accepted his resignation, filled the position with someone else, and called him into my study to explain what I had done and why.

I expected the church to fall apart, but it didn't. Instead, he ended up receiving Christ and offering a public confession before the entire congregation. An elder from another church I served said, "Steve, always do right, and it will come out right. But even if it doesn't come out right, you will feel right having done right."

Second is the principle of **image:** people see you as a representative of God, even if you don't like it, and often will react to you on a human level as they react to God on a spiritual level.

I fully expect to go into an airport sometime and find three rest rooms: one for men, one for women, and one for clergy. Our image—and thus, God's—is sissified.

Paul said we are ambassadors for Christ (2 Cor. 5:20), and an ambassador must truly represent his or her government. If I am sweet when I ought to be angry, weak when I ought to be strong, and nice when I ought to be hard, I do not adequately represent the government. And people might start picturing our "terrible" Lord the way I have allowed them to caricature me.

Peter Cartwright, the early Methodist circuit rider, didn't allow that problem. When he came into a town, he would often stand on the outskirts, turn to his friends, and say, "I smell hell." The stench of sin bothered him. How easy it is to try to cover the smell of hell with the perfume of platitudes, but if we will be true to the image we represent, we cannot.

A couple came to me asking to be married. After discussing their situation with them, I realized he was not a Christian and she was. At that point I had a problem endorsing their marriage. I said, "I like both of you a lot, but I'm not going to be able to do the ceremony," and I explained the biblical reasons why I could not perform the ceremony.

The young woman began to cry, and the young man got angry. He said, "I thought pastors were here to *help* people, and you've made her cry!"

I said to him, "Son, I *am* helping you; I'm telling you the truth. If you don't like the truth, you should go somewhere where people will lie to you." He and his fiancée left my study angry, but I can live with that. And maybe when they think of pastors in the future, the image won't be the same. They may dislike pastors, but they'll know pastors aren't afraid to speak the truth.

Third is the principle of **mandate:** having been given by God a mandate for leadership, you must lead, or your sin is unfaithfulness.

I love God's charge to Joshua, and I assume it belongs to me and every pastor called of God: "Have I not commanded you? Be strong and of good courage; do not be afraid, nor be dismayed, for the LORD your God is with you wherever you go" (Josh. 1:9 NKJV).

Someone once said about leadership: "Either lead or follow or get out of the way!" Once while completing a building program, I did almost everything wrong. I was afraid to lead because any direction I might take could split the church. So I got in the way. My indecision was causing significant problems until my good friend Jim Baird showed me he cared enough about me to tell me the truth.

"Steve," he said, "if you are not willing to pay the price of leadership, then don't expect anything to happen." That shook me up enough to make me take a stand, to *lead,* and we did complete the project.

Finally, there is the principle of **passing:** hold your church lightly and be willing to leave quickly.

I admit it: I used to play a lot of poker, and I learned (with Kenny Rogers) a lot about life from the poker table. I learned there are times when you need to pass and wait for a better hand. Other times you just need to leave the table. I don't think a pastor should resign at the drop of a hat or over piddling issues, but I do believe there are issues important enough to cause a pastor to leave—and leave quickly.

Jesus knew about us, I believe, when he gave us the sacrament of shaking the dust off our feet. "And whoever will not receive you nor hear your words, when you depart from that house or city, shake off the dust from your feet" (Matt. 10:14 NKJV). You don't do it very often, but when the right time comes, it's effective.

In our city we have an announcer who signs off each morning with these words: "Now, y'all hold on to what y'all have got until y'all get what y'all want." I suspect that's good advice for a pagan, but not for a Christian, and certainly not for a pastor.

I keep an updated resignation in my files, and the fact that I know it is there and I am willing to use it keeps me from selling my soul. I won't capitulate on something important only to stay in my church. The knowledge that I can always go into vinyl repair has covered a multitude of sins.

The tough side

Developing a Christian mean streak is, of course, another name for Christian boldness. "The wicked flee when no one pursues, but the righteous are bold as a lion" (Prov. 28:1 NKJV). Without boldness, we cannot serve God adequately.

I'm angry at the structures that tell me I can't be angry. I'm angry at myself when I compromise in the wrong places. I'm angry when society and the church tell me I am not to be what God called me to be—an obedient ambassador of Jesus Christ.

In *Perelandra,* the second book of C. S. Lewis's science fiction trilogy, the protagonist, Ransom, has been sent to the planet Perelandra to prevent a fall similar to Adam's on earth. The adversary, in the form of a man named Weston, is also on Perelandra, working against Ransom's efforts.

Ransom realizes with horror the evil represented by Weston, and gradually comes to understand he must face and destroy Weston in battle. It is a frightening prospect. In the darkness of the Perelandran night, Ransom considers the fact that he can stand and fight or he can run. Out of the blackness comes a voice that says, "My name is also Ransom."

With Ransom, we face the same decision. We can stand and fight, or we can run scared. It behooves us to act in a manner that honors the name we bear—*Christ*ians. If we are going to carry the name, we must be willing to pay the price. Ransom stood and fought the forces of evil because he was reminded of the name of another who refused to withdraw from the fight.

We also bear the name *Ransom*. If we are only out to be nice, mild-mannered folk, we should either change our name or change our calling.

Now, don't you feel a mean streak coming on?

25

Preaching the Terrors

In practice, we tend to preach the terrors by making them less terrible. But what is lost is the very real terror of obeying God without the least idea how things will turn out in the end—which is, after all, the human situation.

—BARBARA BROWN TAYLOR

Not too long ago, I was invited to address a senior citizens' group on "Women in the Old Testament." They had been studying various biblical characters and wanted me to introduce them to some of Israel's heroines; so I did.

I told them about Jael, "most blessed of women" (Judg. 5:24 NIV), who drove a tent peg through Sisera's temple with a mallet.

I told them about Judith (whose exploits, mentioned in the Apocrypha, parallel Jael's), who seduced Holofernes and then paused to pray—"Give me strength today, O Lord God of Israel!"—before taking the man's own sword and plunging it into his neck (Judith 13:7 NRSV).

I told them about Esther, who won permission for the Jews of her husband's Persian empire "to destroy, kill and annihilate" 75,000 of their enemies (Est. 8:11 NIV).

By the end of my talk, my audience's eyes were very large, and I was feeling a little queasy myself. They thanked me very much and have never asked me back.

Granted, I could just as easily have talked about Sarah, Ruth, and the widow of Zarephath, but there comes a time in every preacher's life when the queasy-making parts of the Bible can no longer be ignored, when it is time to admit that the Bible is not a book about admirable people or even about a conventionally admirable God.

It is instead a book about a sovereign God's covenant with a chosen people, as full of holy terrors as it is of holy wonders, none of which we may avoid without avoiding part of the truth.

On the whole, we do not do so well with the terror part. It does not fit the image of the God we wish to publish; it goes against the good news we want to proclaim. In these days of dwindling numbers, who is eager to remind the congregation how the prophet Elisha cursed a crowd of jeering boys in the name of the Lord and how two she-bears trundled obediently out of the woods to maul forty-two of them (2 Kings 2:23–25)? Or how Ananias and Sapphira were struck dead for withholding a portion of their cash from the early Christian community (Acts 5:1–11)?

Fortunately or unfortunately, there is little reason to tangle with such peripheral texts of terror when we have much more central texts of terror readily at hand. In the Old Testament, God asks Abraham to roast his only son; in the New Testament, obedience to God's will puts another only son on a cross. In these two worst-case scenarios, and all their derivatives, the issue for us remains the same: How do we preach a loving God who does such unloving things? How do we preach the terrors?

Terror at the center

Because I am addressing biblical texts in this article, I am taking the biblical view, which is that God's will is at work in all the events of our lives. While there are good theological reasons and even better pastoral ones to approach the terrors as stray bullets outside God's plan, the Bible leans the other way. "I make weal and create woe; I the Lord do all these things" (Isa. 45:7 NRSV).

In practice, we tend to preach the terrors by making them less terrible. Of course God sent a ram to take Isaac's place at the last moment, we say; of course God raised Jesus from the dead and made him Lord of all. Thus the first story becomes one about how obedience results in rescue and the second one a story about how obedience results in resurrection.

But what is lost while such morals are being made is the very real terror of obeying God without the least idea of how things will turn out in the end—which is, after all, the human situation. Things will turn out according to God's will, certainly, and in faith we confess that to be enough for us. But insofar as God's will is so radically different from our own, there is plenty of room left for terror in our lives.

Every preacher has his or her own canon of terror. My own includes three kinds of texts: first, those in which God sanctions violence—killing every firstborn in the land of Egypt (Exod. 11:5) or ordering Saul to slaughter the Amalekites down to the last woman, child, and donkey (1 Sam. 15:3); second, those in which God aims to separate me from my stuff—suggesting that I surrender my last handful of meal (1 Kings 17:11–13) or sell all that I own to follow (Mark 10:21); third, those texts in which God exercises final judgment—refusing to open the door to the foolish bridesmaids (Matt. 25:12) or banishing the ill-clad wedding guest to outer darkness where there is weeping and gnashing of teeth (Matt. 22:13).

They are terrible to me because they expose my vulnerability. If God can condemn Amalekite babies for the sins of their parents, then there is no hope for me. Nor can I find safety in following Jesus, if selling all that I own is the way. So, of course, I will find myself on the wrong side of the door when the time comes, hearing my muffled sentence pronounced through the latch: "I tell you the truth, I don't know you" (Matt. 25:12 NIV).

These terrible texts remind me how helpless I am, how frail and not in charge I am. While there are clearly things I can do to improve my life and things I can do to cheapen it, my fate is ultimately out of my hands. I cannot control God's disposition toward me, and that is terrifying.

One way to hide from such knowledge is to take refuge in righteousness, suggesting that those who behave properly are terror-exempt. Obey God and avoid the sword. Give generously and prevent misfortune. Be good sheep and dodge the outer darkness. Congregations are relieved to hear sermons like these, and preachers are glad to preach them because they offer some leverage in an otherwise frightening universe, but they finally fail to meet the test either of human experience or biblical witness. Job stands on one side of the pulpit shaking his head and Jesus on the other, both of them confirming our fear that righteousness does nothing to dissuade God from trying the faithful by fire and by ice.

Jesus' own death is the chief terror of the gospel. Here is God's beloved, who has done nothing but right all his life, and what is his reward? Not ripe old age with grandchildren hanging on his sleeves but early, violent death on a cross. This death ruins all our efforts to turn the Bible into a manual for the good life.

No one who has heard the story of Jesus Christ can mistake where following him will lead, which makes the gospel itself a text of terror for all who wish to avoid suffering and death. The good news of God in Christ is heard loudest and best by those who stand on the far side of a fresh grave.

That, finally, is what makes a text terrible to me: not what it exposes about me but what it exposes about God—a sovereign God who is radically different from me, whose mind I cannot read, whose decisions I cannot predict, whose actions I cannot control.

"It is a dreadful thing to fall into the hands of the living God," writes the author of the letter to the Hebrews (10:31 NIV). But it is not as if we had a choice. That is whose hands we are in; our only choice is how we will handle our fear.

Hidden consolations

As preachers we have an additional choice, and that is how we will address the fear of those who listen to us. Jonathan Edwards, the great eighteenth-century American pastor and theologian, was one of the most frightening preachers of all time. In his book *Thoughts on the Revival of Religion in New England,* he rose to the defense of those who were being blamed for "speaking terror to them that are already under great terrors." It was, he said, a matter of saving those who were drowning in full sight of land:

> A person that sees himself ready to sink into hell is ready to strive, some way or other, to lay God under some obligation to him; but his is to be beat off from every thing of that nature, though it greatly increases his terror to see himself wholly destitute, on every

side, of any refuge, or any thing of his own to lay hold of; as a man that sees himself in danger of drowning is in terror and endeavors to catch hold on every twig within his reach, and he that pulls away those twigs from him increases his terror; yet if they are insufficient to save him, and by being in his way prevent his looking to that which will save him, to pull them away is necessary to save his life . . . (from *Theories of Preaching,* Richard Lischer, ed., Labyrinth Press).

It is an alarming image, and yet it is what texts of terror do. They pry our fingers away from our own ideas about who God should be and how God should act so that there are only two things left for us to do with our fear: use it to propel us toward the God who is or let it sink us like a stone.

Preaching texts of terror calls for the same kind of choice. We may try to protect ourselves and our congregations from them by tossing out inflatable bits of comfort and advice, or we may find the courage to forsake those twigs and swim for our lives toward the living God. As fearful as that may be, it is finally less fearful than the alternative.

In a paradoxical way, texts of terror carry their own consolation inside of them. Several nights ago, a friend and I watched Laurence Olivier in Shakespeare's *King Lear.* Neither of us had ever seen the play before, so we were unprepared for the relentless tragedy of it, with fathers rejecting children, children betraying parents, brothers plotting against brothers, and sisters poisoning sisters. By the end of the last scene, the stage was littered with bodies—Lear, Cordelia, Goneril, Regan, Edmund— all dead.

As the lights went down and the credits rolled, my friend turned to me with tears in his eyes and said, "What could be more wonderful than that?"

When I asked him to explain himself, he could not, except to say that he recognized his own life in the play, and that it helped him somehow to see his worst fears acted out. It was *real*—that was the best he could do—and it was redemptive for him to witness real pain suffered in a way that seemed true to him.

In the same way, I believe, texts of terror are recognizable to us. Judgment, violence, rejection, death—they are all present in our world, if not in our lives, and there is some crazy kind of consolation in the fact that they are present in the Bible as well. They remind us that the Bible is not all lambs and rainbows. If it were, it would not be our book. Our book has everything in it— wonders and terrors, worst fears and best hopes—both for our- selves and for our relationship with God.

The best hope of all is that because the terrors are included here, as part of the covenant story, they may turn out to be redemptive in the end, when we see dimly no more but are face to face at last. That is the fundamental hope all texts of terror drive us to: that however wrong they may seem to us, however misbe- gotten and needlessly cruel, God may yet be present in them, working redemption in ways we are not equipped to discern.

Our fear of God's method may turn out to be like our fear of the surgeon's knife, which must wound before it can heal. While we would prefer to forego the pain altogether—or at the very least to perform our own surgery, thank you very much—our survival of the terrors depends on our trust in the surgeon's skill. If we believe the one to whom we surrender ourselves is compe- tent, then "all shall be well, and all shall be well, and all manner of thing shall be well" (Julian of Norwich).

If we are open to this possibility in our interpretation of Scrip- ture, then we open the possibility of its being true in the interpre- tation of our lives as well. Whether the terror is heard on Sunday or lived on Monday, the hermeneutical question remains the same: Do we trust God to act in all the events of our lives, or only in the ones that meet with our approval?

Several summers ago, I spent three days on a barrier island where loggerhead turtles were laying their eggs. One night while the tide was out, I watched a huge female heave herself up onto the beach to dig her nest and empty herself into it while slow salt tears ran from her eyes. Afraid of disturbing her, I left before she had finished her work but returned the next morning to see if I could find the spot where her eggs lay hidden in the sand. What I found were her tracks, only they led in the wrong direction. In- stead of heading back out to sea, she had wandered into the dunes, which were already hot as asphalt in the morning sun.

A little ways inland I found her, exhausted and all but baked, her head and flippers caked with dried sand. After pouring water on her and covering her with sea oats, I fetched a park ranger, who returned with a jeep to rescue her. As I watched in horror, he flipped her over on her back, wrapped tire chains around her front legs, and hooked the chains to the trailer hitch on his jeep. Then he took off, yanking her body forward so fast that her open mouth filled with sand and then disappeared underneath her as her neck bent so far I feared it would break.

The ranger hauled her over the dunes and down onto the beach; I followed the path that the prow of her shell cut in the sand. At ocean's edge, he unhooked her and turned her right side up again. She lay motionless in the surf as the water lapped at her body, washing the sand from her eyes and making her skin shine again.

Then a particularly large wave broke over her, and she lifted her head slightly, moving her back legs as she did. As I watched, she revived. Every fresh wave brought her life back to her until one of them made her light enough to find a foothold and push off, back into the water that was her home.

Watching her swim slowly away and remembering her night-mare ride through the dunes, I noted that it is sometimes hard to tell whether you are being killed or being saved by the hands that turn your life upside down.

Wrestling out the blessing

Our hope, through all our own terrors, is that we are being saved. Whatever we believe about why things happen the way they do, we are united by our hope that God is present in them, working redemption in light and darkness, weal and woe.

To hope this does not mean we lie down before the terrors, however. For as long as we have strength to fight, it is both our nature and our privilege to do so. Sometimes God's blessing does not come until daybreak, after a full night of wrestling angels, and sometimes it takes much longer than that. As preachers and as believers, it is our job to struggle with the terrors, refusing to let go of them until they have yielded their blessings. If we are tempted to draw back from this task and seek an easier way, we are not alone. The world is full of former disciples. "Do you also wish to go away?" Jesus asks the handful who are left with him at one point. "Lord," Simon Peter answers him, "to whom can we go? You have the words of eternal life" (John 6:67–68 NRSV).

26

Expanding the Mind

Study waits quietly, almost helplessly, like a doctor who can't get near a victim because of the frantic activity surrounding the scene of the accident.

—DON MCCULLOUGH

There was a time when pastors worked in studies; now we work in offices. This reflects, at least in part, a change in perceptions about the pastoral role. Jonathan Edwards and his eighteen hours of daily study may still be mentioned in reverent tones by seminary professors seeking to inspire scholarly excellence, but today's pastor will likely find a more congenial model in Lee Iacocca.

The modern church, with its plethora of programs, seems to want administrators more than theologians. Successful pastors' conferences don't offer theological lectures; they provide training in management techniques.

So why study?

It's an important question considering the contemporary expectations heaped on pastors. Why study when you could be developing strategies to attract newcomers? Why study when you could be creating flow charts for more effective congregational communication? Why study when you could be defining goals and honing objectives?

How can you justify sitting alone at your desk to work through a section of Karl Barth's *Church Dogmatics* when Mrs. Brown lies in a hospital bed, terrified of her upcoming surgery? How can you possibly luxuriate on an island of solitude when all around rages a stormy sea of human misery?

Why study?

Simply put, we have no choice: if we've been ordained to the ministry of the Word, we must work to understand both God's Word and the world to which we proclaim it.

John Stott has developed the metaphor of bridge building: "If we are to build bridges into the real world, and seek to relate the Word of God to the major themes of life and the major issues of the day, then we have to take seriously both the biblical text and the contemporary scene. We cannot afford to remain on either side of the cultural divide . . . it is our responsibility to explore the territories on both sides of the ravine until we become thoroughly familiar with them." Only then shall we discern the connections between them and be able to speak the divine Word to the human situation with any degree of sensitivity and accuracy.

Our study of these diverse worlds doesn't simply provide a file of facts for spicing up a dull sermon. Study changes us; it provides a broad context, delivering us from the narrow dimensions of personal experience.

A popular myth holds that personal experience is the only adequate teacher. Fred Craddock points out the fallacy of this notion:

> A soldier in the trenches of the Civil War came to understand war in ways unavailable to noncombatants. However, that experience was also limiting; so limiting, in fact, that the soldier could hardly interpret that war to the nation and to subsequent generations. That task calls for another perspective, that is, another experience. Getting distance from an event and reflecting on it is experience as surely as being plunged into its swirling currents. Study is not an alternative to experience but is itself a form of experience that grants understanding, even expertise, on a range of subjects.

As valuable as my own experiences are, they are too small, too cramped for my ministry. But through Augustine's *Confessions,* I enter into the spaciousness of one of the greatest minds of the ancient world; through Calvin's *Institutes of the Christian Religion,* I have my understanding of God stretched and ordered beyond my own natural abilities; through Tolstoy's *Anna Karenina,* I discover the ecstasy and terrible pain of adultery; through *The Autobiography of Malcolm X,* I become a black man, and have kindled within me the fires of anger over racism. Study lifts me to a higher and wider plane.

Billy Graham addressed a gathering of clergy in London in 1979. He said that if he had his ministry to do over again, he would study three times as much as he had and would take on fewer engagements.

"I've preached too much," said Graham, "and studied too little."

This is a regret we don't want to discover near the end of our own ministries. We want to sink deeply the pylons of the bridge in both the soil of God and the soil of humanity.

Time search

I've pastored both a small church and a large church, and I've discovered little difference: there never seems enough time for study. Opportunities for reading are as scarce as pine trees on southern California beaches. But if you know where to look, the occasional Torrey Pine can be seen; time for study can be found.

When we pastors get together, complaints about our busy schedules surface immediately. Clergy magazines are filled with themes of weariness, burnout, stress. Yes, pastors are busy. But we sometimes forget we have been given a wonderful gift—the gift of time. When we were installed as pastors, most of us were released from the burden of having to earn an income and given great freedom (in general) to invest ourselves in the tasks we deem important.

During the French Revolution, political prisoners were incarcerated in dingy dungeons. There is a story about a state's prisoner who possessed a Bible. His cellmates were eager to hear him read, but the darkness prohibited him from seeing the words. The only shaft of light fell through a tiny window near the ceiling, and this for only a few minutes each day. The prisoners, then, would lift the owner of the Bible onto their shoulders and into the sunlight. There, in that position, he would study. Then they would bring him down and say, "Tell us now, what did you read while you were in the light?"

The church, through ordination, has lifted pastors onto its shoulders and commissioned them to study on its behalf. If we fail in this task, it's not because we don't have the time; it's because we've not made good use of the time we've been given. For me, the real problem has been lack of discipline.

When I started my Ph.D. work at the University of Edinburgh, I was forced to face some uncomfortable tendencies in myself. The first few months were heaven. I had just completed four years as pastor of a church in a challenging setting, and now to do nothing but read and write felt like a wonderful vacation.

But then the Scottish winter rolled in, and it paralleled the gloom in my soul. Study was all I had to do—no preaching, no committee meetings, no lunches with elders, no hospital calls. Suddenly I realized the pastorate had not prepared me for disciplined study.

If the slightest feeling of boredom came over me, I had always had an escape: if reading a chapter of theology began to feel like slogging through knee-deep mud, well, there was always Mr. Smith to visit or a phone call to make or a luncheon to schedule. I discovered that as a pastor I could be busy in an undisciplined, even irresponsible way.

Yet discipline is required for all great endeavors. Louis Nizer, still a practicing attorney in his eighties, was asked if luck existed in trial law. He said yes, but added, "It only comes in the library at three o'clock in the morning. That holds true for me to this day. You'll find me in the library looking for luck at three o'clock in the morning." And that's probably where a lot of inspiration for ministry is found too.

The movie *Field of Dreams* is a whimsical story about a young Iowa farmer who hears a voice in the cornfield say, "If you build it, he will come."

"Build what?" the farmer wants to know. A ballpark, he learns. Who will come? Shoeless Joe Jackson, the Chicago White Sox legend. More important, another player will also come: the farmer's deceased father. So the farmer plows his corn under and marks out a diamond in the field. Sure enough, Shoeless Joe Jackson appears, along with seven other White Sox players and a few old New York Giants—and his father.

"If you build it, he will come." That's also true for the pastor. If we create the right conditions in our lives, our Father will more likely visit with the truth and inspiration needed to speak in his name.

It's not easy to plow an open space in the busyness of parish life. But here are two ways that have helped me.

Establish a routine of time and place. Unless study is made a regular, habitual part of my schedule, it will constantly be postponed for lack of time. Study makes no imperious claims on me; it never importunes with pleas of desperation. Hospital calls, committee meetings, counseling sessions, staff problems, correspondence, telephone calls—these things elbow their way to the front of the line, extorting time by threatening to make me appear uncaring or irresponsible if I don't give way to their demands.

But study waits quietly, almost helplessly, like a doctor who can't get near a victim because of the frantic activity surrounding the scene of the accident. So when I'm wise, I clear a way for study, protecting it in every way possible.

The rhythm of my week has a predictable pattern: the first half is heavily administrative, with time given to staff and committees, and the latter half is reflective, with time for reading, writing, and sermon preparation. I find it helps to be specific on my calendar by writing phrases such as "Read von Balthasar on prayer" or "Get caught up on journals."

Then, when faced with requests for my time, I can say, "I'm sorry, I already have a commitment scheduled. May I see you next Monday afternoon?" It also helps me to think of study not as time alone—for that seems so selfish when purchased at the expense of saying no to individuals—but as time in company with my whole congregation. I imagine their faces, expectant with anticipation, waiting to hear what I've learned. And I remind myself that I won't be able to offer them anything of substance if I don't study.

Many pastors enjoy the benefit of annual study leaves. My own denomination requires congregations to grant at least two weeks a year (cumulative up to six weeks) for this purpose. In addition, some pastors are given extended sabbaticals after several years of service. I seize these opportunities for expanding mind and spirit whenever offered so that I can participate in conferences, continuing education courses at seminaries, travel, and more in-depth research.

But study leaves and sabbaticals are extraordinary events, only frosting on the cake of regular, disciplined study. My ministry must depend upon more frequent feedings of the mind.

Teach the congregation. Once a routine is established, it should be made known. We've all heard the gibe about pastors working only one day a week. Before dismissing such nonsense, we ought to listen to it: it may indicate a genuine lack of understanding about what we do. If we were more intentional about telling our congregations how we organize our time—especially our study time—we might find them more supportive of our efforts.

I periodically mention from the pulpit my need to study; I make certain the staff understands I'm more available earlier in the week than later; I tell those who want to see me that Thursday and Friday are not good days because of sermon preparation. By now most of the congregation know they dare not call me on Friday unless it's a serious emergency.

God's side of the ravine

John Stott's metaphor of bridge building offers me a helpful way to organize my study time: on the one side, God, and on the other, humanity. I learn from both. Here's how I deepen my understanding of God.

Both forest and trees. To communicate the Word of God to the world of humanity, I begin with the biblical text. To organize my time for this task, I remember the so-called hermeneutical circle: the whole Scripture interprets its various parts, and the various parts reveal its whole. I want my study, therefore, to be both general and particular; I plan for reflection on the forest and for detailed study of individual trees.

To keep myself thinking about the broad sweep of God's revelation, I try to read four chapters in the Bible each day. Now, parts of it, I admit, bore me. So to keep from getting lost in the genealogies of Genesis or drowning in the blood sacrifices of Leviticus, I read in four different places. A pattern I have used with profit is Robert Murray McCheyne's *Bible Reading Calendar,* introduced to his Scottish congregation in 1842. The calendar begins the year at Genesis, Ezra, Matthew, and Acts (the four great beginnings), so at the end of the year, I've read the Old Testament once and the New Testament twice.

Staying with it every day can sometimes be difficult (especially if I skip a day because of an early morning breakfast and have to read eight chapters the next day). I feel it's necessary, though, for a clear view of the forest. I'm surprised continually how the various passages interact with each other and with my upcoming sermons; connections I would have never made jump out at me through this daily discipline.

In addition, I set aside a few hours each week (two to four) for theological reading not connected in any obvious way with sermon preparation. To study only for next Sunday leaves me wading in shallow waters, so to stay fit I swim in the depths by working through a volume of systematic theology.

Early in my ministry, I made a choice I haven't regretted, though it would probably cause despair for my seminary language professors: with study time so limited, I decided to spend it with Karl Barth rather than Hebrew vocabulary lists. Consequently, my reading knowledge of Hebrew rapidly died, and my Greek isn't too healthy (actually, it's in the intensive care unit). But I believe a growing ability to think theologically (with breadth and depth) has more than compensated for the deficiency.

Earl Palmer remembers a senior class dinner at Princeton Seminary in which George Buttrick challenged the future pastors by saying, "When you are at Coney Island, don't tell the people of the concession on the boardwalk about which they know; tell them of the mystery of the sea, about which they don't know." Palmer went on: "Don't read only what your people are reading. . . . Read what your people are not reading."

The books that deserve our attention, I believe, are primary sources; leave secondary sources to others. The best books are often not carried by the average Christian bookstore, but most merchants happily order them.

Having a panoramic view of the forest isn't enough; I don't really see its wonder until I've closely examined individual trees. For me, study of the particulars of Scripture happens as I prepare for sermons. I dissect the text, sentence by sentence, word by word, asking a thousand questions and trying to answer them myself before reading the commentaries. I often find myself impatient, not wanting to stay with the text long enough. But I've learned that the best expositors, like Jacob wrestling with the angel, won't let it go until they get the blessing (and often a pain in the thigh too).

Freeman Patterson, a professional photographer, has described the way he approaches his art: "On those frosty mornings when I grab my camera and tripod and head out into the meadow behind the house, I quickly forget about me. I stop thinking about what I'd do with the photographs, or about self-fulfillment, and lose myself in the sheer magic of rainbows in the grass."

The way Patterson surrenders himself to his subject is the way I like to become wholly captivated by a text. I find this difficult, however. Many things distract me before I'm finished seeing the text itself: possible sermon outlines, an idea to comfort the disturbed or to disturb the comfortable, a great story I've been saving for a dramatic illustration. These things—and a hundred more—can seize my attention as rabbits distract a hunting dog. But when I manage to keep my eyes focused on the pheasant, as it were, I end up with more to feed my people.

Only after I've spent time with the text itself do I let myself wander through the commentaries. And I mean wander. I don't feel compelled to read every word of every commentary in my library; I meander through them, checking my own exegesis to make sure I'm not being dishonest with the text and watching for ideas I might have missed. I try to read at least one historical/critical commentary and a couple of expositional/homiletical commentaries.

Dailies to quarterlies. For the task of getting grounded on

God's side of the ravine, there are many periodicals available to update us on recent theological trends, practical advice, book reviews, and news of the Christian world. These can be important resources stimulating our thinking and pointing to what God is doing in our world.

But I'm cautious with periodicals. They can consume a great deal of time, piling up and burying me in a truckload of guilt. So I scan periodicals, occasionally using the last half-hour at the office to get through the accumulated stack. When an article interests me, I slow down, perhaps copying it for my files.

Humanity's side of the ravine

My first task in study is to sink one side of the bridge deeply into the soil of God, the Word of God. But the bridge building isn't complete until the other pylon has been sunk deeply into the soil of humanity, the world. Here's how I do that.

Pay attention to people. Exegeting Scripture isn't enough; I must also exegete human life. Often the people who drain my emotions and distract my thinking are important resources for study. I want to know those with whom I minister, not in the way a salesman knows a client well enough to make a sale but rather in the way a husband knows his wife, with a participatory knowledge that transforms him as much as it transforms her. I don't want my knowledge to be simply utilitarian, for that leads to manipulation; it must be incarnational, for that leads to transformation. I've found the best way to know people is to listen to them.

When Frank and John told me they both had AIDS, I found it difficult to silence my inner voices—judgmental voices, I'm sorry to admit—long enough to hear them. But I tried. I began to hear two stories of anguish. Frank had an identical twin brother who was also homosexual. Both Frank and John said they couldn't remember deliberately choosing this themselves. They lamented their impending deaths. And they spoke of their love for each other. Though I disagree with their life style, that conversation moved me to compassion as I recognized the human dimension to the issue of homosexuality.

Reading to know our world. Thankfully, my knowledge of humanity need not be limited by my circle of friends and parishioners. Through books I can enter into the lives of others. Because reading time is precious, I'm careful about what I read. (I sometimes think I take as much time choosing what to read as I spend reading.) Every year publishers dump 50,000 new books on the market, and even if 49,000 aren't worth the paper they're printed on, that still leaves a good many crying for my attention.

In selecting books, I pay careful attention to reviews (my favorite weekly source is the *New York Times Book Review*) and recommendations from people I trust. Also, if I find an especially challenging and inspiring author, I read her other works, and then I read the thinkers who have influenced her. Good books, then, lead me to other good books.

My goal is to finish at least one book a week. This seems necessary to me, since I'm faced with the weekly task of preaching. I usually juggle four different books at once. In addition to the volume of theology I've already mentioned, I'm always in a novel and a biography. The fourth book shifts between different categories—most often social and political commentaries, religious works (not strictly theology), and psychology.

The daily newspaper consumes large amounts of time, and for me it's rarely worth it, even though I receive one of the nation's finest. I limit my newspaper reading to the front page, occasional editorials, and a quick scan of the sports and arts sections. Most news develops over several days, so a weekly news magazine like *Time* or *Newsweek* offers a good summary. (For many years I've read *Time* cover to cover.)

The electronic media. The people in our congregations, however, do not spend most of their time reading. Electronic media influence them far more than the printed page. The average American spends four and a half hours each day watching television—an increase of 80 percent in the past fifteen years. If we're not watching some television, we're out of touch with an important part of today's world.

As for radio, I don't follow my natural inclinations and turn to the classical music station when I jump into the car. Many of my parishioners—perhaps most—prefer light rock to the music of Bach. So I have my dial set on a popular "top-forty" station and keep it there as long as my aesthetic sensibilities can take it. As with television, popular music reveals much about our contemporary culture. And besides, I've grown to like the beat.

Cultural events. Most communities offer opportunities to experience movies, drama, concerts, and visual arts. Nowadays, even those in rural areas enjoy traveling performances; few pastors are completely cut off from these things. Time and money, of course, may limit taking full advantage of what's available. But when I do see a movie or watch a play or listen to a concert or visit a gallery, I often find my mind stretched and my emotions touched.

Study record

Unless a pastor has a perfect memory, storing and retrieving the fruit of our study will be necessary. Filing systems, I suppose, merit the comment C. S. Lewis made about the devil: the two great errors we make are to think too much or too little about them.

An elaborate system, complete with codes and cross references and computer programs, can create a methodological legalism, causing me to join with the apostle Paul in crying, "Wretched man that I am! Who will deliver me from this body of death?" (Rom. 7:24 NKJV).

But the stories, quotations, and images need to be recorded to be remembered. I keep with me at all times (except in the shower) a small hand-held recorder. It uses a microcassette, which can store 120 minutes of dictation. Many reasonably priced models are on the market, and I would consider myself horribly deprived without one. If the proverbial push came to shove, I would probably trade my entire set of Kittel or maybe even the *Church Dogmatics* for one.

When I come across something in my reading or have a thought I don't want to forget or think of an interesting image, I simply reach for my recorder and speak to my secretary, "Susie, a quotation card . . ." She will then type whatever I tell her on a four-by-six-inch card and add the appropriate bibliographic references I may want to keep.

Before using this method, I might have found something worth remembering, but an argument would immediately ensue: I really should get up, get a piece of paper, and write this down; on the other hand, my shoes are off, my feet are up, and a tired man deserves to relax. The treasure would never get recorded. Now I simply reach for my recorder, push a button, and in seconds it's accomplished.

What do I do with the cards? I do not file them, at least not immediately. I keep a pile growing for about a year, because a good quotation or illustration can almost always be used in a variety of contexts. Just after I've written a bare-bones sermon outline, during the brainstorming part of the preaching process, I shuffle through the stack. This doesn't take much time; after a few weeks, a card is so familiar that one glance reminds me of its content.

About once a year I force myself to categorize each card and file it according to a specific subject. Through the years the file boxes have accumulated. In the event of a fire, I would probably risk my life to carry them to safety before anything else.

Building the bridge between God and humanity requires disciplined study. The work isn't always easy, but we have no choice. The Lord deserves our minds as well as our hearts in his great enterprise.

Leonardo da Vinci was once hard at work on a great painting. It was nearly complete when suddenly he called a student to him, gave him the brush, and said, "You finish it."

The student protested, feeling unworthy.

But da Vinci said, "Will not what I have done inspire you to do your best?"

God's masterful work of creation and redemption through Jesus Christ inspires me to excel in the difficult task of enlarging the mind to expand the ministry.

PART 9

Stepping Up

27

What I Want to Be
When I Grow Up

*Growth cannot happen without a powerful respect for the reality
of indwelling evil and its insidious work through self-deceit.*

—GORDON MACDONALD

When I was in college, I participated in a campus ministry
whose aim was the evangelization of the whole world. The audac-
ity of the dream ignited new passion within my personal faith,
and for that I'm grateful. But sometimes, I suspect, the motiva-
tional approaches went a bit too far.

One day, for example, a staff member read us a story from the
biography of C. T. Studd, one of the great English missionary
pioneers of the nineteenth century. We'd all come to revere Studd
as one of those who gave up everything—including a great sports
career—to evangelize the nations. We listened intently for further
insights that would enable us to imitate this man and his faith.

As I recall, Studd went off to Africa and remained there seventeen years without seeing his English homeland. He never saw his
wife, either, since she remained in England to assist the supporting mission organization. For reasons I cannot fathom now, we
assumed this willingness to accept marital separation was admirable, the epitome of commitment.

Now here's the story we heard that day: Studd's wife eventually
came to Africa. But only because it seemed prudent for her—get
this—to visit the various outposts of the mission's work. So her
husband's mission station became part of the itinerary.

As I remember the story, she came up a river by boat to the
place where Studd was living. He met her and walked her to the

front porch of his house. There they stayed for thirty or so minutes, visiting about the progress of "winning the lost" and then
having a time of prayer. Then she returned to her boat and continued her tour.

We students were breathless when we heard this story. "What
extraordinary dedication!" we said to one another. "This is what
it's all about. If God is to use us, these are the kinds of people
we've got to become."

As far as I know, none of us ever became those kinds of people,
and that's probably good. I still admire C. T. Studd, but not his
perspective on marriage.

Occasionally, I've pondered the wisdom we employ in choosing role models for ourselves or for impressionable young people.
In this case we simply didn't know the whole story. We selected a
"sound bite" out of a good man's life and used it to exemplify
sacrifice and dedication. The possibility never occurred to us that
C. T. Studd may have had a substandard marriage. Or that what
Studd and his wife did might have been just plain wrong.

Maybe the fact that he didn't rush to the river—after all he had
been an athlete—and scoop her up in his arms and smother her
with kisses (even though we are talking about a Victorian culture) says something that's sad. At age fifty-three I now know
something that I didn't know at nineteen: there's no way I would
leave my wife for seventeen years. And if something had necessi-
tated a separation of that period of time, I wouldn't have chosen
to spend the only thirty minutes we had together sitting on a
front porch talking about missions.

The faith tradition in which I was raised was built on the
crusader model. It is shaped, first and foremost, by the belief that
we have a message of salvation to give to the nations, which must
be proclaimed at all costs. It follows, then, that the heroes are
those who proclaim that message at whatever necessary sacrifice.
Studd is an example of this apostolic life style: preach the gospel
with nothing held back.

Our teachers seldom made clear to us that apostle-types tend
to be strange (if wonderful) people. They are not always good
husbands or wives, good parents, or specimens of good health.
They are often poor at team-building or team-playing. Get too

close to them, and you discover that their strengths are awesome
. . . but so are their flaws.

But since we rarely hear about the flaws—and those brave
enough to tell us about them have usually found their comments
unwelcomed—we conjure up these images of superlative people
that set the standard of what we have to be like.

And we grow discouraged when that doesn't happen. We want
to be like C. T. Studd, but then we also want to be a good spouse,
a good parent, a good team player, a good preacher, a good
caregiver, and on and on. It doesn't work, because there is probably no such thing as a well-rounded hero. So many of us live lives
of quiet dissatisfaction because we do not measure up to the
standards we've set for ourselves.

Today, the heroes may be different: not the missionary pioneer
of yesterday but the entrepreneurial leaders who have unusual
gifts and build megachurch institutions that attract, evangelize (I
think), and mobilize thousands of people. Some of these I am
fortunate to call my friends. I admire them; I don't think I envy
them. But I must be candid. I would have twenty years ago.

At the age of thirty, I would have hungered for that sort of
effectiveness. I would have brooded on what it might take to offer
such leadership. I would have studied these entrepreneurial leaders as carefully as possible so that I could be like them and experience their success.

If there are virtues to growing older, one of them is to slowly
lose the need to be like everyone else—especially the most successful heroes. To gain a bit of maturity is first to see that the
Spirit gives gifts to whom he will, and to see that with all the
success and privilege comes significant "bondage." Being a leader
is wonderful. But it is not without its price.

There is enormous spiritual pressure to the seduction of pride
and competition. There are potential "soft addictions" of sensation, excitement, applause, and being the center of attention.
There are the desperately lonely moments when one in the spot-
light realizes that there are many acquaintances but few friends
and little time for friendships.

For leaders there is the anxiety of wondering what this notoriety is doing to the family, especially the children. The bondage goes on and on.

No, there is little to envy or copy among the heroes. God knows which ones are his, and he knows why they are successful. And most of the time, I'm glad it's them and not me.

I measured myself against the heroes of the past and the present. Then I remember realizing one day that there were one or two young men measuring themselves against me. I wasn't measuring up to *my* models, and they were upset because they weren't measuring up to me.

This measurement stuff—when the criteria is someone else's achievements or personality—has to be seen for what it is: a sure menu for misery.

Perhaps we've made a dangerous move by sizing up ourselves on the basis of our ability to grow large, impressive organizations. We hear less and less about the quality of a leader's spirit. The conferences—for the most part—are all about the "market," the institution, the program.

Perhaps this is not all bad except when it is compared to the amount of time spent on the subject of the soul and its capacity to be prophetic, perceptive, and powerful.

My illusion

For two of the years I was in seminary, I pastored a tiny country church 175 miles east of Denver. For a year, Gail and I saved money by living in the church's small parsonage. That meant on Tuesday at 4 A.M. I would leave the house and make a three-hour drive in our Volkswagen Beetle to Denver.

The drive along Route 36 from the Kansas border to Denver was almost a straight shot. As you looked westward to the horizon, you sensed that the car could go in any direction and never run into a barrier. It was smooth sailing.

Life is sometimes like that. No barriers. You feel, *I can do anything I want if I am willing to work hard enough. And pray hard enough. And study hard enough.* I once believed that myself.

But back to Route 36. Just beyond the town of Last Chance,

Colorado, you suddenly see three mountain peaks on the horizon—Pike's Peak to the south, Long's Peak to the north, and Mount Evans directly to the west. Instantly the illusion of a barrierless journey is pricked by the realization that three solid and rather large obstacles represent a reduction in options.

Sometimes in ministry we also reach a "Last Chance." The day comes when you discover personal barriers and limits: *I cannot do this as well as . . . I don't actually have the gift of . . . This task requires something that simply isn't my strength.*

Obligations are accrued. Perhaps a spouse. Maybe a child or two. Perhaps responsibilities to extended family members. They wouldn't be complimented by being called barriers. But they nevertheless cut down on other options.

This can be a tough moment for some young leaders. The once dizzying dreams are slowly modified by reality. And little by little, we discover why we're really in this "business" of serving God. We're probably not going to be heroes, and the world is not going to beat a path to our door begging for our insights. And that's okay.

But let me finish my parable.

On the trip to Denver, as you near the city, there comes a point where the long stretch of the Rocky Mountains rises up like an impenetrable wall. Where once only three barriers, evenly spaced apart, interrupted the horizon, now barriers fill your vision. You get the feeling you can't go anywhere. You're *trapped*! The illusion of barrierlessness is inverted.

That's the perception of more than one midlifer in the ministry. The freshness is gone; the fears of mediocrity, of ineffectiveness, of being lost in the shuffle are malignant.

Penetrate the curtain of quiet thought of many forty- and fifty-year-old pastors, and you will find this wall is a very real perception: *Where can I go? And who can I tell that I fear I can't go anywhere? And why do I feel ashamed that I even worry about these things? Would my heroes, then and now, worry about walls? What's wrong with me?*

When you get to the "Denver" of my parable, you have three choices: (1) try going back to your point of origin, "youthfulness," where the dream of no limits still exists, (2) try driving in circles, cursing the wall and moaning that it's impossible to go back, or, and this is the important possibility, (3) try going up to the wall and find the passes or tunnels that lead to a healthy, spiritually vigorous, and personally effective last forty years of life.

I'm at the point in life where I'm traveling through the wall and enjoying the process! Now I know that life in the "barrierless" days was nice but terribly unrealistic.

No wonder that in those days the older men never sought me out for wisdom and counsel. They were kind to me, listened to my sermons, followed me when I had good ideas and enthusiasm. But now I know what they were thinking: *He's a good kid who needs to grow a little before he's ready to know our hearts.*

I took my turn driving in circles. In a moment of great personal failure and sadness, I had to drive in circles while Gail and I sought the voice of the Lord about our future—whether one actually existed or not. Some of the darkest days of my life. But days of unforgettable tenderness as God taught us some things through pain that we might not have learned otherwise.

Because God is a kind and gracious God, and because I was surrounded by some men and women who believed in restorative grace, I discovered the future up in the passes and tunnels that lead through the wall.

Elsewhere I've written about the day I was hit with the question: *What kind of an old man do you want to be?* And I opted for growth and grace as my old-age life style. I love the words of Tennyson in his poem "Ulysses." He imagines the old, travel-worn Ulysses brooding on what one might do for an encore after having seen the world:

> *Tho' much is taken, much abides; and tho'*
> *We are not now that strength which in old days*
> *Moved earth and heaven; that which we are, we are;*
> *One equal-temper of heroic hearts,*
> *Made weak by time and fate, but strong in will*
> *To strive, to seek, to find, and not to yield.*

That spells it out for me—"strong in will to strive, to seek, to find, and not to yield." Here's an old man who has chosen growth for an old-aged life style when other old men were opting to go to Greece's version of Florida and the shuffleboard courts.

Or perhaps I could have used Paul's words—"Though our outward man is perishing, yet the inward man is being renewed day by day" (2 Cor. 4:16 NKJV). Again, "I have fought the good fight, I have finished the race" (2 Tim. 4:7 NKJV). I love the enthusiasm of Tennyson's Ulysses and Paul's feistiness.

So at midlife, I asked God for a rebirth of spirit and mind. And I found a wonderful liberation. Liberation from feeling that I always had to be right and to please everyone's definition of orthodoxy; liberation from always having to be more successful this year than last year; liberation from fearing that some people wouldn't like me; a slow and certain liberation that said, *Be content to be a pleasure to Christ, a lover to your wife, a grandfather to your children's children, a friend to those who want to share life with you, and a servant to your generation.*

In part, that liberation came from the grace and kindness of Jesus and, also, from having to clean up after failure. Those who knew me now knew my worst moments, my most embarrassing failures. I was free now to open my life and be what I was: a sinner who survives only because of the charity of Christ.

Now there is freedom to talk about fears, doubts, disappointments, and weaknesses. Because anything good that comes from someone like me actually comes from God. Paul said it best: "When I am weak, then I am strong" (2 Cor. 12:10 NKJV).

So when you decide to go through the wall, where do you start?

My mission

I continued to wrestle with the question, *What sort of an old man do you want to be?* I looked around and discovered I didn't know many old men who impressed me with the same traits mentioned by Tennyson's Ulysses.

Why? Maybe because most men and women never build a

growth plan for the old years. And if you don't plan for the kind of man (or woman) you want to be when you are eighty (God willing) and begin building that when you are forty or fifty, it's not likely to happen.

That's what drove me to define my personal mission. Without a mission, people live by reaction rather than initiation. I'd written a few mission statements for organizations; why not one for myself?

Today my mission statement sits on page 2 of my journal where I read it each morning as I start my day. It defines my direction and channels my enthusiasm:

> My life is focused on serving God's purposes in my generation so that the kingdom of Christ might be more firmly established wherever I go. In my dealings with people, I want to be a source of hope, encouragement, enthusiasm, friendship, and service. As a man I seek the daily enlargement of my spirit so that it might be a dwelling place for Christ, a source of wisdom and holiness unto the Lord.

It is a functional statement, describing in broad, macro-terms what I want to do with my life. It calls for me to grow by being on a constant search for the purposes of God for the times in which I live. And it puts me squarely on a mission of kingdom building: calling people to the kingdom conditions in the world in which I live.

It is a statement of quality, reminding me every day of what kind of man I want to be, what I believe Jesus has called me to be: a servant. I know the words are lofty. They're meant to be. A mission that isn't lofty isn't worth pursuing. I want my mind and spirit to be rechallenged every day with what Paul called "the high calling of God in Christ Jesus" (Phil. 3:14 KJV).

It is also a relational statement. It calls me to high standards as I interact with people, and it describes some of those standards. It outlines what I want to offer in my relationships. More than once I've awakened in a less-than-best mood and grumped a bit at Gail. And then, having successfully grumped, I have turned to my mission statement about hope, encouragement, enthusiasm, friendship, and service. Repentance usually follows.

I've heard people groan about mission statements. "Too managerial," some say. "Not my temperament," says another. "Too broad, too general, too ethereal." But I'm fascinated by a little-known instruction in Deuteronomy 17 where Moses spoke of future kings. Kings, he said, should be careful to do certain things and not do other things (such as have many wives, acquire horses, accumulate gold and silver, or send people back to Egypt).

Then, having issued that warning, Moses said this: "When he takes the throne of his kingdom, he is to write for himself on a scroll a copy of this law, taken from that of the priests. . . . It is to be with him, and he is to read it all the days of his life so that he may learn to revere the LORD his God and follow carefully all the words of this law and these decrees" (Deut. 17:18–19 NIV).

Isn't that describing a mission statement? Interesting that he would say the king should "write for himself." He is to read what he's written every day. Why? Because a king's life is open to all sorts of internal and external seductions and deceits. He needs reminders of where he's supposed to be going and what he is to avoid. Both kings and Christian leaders should construct for themselves such a statement, a covenant of growth.

My sub-missions

But a mission statement may not be enough. Early in this quest, I began to think about "sub-missions," equally lofty goals for each major area of my life. I identified seven areas needing discipline.

Physical: My sub-mission is to keep my body healthy, through good habits, regular exercise, prudent nutrition, and weight discipline.

Relational: My sub-mission is to love my wife in the pattern of Christ's love, to enjoy her friendship, and to make sure that her quality of life is the best I can make it. It is to be as faithful a family man as possible to my children and my grandchildren.

And, finally, to be a vigorous friend to a small circle of men and women to whom I'm drawn in community. Beyond that I want to be a contributing member to my generation, always giving more to people than I take.

Intellectual: My sub-mission is to steepen my learning curve whenever possible through reading and exposure to the thinking people and disciplines of the day.

Financial: My sub-mission is to be generous, debt-free, moderate in expenditure, and careful to plan for the years of my life when income production may be difficult.

Vocational: My sub-mission is to represent the purposes of God for my generation and to teach/write as well as model all aspects of "quality of spirit." I would like to make this happen both inside and outside the Christian community.

Spiritual: My sub-mission is to be a focused, holy, obedient, and reverential man before God and his world; to discipline my life so that it is controlled by the Spirit within me and so people are drawn one step closer to Christ because of me.

Recreational: My sub-mission is to seek restoration in this world by enjoying creation, caring for it, and seeking its reconciliation to the Creator.

I read these statements almost every morning as part of my personal meditations. Several comments about them:

First, they reflect what I personally think God wants from me. I don't compare myself with the apostles and the heroes anymore. Their achievements were and are unique; but so are mine. My sub-missions excite me. I seek a certain nobility in them. They motivate me to a higher way of living.

Second, they represent a variety of dreams, reflecting my life as a whole person: in touch with my body, my friends, my mind, my skills, and my world.

Third, they're flexible. Over the years, I've fine-tuned these statements as I've discovered new interests and abilities.

Finally, they're not crippling dreams. They are open-ended. And they do not produce guilt when I slip backward a bit. But you can be sure that I'm sometimes chided and rebuked when I read them.

My journal

Over the years I've introduced several other activities to my spiritual disciplines. The first and foremost is journaling.

My journal carries a starting date somewhere in 1968. And since then I've managed to keep a record of almost every day of my life.

I began journaling because I discovered that many saints found it profitable. This is one of the times I copied my heroes. The saints and mystics lived without TV, phones, and all the other scintillating interruptions we've allowed into our lives. A commitment to keeping a journal forced me away from the distractions. And it pressed me to think, to evaluate, to reflect, and to remember. It provided a way to look at events and impressions and interpret the presence of God in it all.

Today I write my journal on a laptop computer, a concession to technology. It enables me to write more, do it faster, and to overcome my repugnance toward my own handwriting.

The journal becomes a tool for measuring short-term and long-term growth. The short-term measurements are daily. I frequently end a daily entry into the journal with: "Results today will be measured by . . ." And then I list the things I believe I should accomplish and what it would take to consider those accomplishments as finished. There is a sense of well-being when I go back to that list the next day and type in "done" after each one.

Sometimes I write simple goals like "Enjoy a great afternoon with Gail," or "Review travel schedule, and make sure your calender is up to date."

For long-term growth, I use the journal—using older language—to inquire of the state of the soul. What has Scripture been saying to me? What is God saying through my meditations? What feelings, themes, attitudes are predominant these days? Am I fearful, preoccupied, moody, angry? What sensitivities are being stimulated? What new thoughts, new concerns might be God's way of directing my life? This stuff has got to be written down in my world, or it just sails right through the conscious mind and leaves, having no effect.

Then I use the journal approximately every four months to

evaluate growth and progress. New Year's Day, my birthday (in April), and the end of vacation (August 30) are usually times to look over the past months and ask the great Sabbath questions: Where have I been? And has the journey been fruitful? Where should I be going? And do I have the resources to get there?

After all these words about pursuing growth, I must admit there is no guarantee against failure. Some of the very best people in biblical history failed—terribly. What set them apart, more often than not, was not their great achievements but their repentant and broken spirits. And wasn't it a broken spirit that God said he loved best?

I need to go one step further and note some things about personal growth that seem at first to be bleak. I've learned the hard way that having a mission statement, a series of sub-missions, a process of journaling and evaluation is not a promise of success. I know failure, and I've found no human way to ensure against it.

The older I become the more I realize my condition as a barbarian loved by my Father. And this may be the most important insight that comes with aging. Almost all old people who are growing have certain common traits. One of them is that they know without equivocation that they are sinners. And they've come to appreciate the central importance of grace.

I once had a friendship with a man in his seventies and eighties. Lee was a godly man who brought the most unusual people to Jesus.

One day we were having breakfast, and Lee began to tell me about a recent trip he'd taken to Boston. "As I drove toward the city," Lee said, "I realized that I was going to be parking my car and walking through the combat zone (Boston's notorious redlight district). So I pulled into a rest stop and had a time of prayer so I could ask God to protect me from temptation when I walked past all those pornography stores and massage parlors."

"Wait a minute, Lee," I interrupted. "I don't want to offend you, but you're seventy-eight years old. Are you telling me that you're concerned about sexual temptation at your age and after all these years of following the Lord?"

Lee looked at me with an intensity. "Son, just because I'm old doesn't mean the blood doesn't flow through my veins. The dif-

ference between us old men and you young men is this: we know
we're sinners. We've had plenty of experience. You kids haven't
figured that out yet."

Now, years later, I understand a bit of what the old man was
saying. And I understand why old men and women who are
growing are among the most gracious and forgiving people there
are.

Growth cannot happen without a powerful respect for the reality of indwelling evil and its insidious work through self-deceit. It
leads us to lie to God, ourselves, and one another. The spiritual
disciplines are designed not only to lead us into the presence of
the Father but to sensitize us to the lies we can find so easy to
believe.

The leader is constantly the target of the temptations to deceit.
We are never far from the statement King Nebuchadnezzar made
on the walls of Babylon when he said, "Is not this the great Babylon I have built as the royal residence, by my mighty power and
for the glory of my majesty?" (Dan. 4:30 NIV). Look around at
some who have been deceived by the success of media ministry,
success in fund-raising, the sensation found in fast-growing institutions, or the money capable of being accumulated through large
fees and "love offerings."

My questions

Growth cannot happen when the success is superficial and the
heart is deceived. In the Bible, deceit was almost always challenged by the power of hard questions. To Cain: "Why is your
face downcast?" (Gen. 4:6 NIV). To Hezekiah: "What have [the
Babylonians] seen in your house?" (2 Kings 20:15 NKJV). To Judas:
"Why are you here?" To Ananias and Sapphira: "Why have you
lied to the Holy Spirit?"

Gail and I have compiled some tough questions to ask ourselves when we think about growth. Questions like:

1. Am I too defensive when asked questions about the use of
my time and the consistency of my spiritual disciplines?

2. Have I locked myself into a schedule that provides for no rest or fun times with friends and family?

3. What does my Daytimer say about time for study, general reading, and bodily exercise?

4. What of the quality of my speech? Am I whining and complaining? Am I frequently critical of people, of institutions, of those who clearly do not like me?

5. Am I drawn to TV shows or entertainment that do not reflect my desired spiritual culture?

6. Am I tempted to stretch the truth, enlarge numbers that are favorable to me, or tell stories that make me look good?

7. Am I blaming others for things that are my own fault, the result of my own choices?

8. Is my spirit in a state of quiet so I can hear God speak?

In *Rebuilding Your Broken World,* I recounted the story of Matthias Rust, the young German who piloted a rental plane into the heart of the former Soviet Union and landed in Moscow's Red Square. I've always thought that to be an apt illustration of what can happen to any Christian leader at any time.

The Soviets were sure they had the best systems of air defense in the world. And a teenager penetrated their airspace and taxied up to the front door of the Kremlin. No Christ-following man or woman can feel the confidence that they are growing if they are not living in a perpetual repentance, a holy sorrow that acknowledges that, apart from the power and grace of Christ, we will succumb to the evil that abides within until the day Christ returns.

Mastering pastoral growth depends largely not on our measuring ourselves against the saints and heroes. There is value in learning from their lives and witness. But they are among the cloud of witnesses about whom the writer in Hebrews spoke. They remain in the stands as we run our leg of the race.

We cannot match ourselves against their performances. Rather, our eyes are to be upon the One who runs with us. Thanks be to God who is alongside when we run, who hoists us back up when we fall, who redefines direction when we are lost, who cheers us on when we grow fatigued, and who presents us to the Father when we finish the race.

28

Being Holy, Being Human

The tension between living out the pastoral role and being genuine will be played out differently. For me, the decision hinges on the answer to this question: "Which will better enhance the ministry of Christ in the church?"

—Ben Patterson

I felt a little ashamed of myself for doing it, but not enough to stop myself.

It was my day off; my wife and I had taken our usual long walk, had breakfast together, and stopped in a clothing store to shop. When I saw two church members in the boutique, I quickly ducked behind a mannequin. I was tired, it was my day off, and I didn't feel like extending any greetings. Making sure they weren't looking, I slipped out of the store and made my escape.

It wasn't pastoral of me, but it was honest. And it illustrates a struggle I face in the pastorate—trying to balance the tension between the personal and the professional—being the person I am and being that person called a "pastor."

Other professions live with the same tension, but they can handle it more efficiently. In *The Christian Century,* columnist Martin Marty once wrote about the schizolike attitude of flight attendants. On airplanes we find attendants gracious, sometimes to the point of gushiness. They look us in the eye, give us a big smile, and extend plenty of hospitality.

But when our flight lands and we spot these same attendants in the concourse or baggage claim area, they simply walk by, avoid eye contact, and ignore us. Marty calls that "civil inattention"— they step out of the flight attendant role and become themselves, no longer obligated to look after us.

Pastors must be pastors. But we are also people. Do we have a right to step out of the professional role? Although we can't divide our roles as cleanly as a flight attendant, we still must figure out why and how to live with this tension. Here are some insights that have helped me.

Beyond genuine

As a child of the 1960s, I wanted no part of the institutional baggage of the church. Even when I attended seminary, I intended to go into youth work. Ministry to me meant parachurch, non-ordained ministry.

Like Father MacKenzie, one of the "all the lonely people" in the Beatles' song "Eleanor Rigby," the pastors I knew seemed to be lonely, hollow men trapped in ecclesiastical roles, creatures weighted down with the expectations of their congregations' collective psyches. I believed what they were forced to be kept them from what they ought to be—themselves, whatever that was.

I've gone through a few changes since then. I've learned that ministry is more than simply being myself, that in fact, ministry is often enhanced when I accept the pastoral role. In particular, there are five advantages of living in the pastoral role:

It checks individualism. In an effort to be genuine, I sometimes think, *I'm going to say what I think and do what I want, regardless of people's expectations.* But sometimes people's expectations—for example, that pastors be good listeners or that pastors not selfishly pursue their own agendas—are exactly what a strong-headed person like me needs to adhere to most.

Archbishop William Temple once remarked, "I'm suspicious of people who are anxious to tell me what God said to them but don't want to hear what God said to me."

Sometimes when I get excited about a concern, I tend to be less interested in others' agendas. It's shortsighted of me to think I'm the only one who's hearing from God. In short, living out the pastoral role can keep me honest—it doesn't let me run off on a selfish tangent.

It keeps the issue in focus. Being genuine means telling people how I feel about things. But in many instances, sharing my feelings merely sidetracks ministry.

For instance, if the church board is in the midst of a debate and I tell people how I *feel* about the process or the topic being debated—for example, "I feel uncomfortable with the anger being exchanged" or "This topic troubles me"—I merely shift the subject from the topic under discussion to Pastor Ben's feelings. That undercuts the importance of the subject matter and puts off a decision even longer.

It keeps emotions in control. Years ago, when people would treat me badly, I'd get angry and blast them and then try to justify the emotional outburst, muttering things like "righteous indignation," "justice," and "honesty." But the truth was I only hurt the person by satisfying my desire to get even.

The pastoral role, however, can keep such things from happening—protecting me, and others from me. The role helps me realize there is more at stake than my honesty.

Sometimes, of course, even when I'm in the pastoral role, I'll tell someone, "I'm mad at you," or "You've hurt me." But first I've asked myself, *Is what I want to say edifying to this person? Does it build up? What is God's desire for him or her at this time?*

It enables me to love when I don't feel like it. Some afternoons I schedule several back-to-back counseling sessions. Immediately after one session, in which I will have listened to someone in great distress, I'll begin another, yet all the emotions of the previous session are still reeling inside me, making it hard to concentrate.

At such moments, raw authenticity would cause me to say, "Listen, I can't listen to you right now. I'm hurt and concerned about someone who's just been in here."

In extreme situations, I might do just that. But most of the time, ministry is furthered if I fulfill my role, put a smile on my face, nod at the person's concerns, and force myself to give attention to the one who has come to see me.

It focuses the attention on Jesus Christ. Playing the pastoral role points me to something, or Someone, greater than myself. John the Baptist said, "He must increase, but I must decrease" (John 3:30 NKJV). That statement should be my goal in every facet of ministry. My preaching should focus on Christ, not on exhibiting my feelings of the moment. I don't want people to say, "Wow, what a neat guy" but "I see Christ glorified in him."

When I lead the liturgy, I don't want to be an emcee or entertainer, drawing attention to my wittiness or personality but one who draws people's attention to what is being said in the liturgy: Jesus Christ is Lord.

In short, if I'm only interested in my authentic self or baring my feelings, the message is lost; people think more about Ben Patterson and less about the gospel.

Beyond role-playing

One of the longest nights of my life took place at a wedding rehearsal dinner. I felt the guests, none of whom I had ever met before, were either mildly belligerent or even hostile to me. It was awful. But my pastoral role demanded I be pleasant.

Still, I felt as if I were skimming through a mental card catalog, pulling out random topics to talk about: "Well, how about them Giants?" and "Do you believe this rain!" Someone finally would respond, and another long silence would follow. I was glad when it came time to eat; at least it gave me something easy to do.

Fortunately, not all of ministry has to be so endured. Sometimes it's better to step out of the role and be myself. In fact, I've found five advantages to being genuine in ministry.

It helps people—and me—accept my limitations. Every pastor has limitations, and we shouldn't have to hide them, pretending we fit perfectly into every pastoral role.

For instance, my predecessor in this church was, in many ways, my opposite. A marvelous pastor, he got jazzed when he was around people; he served as honorary chaplain of the fire and police departments and town council. He was at home in a crowd.

That role, though, has always intimidated me. I don't like being the community chaplain—cutting the ribbons, speaking at parades, keynoting the anniversary celebrations. I realize these occasions can be important, that chitchat builds bridges, and that ceremonies can lead to significance, but being a "public person" doesn't come naturally to me.

It's been a great relief to acknowledge publicly that I am an introvert, that I get physically weary from being around large groups of people, and that there's nothing wrong with me when I do.

I recognize in order to fulfill my pastoral responsibilities, I have to be in many such settings. But I don't have to agonize about my discomfort or doubt my calling. It's one part of ministry where I'll never be comfortable.

Sharing the fact can also help my congregation understand when I don't get involved in community affairs as did my predecessor—and when I don't come off as well when I do.

It short-circuits loneliness. I hate going to presbytery, the bimonthly gathering of pastors and elders of local Presbyterian congregations. It's such a lonely time. Everybody's playing the professional role, especially the pastors. We're a competitive lot; it's hard to let our guard down. But I can't perform ministry that way. If I keep my feelings inside all the time, then I isolate myself from the Christian community. It's only when I express what's in my heart that people draw closer to me.

For me, it's especially important I feel at home in my church. If I can't mess up or say what I think about things there, then I become isolated in my role.

It keeps ministry moving. The stress of a board member's day can easily interfere with the business of the board meeting at night. The issue in question can become an occasion to work out the fight someone had with his wife or the lousy day another had at the office.

Before every board meeting, then, we spend an hour in worship, sharing, and prayer. When I participate in this time, it breaks down the pastoral persona so that others feel more free to let down their various personas.

That allows us to deal with the hurt and frustrations we've experienced during the week. The result: when we deal with the business of the church, we deal with only that and so finish our business before midnight.

People encounter a real gospel. People are much more interesting than any function they serve. I can play a role and even play a crowd, but I will not connect with people if I do. It's only when I reveal my humanity, confessing some of my faults and weaknesses publicly, that people relate to me. And then they can relate better to the gospel. When people see my humanity and the gospel as a vital part of their pastor's life, they're more likely to think Christ can be a vital part of their lives too.

"The Word became flesh" (John 1:14 NKJV). The Word became a real human being; he didn't just play the role of a human being (which, in fact, was an early heresy). And it was as a human being that he connected with people.

Discretion—the better part of honesty

The line, then, between the pastoral persona and who we genuinely are may never be as clear and distinct as we'd like. However, when I find myself consistently on one side of that line, something is wrong. It's not one or the other—I must incorporate both.

How and when I do that is another matter. In fact, each area of ministry—counseling, administration, community chaplain—requires a separate discussion. Let me suggest here how I handle the performance factor from the pulpit.

As much as I believe in saying what's on my heart and mind, only some things are appropriate for a pastor to share from the pulpit. Here is how I handle sensitive areas with care.

Discouragement. I don't publicly confess I am discouraged when I am discouraged. Although I might tell a close friend, I wouldn't say to my people, "I'm really down. I don't know if I'm going to make it."

In becoming leaders, I believe, we relinquish our right to be publicly discouraged. Being a leader means being up, positive, and definite. When we announce that we aren't, it can have a devastating effect. Our people begin to wonder and worry. They begin to lose confidence in the future.

It's important, though, for people to realize we're not constantly up; otherwise they may wonder if we're all there, if life really affects us. So I share discouragement, but only after the fact: "During our building program five years ago, there were many moments when I didn't feel we'd find the money to keep building."

Lust. In front of men's groups, I've admitted feeling lustful. It's something men struggle with, so when a pastor mentions he is tempted, but in Christ struggles with it, the reality of the gospel comes through strong.

I don't, however, admit to such before a mixed crowd. It would send the wrong signals. It may, for instance, make some women wonder if I've been thinking about them sexually. That would only clutter our pastoral relationship.

Even with men, I've learned to check my confessions of lust. I used to be very transparent. But when I was, I subtly and inadvertently communicated lust wasn't so much wrong as it was "natural"—in effect, acceptable. Now I try to share such weaknesses only to the point that it will show others I, too, struggle, but I don't share so much that giving in to temptation sounds okay.

Anger. It's not appropriate to vent in the pulpit unless it's clear my anger is focused outside the congregation, and even then only on something relatively abstract—like sin or injustice or the pornography industry. I've not seen many instances when anger directed at my congregation has done any good. Further, declaring my anger at prominent individuals or institutions respected by my people only puts my people on the defensive.

I can, however, talk about my own struggles with anger. In fact, I did that in a sermon some time ago. I told the congregation, "I am an angry man, and I haven't licked it yet. Some of you may not have a handle on it either." I got more response from that sermon than anything I had preached in a long time.

I didn't find anger an easy subject to talk about, but it's a topic people want to hear about, because anger is something they are anxious to control.

Ambition, pride, competitiveness. In our culture, these are socially acceptable faults. We may formally acknowledge them as wrong, but we secretly admire people who acquiesce to such temptations, because these people are usually "successful."

The danger for me, then, is acknowledging these faults, yet

using them as a subtle means to brag. When I do admit them, I don't candy coat the harm they do to me or others.

Failure. As a leader, I can't go around admitting every little administrative blunder. But if the mistake is big, and if everyone knows it's a mistake, I've got to admit it, at the time it happens or soon after.

When at Irvine, California, I was looking over the worship attendance numbers and, feeling ambitious, decided to recommend to the board we increase our Sunday morning services to three. I presented my case, twisted a few arms, and finally convinced the board.

But I hadn't done my homework. The numbers were wrong, and my growth projections were a couple of years premature. Within a couple of months of trying the new schedule, the strain was becoming apparent—it was difficult to find people to pull off each worship service—ushers, greeters, lay readers, and so on. It was especially hard on our choir, who found themselves shuttling through additional services.

I went to a dear friend in the church and said, "Bob, I made a mistake."

He laughed and replied, more quickly than I would have liked, "You really did." With that confirmation in hand, I went to the board and told them I was wrong, admitting it was all my fault. I could have let the board take the rap since they gave me the go-ahead, but my blunder ate at me. It was my information and vision, not theirs.

Some say we shouldn't talk about our failures unless they are moral ones, and even then only discreetly. They argue that people who really need to know we failed probably already do. The best move is to make steps to correct the problem.

I disagree. If we're going to announce our successes, we should be willing to admit when we've made a big mistake. Nothing can hurt a pastor's credibility more than an inability to admit he or she is wrong. It's nice to always be right, but it's not reality.

Depending on one's personality and the nature of the church we serve, the tension between living out the pastoral role and being genuine will be played out differently. But for me, the decision hinges on the answer to this question: "Which will better enhance the ministry of Christ in the church?" When I seek to answer that question, my reservations about playing the role and my enthusiasm for authenticity pale, and the glory of Christ better shines.

29

Renewing Your Sense of Purpose

Sometimes it's hard to remember why we're in ministry, or whether it's worth it. So periodically, we need to think about our call afresh.

—ED DOBSON

The week after Easter, I received this letter: "This was [written] after considerable prayer. My husband and I are submitting to the will of God and the urging of other Christians by walking away from your church.

"While we could easily slip out unnoticed and certainly never be missed, which is definitely one of the problems here, I feel that our reasons for leaving are important enough to share with you.

"From the pulpit recently we heard you comment that there's not enough unity between our church and other denominations. This, Pastor Dobson, is ecumenism, and ecumenism is of the Antichrist. . . .

"With which of these apostates would you suggest we unite? Our church in one broad sweep is trampling the grace of God and mocking the gospel. The church is the body of Christ, Pastor Dobson, not the unsaved masses of humanity you're trying to attract. Our church offers a program for every aspect of society that sets its foot in its walls—single moms, single dads, fatherless children, divorced women, substance abusers, but virtually nothing for believers.

"Although the church may be growing, you are losing the true saints of God. If this has been your goal, you are to be congratulated because you're achieving it. If not, there's still time to turn away."

It was signed, "In Christ, a saint."

At the bottom of the page, it read, "And thou, Capernaum, which are exalted in the heaven shall be brought down to hell. For if the mighty works which had been done in thee had been done in Sodom, it would have remained until this day. But I say to you it will be more tolerable for the land of Sodom in the day of judgment than for thee."

The same week I received another letter, a response to my sermon, "Smile; It's Easter, and God Loves You."

The letter said, "Greetings. Visits to your church have left the following impressions. . . . [There was] a vapid, soft, and comfortable presentation on Easter with the emphasis on smile rather than our sinfulness driving the Suffering Servant to the Cross. This was so irreverent and out of place as to make one ashamed, not of the gospel, but of its hapless, harmless, one-sided view. . . . God help us. Whatever happened to the offense of the Cross?"

It was signed, "An Unhappy Camper."

After the high of Easter Sunday, this was not pleasant reading. Sometimes such criticism makes us wonder, "Is this job worth it?"

Add to those times in ministry when nothing seems to be happening, and we're sure it isn't worth it. Now add our culture's presentation of clergy on TV, movies, and in magazines—meek, mild, and out of touch—and our calling can be thrown into sudden and wrenching doubt: "Is ministry something I should be investing my life in?"

Yes, sometimes it's hard to remember why we're in ministry, or whether it's worth it. So periodically, we need to think about our call afresh.

Sacred history review

"My spirit grows faint within me," wrote David. "My heart within me is dismayed." So what does he do? "I remember the days of long ago; I meditate on all your works and consider what your hands have done" (Ps. 143:4–5 NIV).

This is how David renewed his sense of call. It's not a bad idea for pastors: to remember what God has done in their lives and ministries.

I find it especially helpful to remember the origin of my call to ministry. I grew up in a pastor's home, so there were subliminal expectations from church people that I would follow my father. Though my parents never pushed that agenda on me, others did, and I reacted to it. As far as I was concerned, it was none of their business what I did with my life.

I was sixteen when I went to Bible college, with the understanding that after two years, I would transfer to a state university and pursue medical school. I had my sights set on being a surgeon.

But at college I was continually confronted with the question, "What does God want you to do?" I had never really given the notion much thought. Then passages of Scripture that dealt with preaching and ministry began to stand out during my devotional times. When individuals spoke in chapel on the subject of ministry, something would stir in my heart.

Halfway through my sophomore year, my struggle became more intense. It reached a crisis one evening when I attended a little church outside of my denominational background. The pastor spoke on Jonah. His thesis was simple: Jonah was called to preach, but he ran away from God. The message seemed to point straight at my life.

He then invited people who believed God might be calling them into ministry to come forward. I disliked public invitations, so I didn't budge. But later that night, I met the pastor in the basement of the church. By then I had made my decision. I said to him, "If the Lord wants me to preach, I'll preach. Whatever he wants me to do, I'll do."

Though the shape and nature of that call has changed over the years, this remains my call: to preach. When there have been harrowing storms to weather, the remembrance of this call has helped me stick to it.

Myth busting

Another tactic when my call seems in doubt is to remember the four myth-busters of ministry. The first three I heard from Truman Dollar; the last I added.

1. *It's never as bad as you think it is.* Even when things seem darkest, circumstances are usually not as hopeless or as awful as they first appear. For example, after one particularly tough committee meeting I was left with the impression people didn't trust me. Then I received a call from my wife. "You won't believe it, Ed, but you just received a beautiful bouquet of flowers," she said. "Let me read the card to you. 'To Ed Dobson, Pastor of the Year.' " The flowers had been sent by a couple who had been separated for nearly two years. Through the church's ministry, they had been won to Christ and had decided to be reconciled. I had conducted their marriage renewal service.

The bouquet was a dramatic reminder that I should never let church politics or conflicts obscure my vision of the bigger things God may be doing.

2. *It's never as good as you think it is.* There are times in church ministry when everything seems to be going marvelously. That's when you need to be careful. As Jerry Falwell used to say, "In ministry I've never had two good days back to back."

3. *It's never completely fixed.* Ministry is a process; it's people. To say, "I've taken care of this problem; it won't recur," is foolish.

4. *It's never completely broken.* Not long ago, a pastor from Kenya spoke in our morning worship service. He pointed out that during the first thirty years of missionary efforts in Kenya, more missionaries died than the number of converts who were won. In the remote inland regions of the country, missionaries sometimes arrived with their belongings stored in coffins. They were resigned to the fact they would never make it back to the coast.

In spite of the difficulties, these men and women were called to reach Kenya, so they kept at it, knowing someday their work would bear fruit. They were right. Thanks to their efforts, today 82 percent of Kenya is at least nominally Christian. Evangelicals alone number nearly nine million. No matter what it looks like, God's work has not stopped.

Criticism management

When I was younger, during times of criticism, I used my call as a baseball bat to confront my critics. Part of that was because of my training. It had been drilled into me during college that regardless of the cost, you have to take a stand. If the whole world is against you, take a stand. So during my first pastorate, I interpreted that to mean I should stand up to my critics.

When I encountered conflict in board meetings, I would bring up the issue in my sermon the next Sunday. "God called me to start this church," I would remind the congregation. "If you don't like it, there are a number of other churches in this town you can attend." I declared the authority of the pastor and expected that to end the issue.

That was stupid. While we ought to stand for what we believe, Paul says we are to teach and admonish others in a spirit of patience and gentleness. Many pastors run aground in ministry not because they lack a legitimate call. Rather it's because they haven't been adequately prepared to work with people. They may have been trained to handle the Greek and Hebrew texts, but they aren't equipped to deal with imperfect people in an imperfect world. Sometimes, opposition isn't a sign you don't belong in the ministry, it's simply part of the call to "Deny yourself, take up your cross, and follow me."

Today, I try to accept criticism as part of the package. Paul was realistic in his description of the ministry: "We are hard pressed on every side, but not crushed; perplexed, but not in despair; persecuted, but not abandoned; struck down, but not destroyed" (2 Cor. 4:8–9 NIV).

The ministry is sometimes pressure, discouragement, disappointment, heartache, criticism, and conflict. I try to communicate that to all who are considering the job. If they don't believe me, I just show them my mail.

Also, when criticism comes now, I try not to believe everything I hear. Recently a woman shook my hand after one service and said, "Good grief, Pastor! Your hand is soft. I bet you haven't seen a good day's work in your entire life."

She grinned and walked off. She obviously didn't know how

such a statement can hit pastors. I just stood there thinking to myself, *Thank you very much. Good day to you as well!*

A lot of criticism is based on ignorance or misconceptions. When it's appropriate, I try to educate people. But when it's not, I find it best just to forget the comment.

When I encounter opposition, I ask, *Is God trying to show me something in this? Is this a process of character development in my life?* I may pray, "This is what they've said about me, Lord. Is it true? Help me to be honest with myself and determine what truth, if any, lies behind their comment."

I will actually read to God the letters critical of me. Sometimes I discover God is trying to say something to me. Other times, he reassures me that I'm on the right track and not to become discouraged.

New direction indicators

Sometimes when we're doubting the call, we're merely doubting the call to a specific ministry. And sometimes the doubt is justified: God wants us to move on.

How we know that, of course, is no simple process. I listen to my journal. For years I've taken time to write out, several times a week, what I'm learning from my study of Scripture, my circumstances, and my ministry experiences.

As I was considering Calvary Church in Grand Rapids, I was also contacted by a church in New York City. New York looked attractive; I would be downtown in the midst of several million unchurched people. During that period, I spent a lot of time reviewing my journals. I noticed entries like, "I'm going to delay Grand Rapids. New York is really where I want to go. Logically, it seems the right place." Then I'd go home that night and get a call from the board chairman in Grand Rapids, inviting me to fly in the next day. Being caught off guard, I would say, "Okay. I think I can do that."

In fact, I noticed that every time I decided to close a door to Grand Rapids, something unusual would open it wider. At the same time, the church in New York would ask me to jump through one more hoop: get another reference, send another sermon, whatever. As I reviewed my journal, the pattern became obvious, and eventually I followed God's leading to Grand Rapids.

In addition, I think it's appropriate to "lay out the fleece," not to test God but to assure myself that, in fact, God is leading. For example, before coming to Grand Rapids, I decided I needed to have 95 percent of the congregational vote if I were to come. "We don't vote unanimously for anything," a board member had warned me. Nonetheless, that was the percentage I needed to feel secure in accepting the call.

I ended up with unanimous calls from the committee and the board and a 99.7-percent vote from the congregation. I've never seen that happen again in this church, even when we have voted on mission candidates or on ordaining someone to the ministry. That helped me move forward with confidence and face conflict that would surely come.

I've also begun praying with my wife about such decisions. That's not the way the previous generation often went about it. My father believed God speaks to the "priest" of the family (the man), and he leads with or without the spouse's consent. At the beginning of our life together, Lorna and I agreed that wherever God called me, we would go together. I have felt it important, though, to bring her more and more into the decision-making process. When the moment of truth arrived regarding Grand Rapids, she said, "Ed, there's no need even to pray any further about this. Calvary Church is where you belong."

Finally, sometimes we just have to go out on faith, and if we've misread God's will, then that too can lead us to the real calling he has for us. When I started in ministry, I believed God had called me to be heir apparent to Billy Graham. I honestly believed I was going to one day take over for him, so right out of college, I set up the Eddy Dobson Evangelistic Association. My wife and I sent out hundreds of letters advertising our availability. If I could summarize the general response, it was, "Paul we know. Jesus we know. But who are you?"

The end result was that we moved into a one-bedroom apartment, and I took a job digging graves. My wife went to work for a

temporary employment agency. I was severely disillusioned by
the response to what I perceived to be my call. But this turn of
events eventually led to my being offered a position at Liberty
College working with Jerry Falwell, and that, in turn, led to my
becoming the pastor of a small, mountain church in West Virginia, my first full-time pastoral experience.

We need others to help us hear God's leading. At any given
time, sitting in our congregation are a half-dozen pastors recover-
ing from burnout. Ministry has temporarily overwhelmed them. I
encourage hurting and tired pastors to find renewal inside a
church. Seek out the leaders of a church, admit your need, and
ask to come under the church's care. After a period of healing and
renewal, you will be able to draw on this group's affirmation that
you're spiritually and emotionally ready to reenter pastoral ministry.

Prevention medicine

Pastors sometimes feel frustrated in their calling because
they're waiting for someone to help them. They honestly believe
the board will one day approach them and say, "Pastor, you need
to take some time off with your family for personal and spiritual
renewal." It won't happen.

Fortunately, I was given this blunt but lifesaving advice when I
arrived in Grand Rapids. Our city has a strong Dutch community,
so my first year a board member met with me weekly to help me
understand the Dutch people and the culture of our church.

"One thing you need to know," he said, "is that we will sit in
board meetings and discuss the tremendous pressures you face,
how hard you work, how you are away from your family too
much, how you need to slow down, and how important it is for
you to take regular days off and get away for your full vacation
each year. Then we'll go home saying to ourselves, 'My, aren't we
taking wonderful care of Ed Dobson!' "

Then he leaned forward and said, "The truth is, Pastor, despite
our pious lectures and good intentions, we won't stop you from
overworking. We will cheer you right into your grave. We will

bury you and then get someone else to replace you, just as we always have."

He was not being cynical. He was simply warning me that if I didn't take care of my physical, spiritual, and emotional health, no one else would. I was struck by an interview with Billy Graham in which he said if he had it to do all over again, he would travel less, study more, and spend more time with his family.

I need to watch proper exercise and diet. I run between three and seven miles a day, and that leaves me refreshed for preaching or teaching, particularly midweek when my energy can lapse. Further, I know I need seven or eight hours of sleep each night to function well. When I traveled with Jerry Falwell, I noticed he rarely needed more than three or four hours of sleep a night. Though he did all the interviews and speaking, I came back from those road trips dead tired. If I tried to keep that same schedule, I'd get sick.

I also watch my emotional gauges. I work hard to keep from having one emotionally draining situation after another. Sometimes I plan golf games between stressful meetings. I also accept the fact that on Mondays I'm drained from the day before, so I don't accept any appointments other than lunch. I read and avoid seeing people or dealing with tough issues. It's a day I use to study and begin preparations for the next Sunday.

Part of guarding my call also means I try to operate primarily in the realm of my giftedness. My limitations are in counseling and administration. As much as my board would love to see me be more assertive in administrative matters, I've told them, "If you want to make me miserable, make me an administrator." They understand my limitations.

Billy Graham said not long ago that he believes he did the one thing God called him to do—preach the gospel. My hope is that forty years from now I can look back and say the same thing.

30

Role Call

*Our aim as pastors should be to produce people whose lives will
either make Jesus appear to be incredibly crazy or amazingly able
to produce the sort of people he demands.*

—WILLIAM H. WILLIMON

"I want to do well as a pastor," said the seminarian, "but I never
want to lose sight of the fact that I'm a person. My personal needs
are more important than my pastoral duties."

At first hearing, this young man's attitude sounds charmingly
modest, appropriately suspicious of his new clerical role. He
wants not to be the pompous preacher. He wants to be just a
person. Yet this is a strange view of a "person." Can any person be
detached from his or her commitments?

A pastor is not merely a person. A pastor is a person who has
had hands laid upon his or her head, made public promises before God and the church, willingly yoked his or her life to the
demands of the gospel. This marvelously empathetic seminarian
has unwittingly subordinated church tradition, theology, and
ordination to his own needs. How can he be sure that his desire to be "just a person" is not simply another means of self-
centeredness (what we once called *sin*)?

The romantic rebel

In our attempts to be empathetic and ordinary people above
the limitations of the pastoral role, we fall into what Mercer law
professor Jack L. Sammons, Jr., has called "Rebellious Ethics."

Following such ethics, we stand apart from our professional roles in judgment of them. The worst moral danger, according to Rebellious Ethics, is for pastors to be captured by their professional roles. The goal of this ethic is to be the sort of pastor who doesn't take himself or herself too seriously, to be more a person than a pastor. In fact, says Rebellious Ethics, the more we summon the psychological courage to rebel against our socially imposed roles, the more ethical we will be.

Listen to the cynicism within the conversation of the Ministers' Monday Morning Coffee Hour. Clergy sit around making cutting comments about their flocks, or regale one another with sacrilegious jokes—an ersatz rebellion from the clerical roles they find so confining. It is an attempt to deny clerical demands by making fun of being a cleric. We adopt the stance of the romantic rebel, the fiction of the roleless person.

In rebelling against traditional expectations for pastors, we have not rebelled against cultural expectations. We have succumbed to the most ethically debilitating of those expectations. We have fallen backward into the clutches of the dominant ethic—you stay out of my life, and I'll stay out of yours.

Chaplain to the personal

The contemporary pastor attempts to achieve power by being so nice, appearing to be caring, empathetic, and kind, all the while conveying this culture's officially sanctioned ethic: there is no point to life other than that which you personally devise. You don't intrude on my comfort; I won't intrude on yours.

It is not that we have been too good at being pastors and not good enough at being people; rather, we have not been good enough at being pastors. True morality, the ability to judge our self-deception, the gift of seeing things in perspective, comes from practices outside those sanctioned by the system. It comes from being forced, Sunday after Sunday, to lead and to pray the Prayer of Confession followed by the Words of Absolution. It comes from being ordered, Sunday after Sunday, to "do this in remembrance of me."

Our ecclesial claim is that through obedience to these practices, Jesus gives us the resources we need to be faithful disciples. And we will never know whether Jesus was speaking truthfully if we refuse to hold ourselves and our people accountable to Jesus' demands.

Our aim as pastors should be to produce people whose lives will either make Jesus appear to be incredibly crazy or amazingly able to produce the sort of people he demands.

Just one of you

During a lunch with the chair of our chemistry department, he noted that ministers could profit from the ethics of chemists.

"The ethics of chemists?" I asked.

"Sure," he replied. "It is impossible to be a good chemist and a liar at the same time. The chemist's honesty about experimental results, openness with other chemists, and commitment to standard methodology would enhance the practice of ministry."

Which suggests Jack Sammons is correct: we don't need to be better rebels from the virtues and practices of our craft; we need to be more deeply linked to them. Separated from the skills and commitment of our craft, we are left morally exposed, victims of conventional wisdom. For pastors, the worst form of self-deception may be the deceptive idea that we are without power, just one of the boys (or girls), not taking ourselves too seriously, a person.

Consider the ethics of preaching. The morality required by the craft of sermon preparation, the self-criticism, obedience to the text, confidence in the congregation, and weekly hard work are moral disciplines. In fact, that may be a good test whether ordinances are morally ready to be entrusted with a congregation: Have they mastered the craft well enough to write fifty-two Sundays of sermons without lying too often?

Sportscaster Red Barber recalled that the chief ethical crisis of his career occurred when the manager of the Dodgers, Branch Rickey, called to prepare him for the fact that in the next few days, baseball's color line would be broken and black players would join the team. Barber's small-town Mississippi roots caused him great consternation. *What should I do?* he asked himself. *Should I resign rather than be part of this?* "Then a voice said to me, 'You are an announcer. You will announce!' Scales fell off my eyes. I knew what I was to do. The next week I announced to the world the arrival of Jackie Robinson. There was no problem." Freedom came from accepting his role.

The notion that we are most fully ourselves, most fully ethical, when we have freed ourselves from the demands of Scripture, tradition, and church, merely demonstrates that we are held captive by the belief that the individual is the basic unit of reality, the sole center of meaning. We live under the modern presupposition that none of us should be held to commitments we have not freely chosen. If I explain my actions on the basis of tradition, community standards, my parents' beliefs, or Scripture, I have obviously not decided for myself, have not been true to myself, have not been moral. I am less than a person.

Ironically, we jettison the older, traditional story—that it is my duty as an ordained leader of the church to bear the church's tradition before the congregation—for a more socially acceptable one—my duty is to my individual feelings and standards in order to free my parishioners to be dutiful to their individual feelings and standards. In effect, all we do is serve the status quo, become chaplains to the present order, urge people to feel sincerely and make up their own minds. Clergy are thus fated to be nice. We hope that nobody will get hurt doing that. Of course, nobody will get to be a true saint, either.

The mother of modernity

In *Sources of the Self: The Making of Modern Identity,* Charles Taylor notes that the Reformation rejected the historic Catholic presumption that some within the body of Christ could be more dedicated to the faith, and thus more capable of winning merit and salvation, and others could be less so.

Now everyone is a saint. God is not more present through specially dedicated people than God is present through everyone.

Thus, the Reformation made its own distinctive contribution to the individualism of the modern world. Despite what we Protestants may think of Taylor's observation, we should pause for thought. Taylor claims that the Reformation's effort to deny special mediation of God's grace through peculiar institutions or special people ultimately destroyed the church's christological center. Everything gets flattened to "what seems right to me," and any person can deliver that.

However, to be a Christian is to be someone who is baptized into practices and virtues based upon the claim that in Jesus Christ, God is busy saving the world, not on our terms, but on God's terms. God's principal way of saving the world appears to be persons, but not just any old person—saints are needed.

Therefore the church calls persons to be pastors to help the rest of us be more than the persons we would be if we had been left to our own devices.

A Baptist friend of mine felt compelled to speak out in the middle of a recent racial crisis in his small southern town. In a sermon, he charged his congregation with being more influenced by their surrounding southern culture than by the Bible they professed. When his board of deacons complained to him about his sermon, his reply was, "Look, I'm a preacher. You pay me to preach the Bible, not what you (or I) think. You think I *enjoy* preaching like this?"

His board sat there in a moment in silence. Then they applauded him and went on to their business. Their pastor had reminded them that for him to be "ordained" meant that he was "under orders."

Both pastor and people are ennobled by being accountable to something more substantial than their "felt needs." Vocation, in a Christian sense, means no one is "just a person." No one is "just" an anything after God's claim upon our lives.

p. 131 - Knapweed - Stunts & kills other plants in vicinity; overtakes area.